IMAGES
of America

MARSTONS MILLS

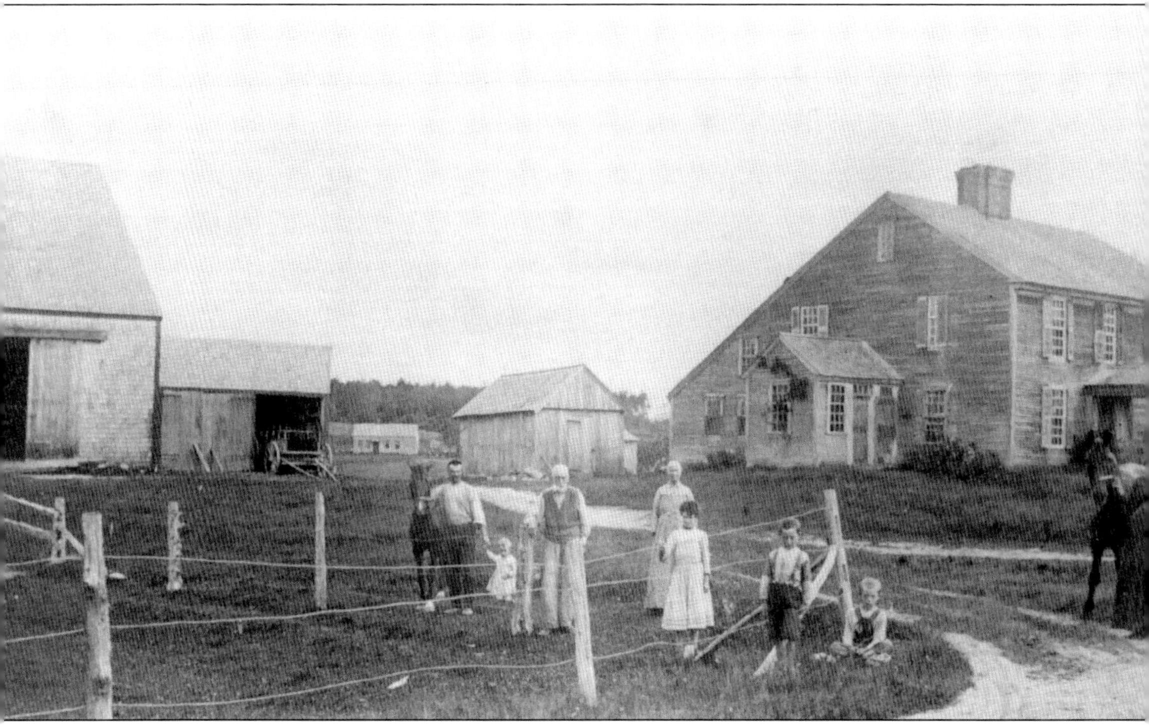

On the Cover: The Nymphas Marston house was later owned by Heman Thomas. In this c. 1889 photograph are George Thomas, William Pierce, Heman Thomas, his wife, Olive, their grandchildren Nora, Heman and Raymond Pierce, and daughter Lucinda Thomas. When patriot militiamen returning from battle at Falmouth in 1778 were invited in by Judge Nymphas Marston for a celebration, a soldier set his musket down in the dining room and blasted a hole in the ceiling. The judge kept that scar as a symbol of his patriotism. (Courtesy of Marstons Mills Historical Society.)

IMAGES
of America

MARSTONS MILLS

James Gould and Vivian Cushing

ARCADIA
PUBLISHING

ISBN 978-0-7385-9820-8

Published by Arcadia Publishing
Charleston, South Carolina

Printed in the United States of America

Library of Congress Control Number: 2012945464

For all general information, please contact Arcadia Publishing:
Telephone 843-853-2070
Fax 843-853-0044
E-mail sales@arcadiapublishing.com
For customer service and orders:
Toll-Free 1-888-313-2665

Visit us on the Internet at www.arcadiapublishing.com

Contents

ACKNOWLEDGMENTS

The photographs in this book are principally based on the collection of the Marstons Mills Historical Society. Unless noted, all photographs are in its archives.

Special thanks are dedicated to Barbara Hill, who was president of the Marstons Mills Historical Society for two decades—from 1984 to 2005. The collection of historic photographs became part of the Living History project, which recorded the memories of the village's oldest residents.

To the society's founders—Wilbur and Vivian Cushing, Robert McClusky, Arnold and Irene Hadfield, we are grateful for beginning the long process of gathering, identifying, and carefully preserving most of the photographs that are presented here.

We owe particular thanks to the librarians of Marstons Mills Library, who gave a protected space for the collection of archives and photographs. Renee Voorhees, the current librarian, is thanked for providing a space for work.

Thanks also go to Nancy and Douglas Clark, and to Kevin Galvin, who were caretakers of the photographs.

The process of assembling and formatting photographs was greatly helped by our go-getters Holly Hobart, Donna DeFlorio, Nancy Wong, and Sandra and William Bolton.

Robert Frazee, who took over the presidency of the Marstons Mills Historical Society in emergency conditions, not only gave essential support and encouragement for the project, but also helped to reproduce maps and posters.

To Paul Rifkin, we owe thanks for technical support.

For loans of precious photographs, we thank John Aalto, Connie Austin, Al Baker, Alex Bally, Barnstable County Fair, Mary Jo Boden, Wendy Brown, Veronica Canning, Lena Childs, Mark Cote, Lindsey Counsell, Charles F. Crocker, Joanne Cunningham, Kay Dick, Justine Dionne, Jacqi Easter, Holbrook and Joel Davis, Mary Lou Fair, Harold Fuller, Judy Galvin, Charles E. Hamblin, Reid Higgins, Vercille Johnson, Susan Leach, Diane Aalto Long, David and Sue Martin, Robert McClusky, Betsy McIntyre, Maureen McPhee, Claire Melix, John D. Meyer, Julia Miranda, Betty Nilsson, O'Donnell family, Gretchen Perry, Loyse Perry, Mary Perry, Gerda Reid, Chris Siderwitz, Crocker Snow Jr., David Still of the *Barnstable Patriot*, Edward Thew, Arthur Thifault, Anne Thomas, Cindy VanWagenen, Rick Wheeler, and Cathy Wright of Osterville Historical Society.

To our faithful acquisitions editors at Arcadia Publishing, Abby Henry and Rebekah Collinsworth, we owe thanks for the final quality of this work.

Finally, but most importantly, we thank the members of our families who put up with our preoccupation with this project and lent important editing and technical support.

INTRODUCTION

Marstons Mills is a village that has preserved much of the rural charm of old Cape Cod. It still produces most of the Cape's cranberries. Its saltwater marina on Prince's Cove is a gateway to the sea, and many of its sons made their fortunes in whaling and large coasting-trade schooners—or were lost at sea. The three Mystic Lakes are among the largest bodies of freshwater on the Cape, feeding a river that is a pathway for herring. The quiet, tree-lined roadways pass by classic Cape Cod cottages, many 200 years old. Here, too, is the Cape Cod Airport, the first in the region, with planes still taking off from grass runways. Although the village has taken on a suburban character in the last 50 years, Marstons Mills is one of the rare places where rural 19th-century America still exists.

Indians have lived in Marstons Mills for 8,000 years, as shown by a major archaeological survey. The Wampanoag Indian name for the area was Mistic, which probably refers to the large lake and its downstream ponds and river. The attractions of the tidal river were the abundance of fish, oysters, and clams, and the annual run of herring and alewives, which provided not only food, but also fertilizer for their crops of corn and squash. When the first white settlers arrived, the Wampanoag sachem Paupmumuck was living on Broad Nook, what we now call Prince's Cove. He, his brother, and two other Indians "sold" the whole southwest quarter of Barnstable in 1648, reserving 30 acres east of the mouth of the river. Around half of it, the white men promised to build a fence, presumably to protect the Indian corn from the newcomers' cattle, but they failed to do so. After Paupmumuck died, about 1665, a woman called Syucy became sachem, and Indians continue to live here to this day.

The first white settler, Roger Goodspeed, built a house in 1653, probably at the mouth of the river, next to the Indians' reserve. Here, Goodspeed found the most valuable asset, fields of salt hay, which he fed to cattle, as he had done on the north shore. We do not know when he was born, or where, but he arrived from England to become a pioneer settler of Barnstable village in 1639. Goodspeed built his second house upriver, perhaps near where his son Ebenezer's house still stands.

Marstons Mills was a major industrial village before the American Revolution. The fulling mill, authorized in 1687, was one of the earliest in America. It was the second on Cape Cod and in southern Massachusetts. A Barnstable town meeting of February 11, 1686/7, gave John Andreas 8 or 10 acres of upland next to John Goodspeed's property on the river "to full Cloth provided he set up and keep a fulling mill and full and Dress ye Towns Cloth Upon Reasonable Terms or Prices." This was never built. Eleven residents, including Roger's son John Goodspeed, built the mill in 1689. It was maintained for 20 years, providing the service to any townsperson who brought his raw wool to the site. Located on the east side of the Herring River (then called Goodspeed's), the mill was well above today's Fulling Mill Lane. In 1705, the town gave John Stacy permission to dam the river below the fulling mill and erect a gristmill. This mill served the local area for 200 years, until 1916 or so.

The resident owner of the mill, John Goodspeed's niece Lydia, married Benjamin Marston in 1716. He was a clothier from Salem, who may have rebuilt the fulling mill on the model of those already operating on the North Shore. Before his death in 1769, he had added spinning and weaving machines in buildings below the mill. By 1738, the village became known as Marston's Mills, with the apostrophe that stuck until the 1880s.

Public schools in Marstons Mills go back more than 250 years. In 1732, the town supported a "Squadron School" whose male teacher, usually a college graduate, taught in private homes, in this case 15 weeks at Benjamin Goodspeed's. For over 60 years, the itinerant teacher was Joseph Lewis (1702–1788), who graduated from Harvard in 1724. In 1742, Marston's Mills pupils got four months instruction near Benjamin Marston's. Town leaders like Judge Nymphas Marston, a Yale graduate, would have been educated in this way.

In 1793, the town created three schools in what is today Marstons Mills: Precinct VII in the Plains with 39 children, Precinct VIII in Jones's neighborhood (Newtown) with 38 children, and the village center Precinct IX with 48 children—125 children all told. Local citizens taxed themselves and usually built a one-room schoolhouse. The most remarkable teacher in early Marstons Mills was Amos Otis Jr. (1801–1875), the author of the authoritative *Genealogical Notes of Barnstable Families*. He taught here for 15 years, walking eight miles from his home in Barnstable village to school and back.

Although Marstons Mills was mainly farming country, its young men were already going to sea in the 1700s. In 1737, we learn of the loss of Benjamin Hamblen, who was killed when the blubber of a whale caught in the Arctic Sea fell on him. Marstons Mills whalers continued into the Civil War era, when one local captain's ship was burned by a Confederate raider off Cape Cod. Many local sea captains ran coastal schooners that carried most of the bulk freight along the coast. The village had its masters of clipper ships and luxurious steam liners. The most unusual local story of the sea is that of two young men who were born on Race Lane, William Wright and Seth Weeks. In an episode that was the basis of Melville's *Moby Dick*, they survived the sinking of the *Essex* by a whale. They were stranded on an uninhabited Pacific isle with another shipmate, surviving on birds and their eggs. They were saved from the fate of their shipmates, some of whom resorted to cannibalism.

Nymphas Marston Sr. (1728–1788) played a major role in the early American Revolution. In 1774, as selectman and former justice, he supported the protest of the 1,500-man "Body of the People" against the British government's giving jury selection to the sheriff rather than the people by forcing the closure of the court. He served on the town's committee of correspondence with other towns that objected to British impositions. As town moderator, he represented a conservative view that led the town to resist the early call for independence. Our cover shows Marston's house, where, to show his patriotism, he preserved the hole in his dining room ceiling, accidentally shot by a militiaman returning from the defense of Falmouth in 1778 when he set down his musket to enjoy the judge's celebratory toast.

The Marstons Mills Methodist church began in 1819, under Henry Hazelton's ministry, when a group was gathered in Hamblin Plains at the home of George W. Baker, who lived on Middle Pond. The first church building in Marstons Mills was opened in 1830. When Yarmouthport Methodists built a new meetinghouse, they offered their building to the Plains congregation for $200. Two founders of the first meeting, Lewis Hamblin and Joseph Holway, moved the building over eight miles by oxen to its present site on Main Street.

In the 1840s, Rev. George W. Green "stumbled and fell" in the battle with "Liberal Christianity," according to the official history. Green evidently introduced some of the currently popular doctrines of the Universalists, who took an optimistic view of human prospects that seemed to contradict the pessimistic view of human sin. Universalism had support from the well-to-do Marston and Hinckley families and the village doctor, William G. Bruce. Since Green was locked out of the Methodist meetinghouse, the Universalists built Liberty Hall across the road in September 1859. It became the village meeting hall, open to all. The Universalist congregation faded away, while the Methodist church lasted until 1968, when it merged with the Methodist Church of Osterville.

The church and parsonage were sold. In 1980, Rev. Philip D. Sherman and his wife, Sheila, raised $55,000 to buy the abandoned building and founded the Marstons Mills Community Church, a Protestant nondenominational congregation, which continues today.

Large-scale production of cranberries began in 1875 in Newtown, the western part of Marstons Mills. Local residents like the Hamblins and Joneses had long been growing cranberries on a small scale in the marshes at the source of the Marstons Mills River. It was the Hyannis harness-maker "Cranberry King" Abel D. Makepeace (1832–1916) who began cultivation of large bogs with the funding of George T. Baker. Makepeace moved to River Road in Newtown in 1880 before moving permanently to West Barnstable. The chief engineer of the project was Stephen Crocker Hamblin (1851–1881), who had grown up working his family's bogs.

With the decline of maritime activity in the late 19th century, Marstons Mills benefitted from the discovery of Cape Cod as a summer resort. The first summer home was Willow Dell, built in 1866 by Judge Henry Scudder, a picturesque "cottage" with steeply pitched roofs and cross gables in Gothic Revival style, on the banks of the river. In 1884, Prof. James Metivier (1853–1930) built Silver Oaks next to Cedar Tree Landing on North Bay. Born on the island of Jersey and a friend of Victor Hugo, Metivier came to America as a boy. He became professor of French at Harvard and Clark Universities. In 1906, the concertmaster of the Boston Symphony Orchestra, Felix Winternitz, built a summerhouse and boathouse for his yacht on Warren's Cove. The house later became the summer retreat of the novelist J.P. Marquand, who wrote his Mr. Moto spy stories here. In 1912, the prominent pianist Carlo Buonamici built a summer retreat at the south end of Middle Pond, a building that was later the home of the Tanampo Club. Some old farms were bought by wealthy gentleman farmers, such as the railway wheel manufacturer Franklin Whitcomb (1852–1946) and aluminum producer E.K. Davis.

Early farming featured cattle and sheep and crops of corn, rye, and hay. In 1898, a German immigrant, Louis Kleinschmidt, started a dairy at what is now the Gifford Farm, with a household delivery wagon. Neighbors like the Aaltos and Fullers took up the business. In 1919, the Swedish-born Hilding Hord began the dairy that became the Mystic Lake Dairy Farm, with 150 milk cows and six milk trucks which delivered 1,500 quarts of milk a day.

The arrival of the automobile shortly after the turn of the 20th century changed the character of the village. The occupations of blacksmith, millwright, and wheelwright became obsolete. The mucky and sandy roads were hardened with crushed stone and shells and soon paved. In 1928, a new state highway cut off the village center and filled over the herring run and fish house.

The first airport on Cape Cod opened in The Plains in 1929, featuring a flying school and air shows, an automobile racetrack, and a polo field. Nearby, the Barnstable County Fair flourished from 1954 until 1972.

In the last 50 years, much of the open farmland has been converted to suburban development, with modest homes and green lawns. But Marstons Mills still has its rural character, thanks to working cranberry bogs, large conservation areas around Long Pond, Prince's Cove and the glacial moraine, a golf course on the old fairgrounds, and the green runways of Cape Cod Airfield.

One

Mill Pond and the River

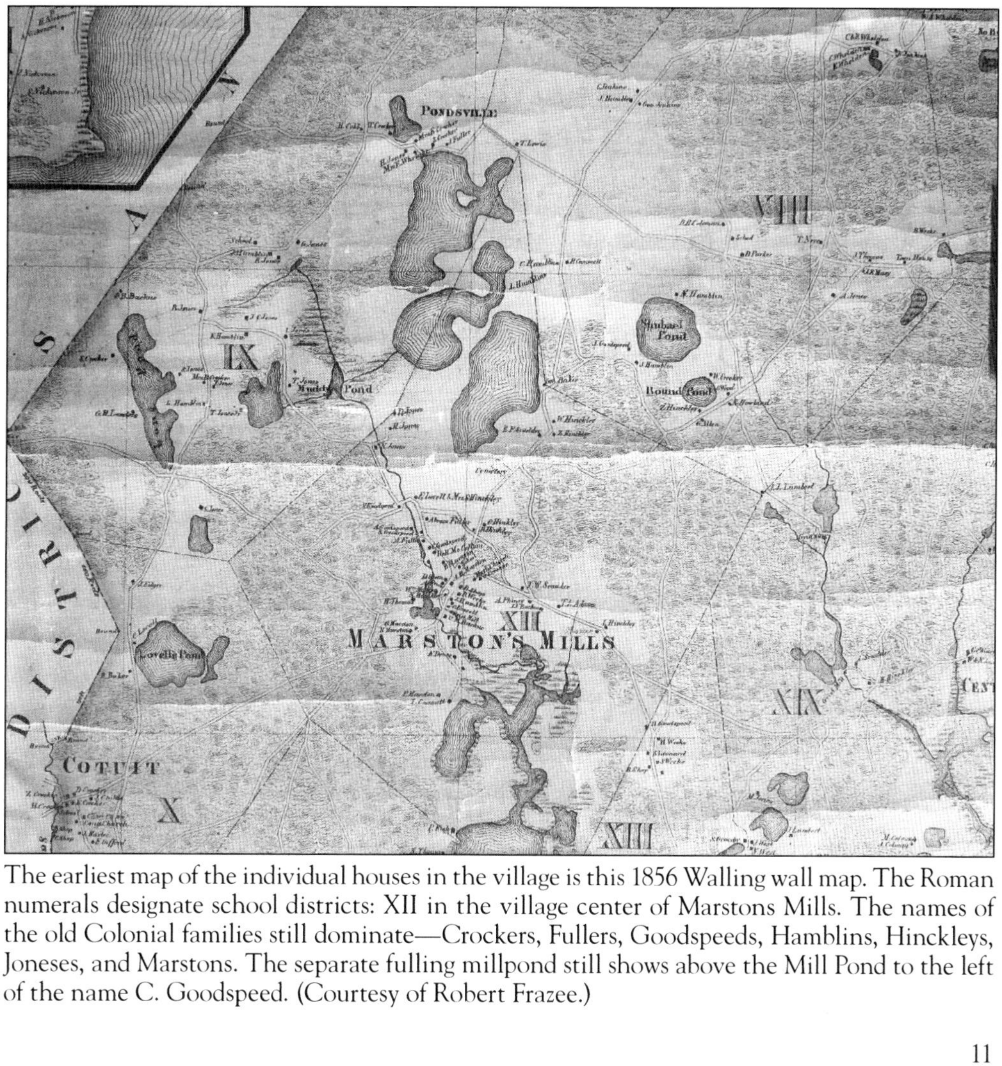

The earliest map of the individual houses in the village is this 1856 Walling wall map. The Roman numerals designate school districts: XII in the village center of Marstons Mills. The names of the old Colonial families still dominate—Crockers, Fullers, Goodspeeds, Hamblins, Hinckleys, Joneses, and Marstons. The separate fulling millpond still shows above the Mill Pond to the left of the name C. Goodspeed. (Courtesy of Robert Frazee.)

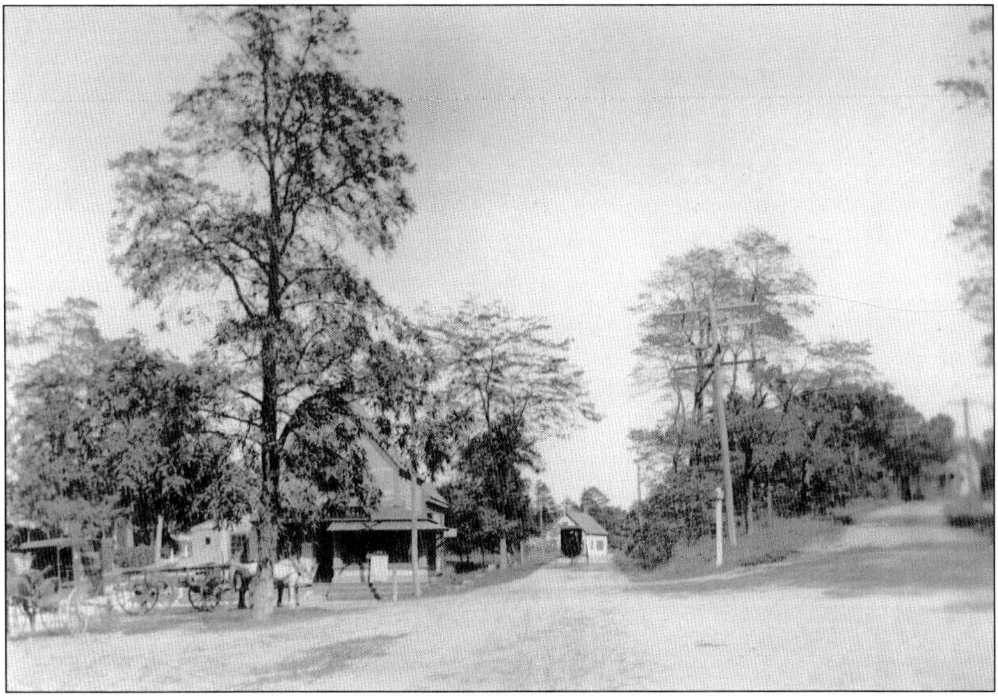

This is a classic scene viewed when entering the village center from the south on the Cotuit Road at the turn of the century. At the left is George Hamblin's grocery store. In the shade of the tall locust tree are waiting wagons, a delivery wagon at the left, and a flatbed drawn by a white horse. In the center, a buggy is going north toward the one-room schoolhouse. Main Street rises to the right toward Liberty Hall.

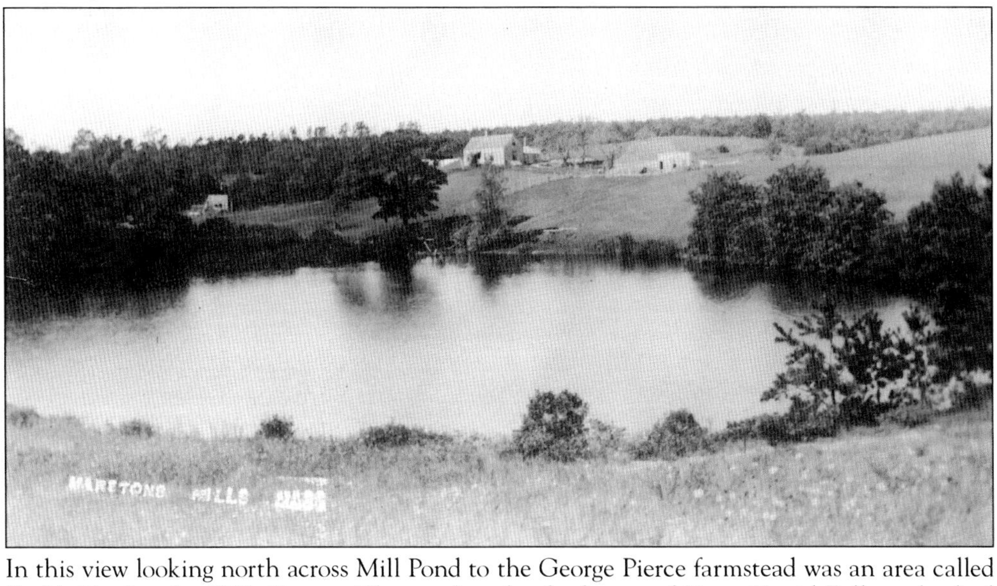

In this view looking north across Mill Pond to the George Pierce farmstead was an area called Zach's Garden. In 1845, Heman Thomas bought the house of Capt. David Fuller, who had inherited it from his father, Zaccheus Fuller, a Mayflower descendant. Fuller and his son George were discovered dead, adrift in their bark *John Potter* off Cape Fear, North Carolina, in 1854. They died of yellow fever, which they caught in Havana.

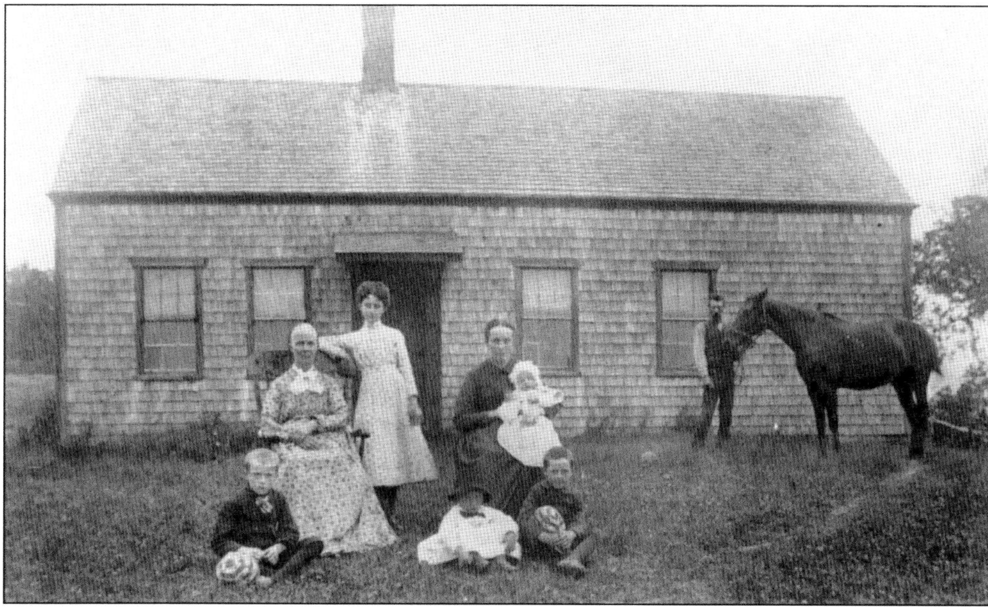

The George W. Pierce family stands in front of their house in 1889. Pictured from left to right are Heman Pierce, Olive Ames Thomas, Nora Pierce, William B. Pierce, Clara Thomas Pierce, Charles Pierce, Raymond Pierce, and George Thomas (holding the horse). George lost an arm when his horse bolted, throwing a scythe off the back of a wagon. When Heman Thomas moved to the Nymphas Marston house next door, this became the home of his son-in-law George Pierce.

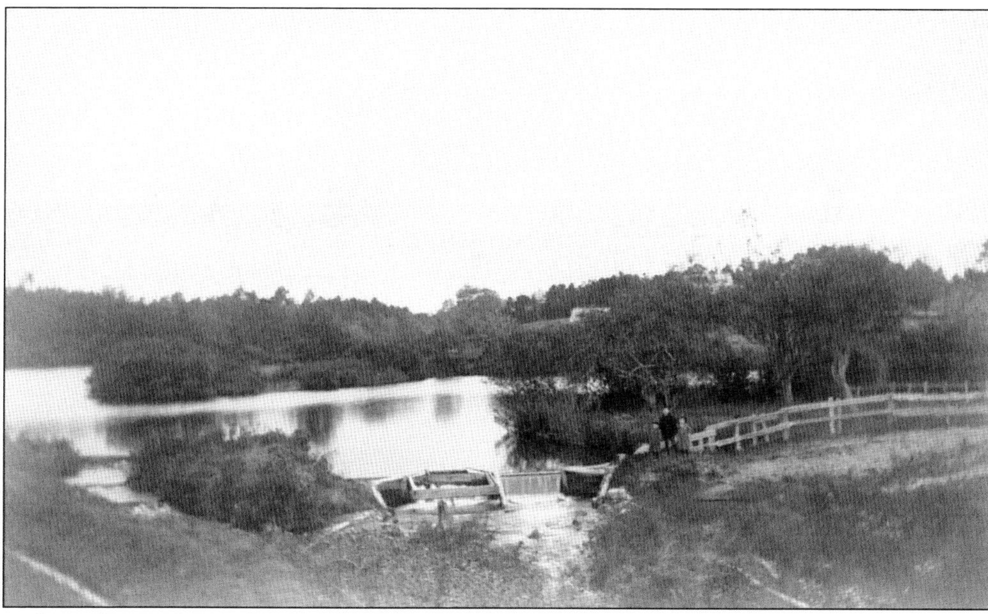

Mill Pond is on the Marstons Mills River, once known as Goodspeed's River, named for the first white settler, Roger Goodspeed, who built his house near here in 1653. Later, it was called Herring River for the large numbers of alewives and herring that passed through here each April and May on their way to Middle Pond where they spawned. Another pond about a quarter of a mile upstream provided the power for the huge hammers of the fulling mill.

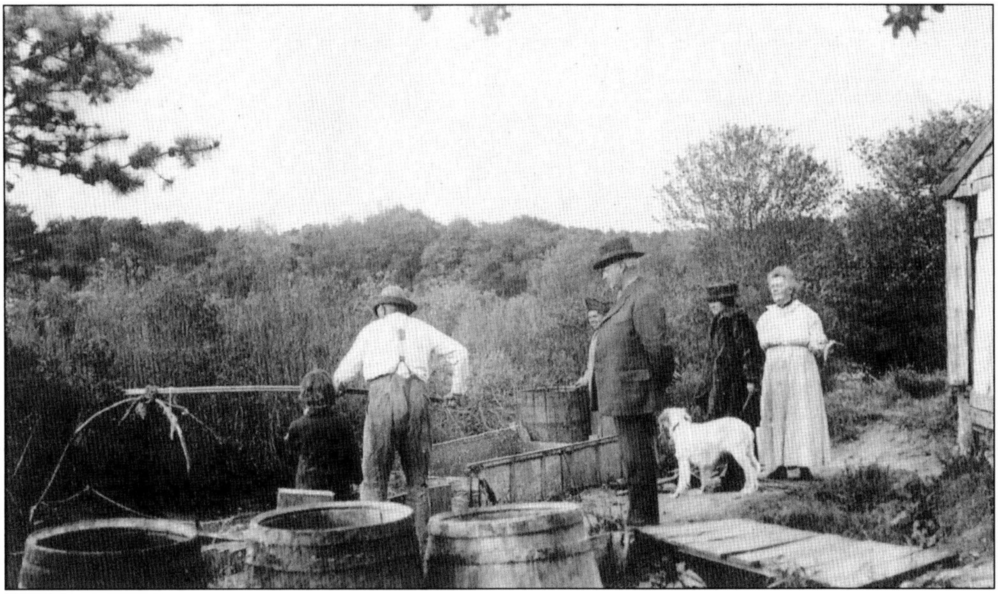

On the Herring Run about 1898, a man is seining for herring. Gear was stored in the fish house at the right. This is one of the most productive herring runs of Cape Cod, with a potential harvest of 600 barrels. Some were "salted and stuck," that is, cleaned, soaked in brine for a week, strung through the eye socket, ready for smoking. In the 1870s, cranberry bogs blocked the herring run to Middle Pond, so a shortcut was dug through a hill in 1880.

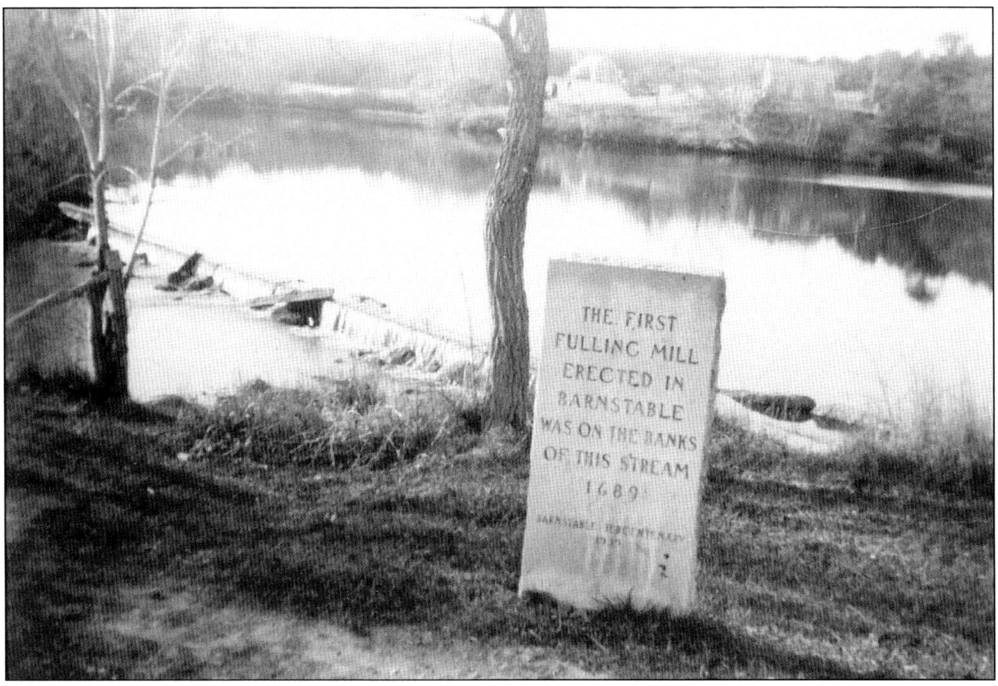

At the tricentennial celebration for the town in 1939, a stone was dedicated to the fulling mill of 1689. The actual site is about a quarter mile upstream, but this location by Mill Pond was visible from the highway. Etched on the stone is "The first fulling mill erected in Barnstable was on the banks of this stream 1689." Thomas Macy was the first to run the mill.

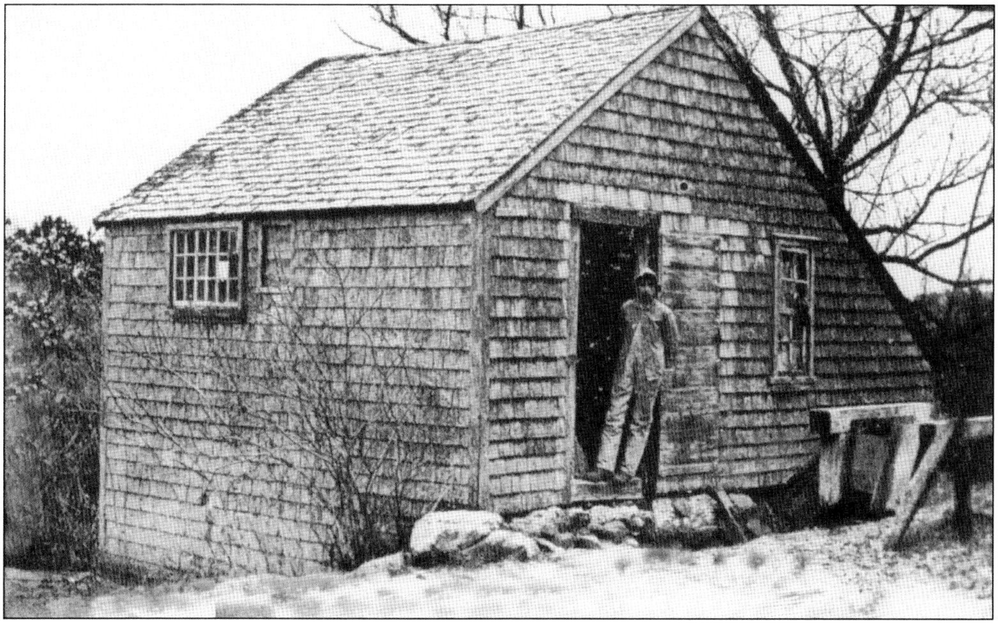

Marston's mill was the last gristmill operating on Cape Cod according to Sandwich historian John Cullity. Here, the last miller, Charles F. Fuller (1861–1936) stands in the doorway facing the street. In 1914, Leonard and Forest Hamblin bought and restored the mill and ran it for a year or so. But low demand, due to supply of industrially ground flour, and greater profit from the Hamblins' cranberry bogs, led to abandonment by 1918.

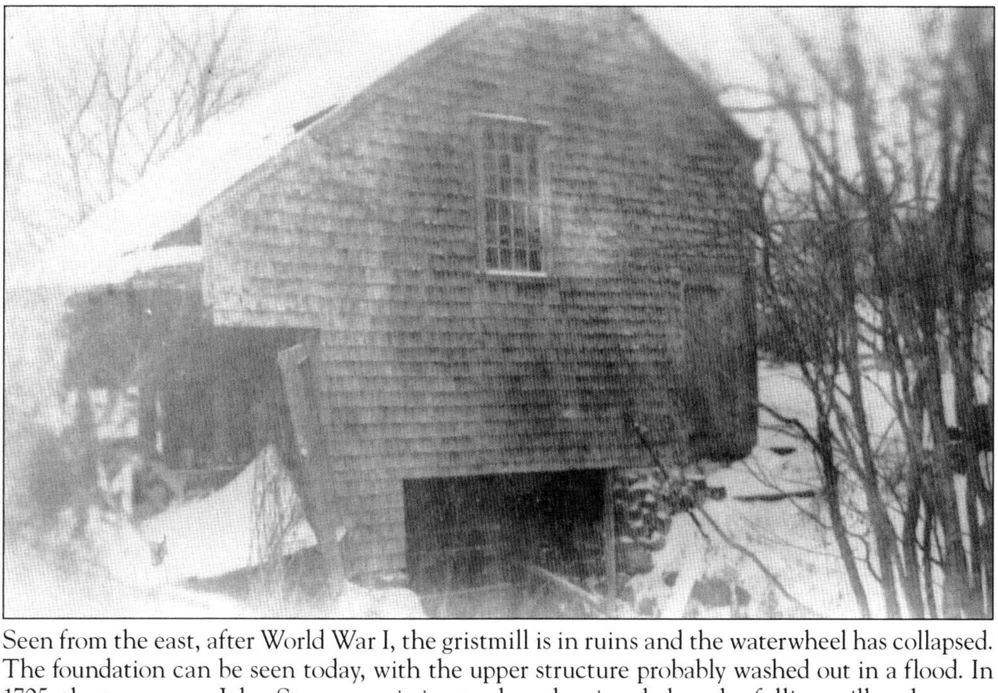

Seen from the east, after World War I, the gristmill is in ruins and the waterwheel has collapsed. The foundation can be seen today, with the upper structure probably washed out in a flood. In 1705, the town gave John Stacy permission to dam the river below the fulling mill and erect a gristmill, with the condition that he not "damnifie or pen back water to hinder ye fulling mill there already set up."

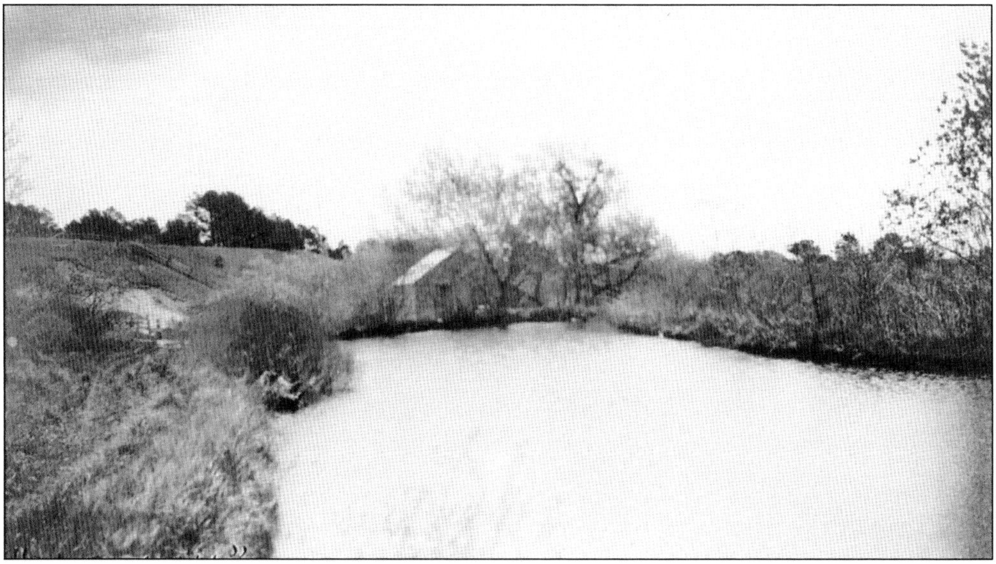

The gristmill lay at the far end of the holding pond, as seen from the east side of the roadway. Wooden gates at the end regulated flow to the waterwheel. This photograph was taken in 1909, when it was owned by the Ryder brothers, Cotuit cranberry farmers. Today, the area to the right is preserved as conservation area of the Barnstable Land Trust, a gift of Cape Cod Savings Bank.

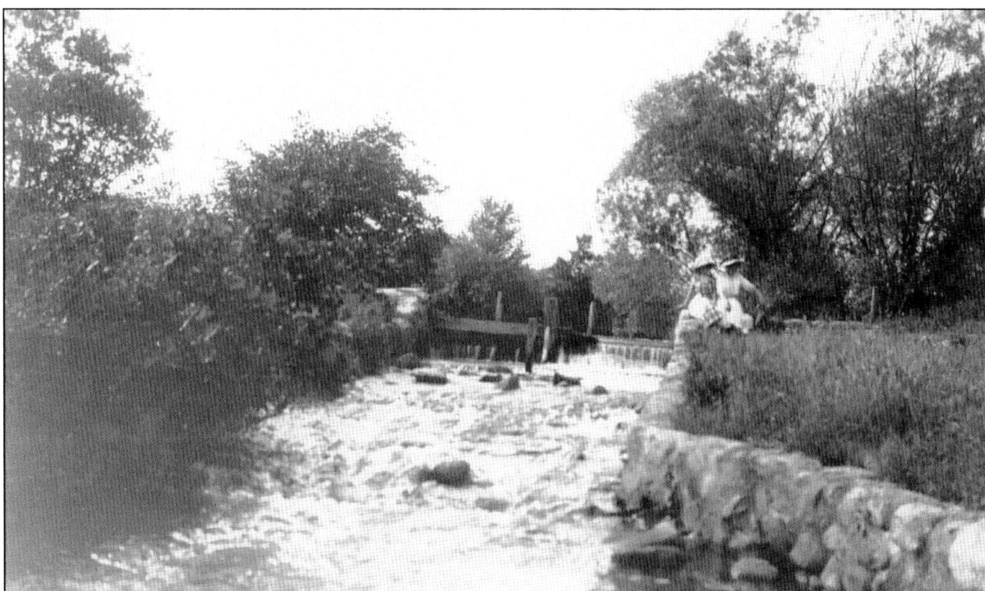

Two ladies are on an outing on the herring run about 1900. There is a peek at Mill Pond in the distance. Once a quiet picnic spot, now the noisy traffic on Massachusetts Route 28 races at the intersection with Route 149, drowning out the music of the water rushing over the rocks on its way to saltwater, only half a mile downstream.

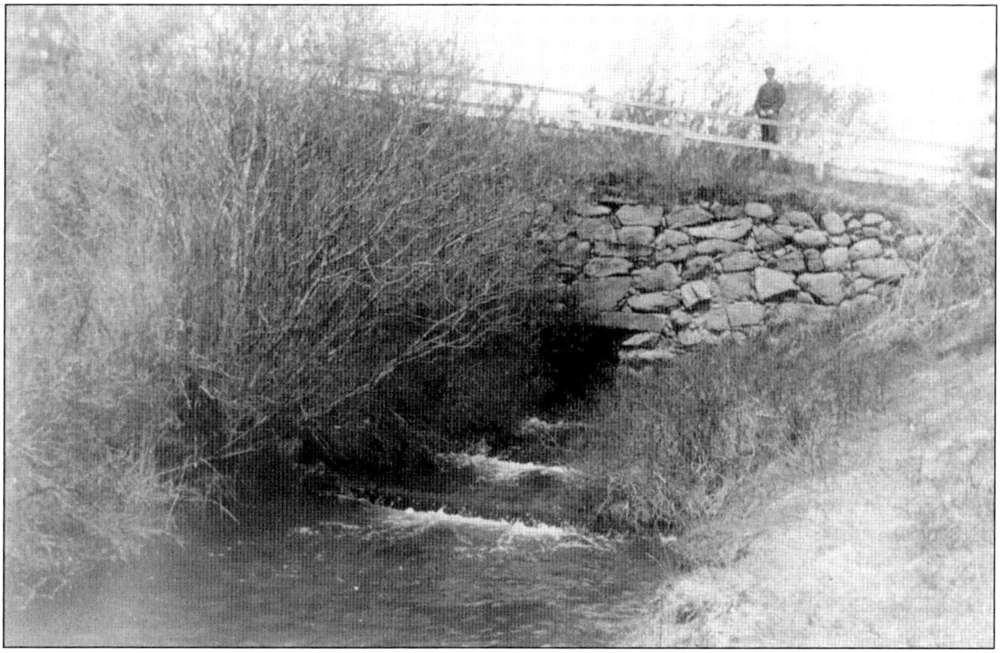

Few people today remember the great stone bridge. A man is standing on the bridge of the main highway across the Marstons Mills River. This image was taken from the east side, where the river runs out of Mill Pond. The bridge is now buried under many feet of sandy fill taken to lessen the dip in the Route 28 in 1928.

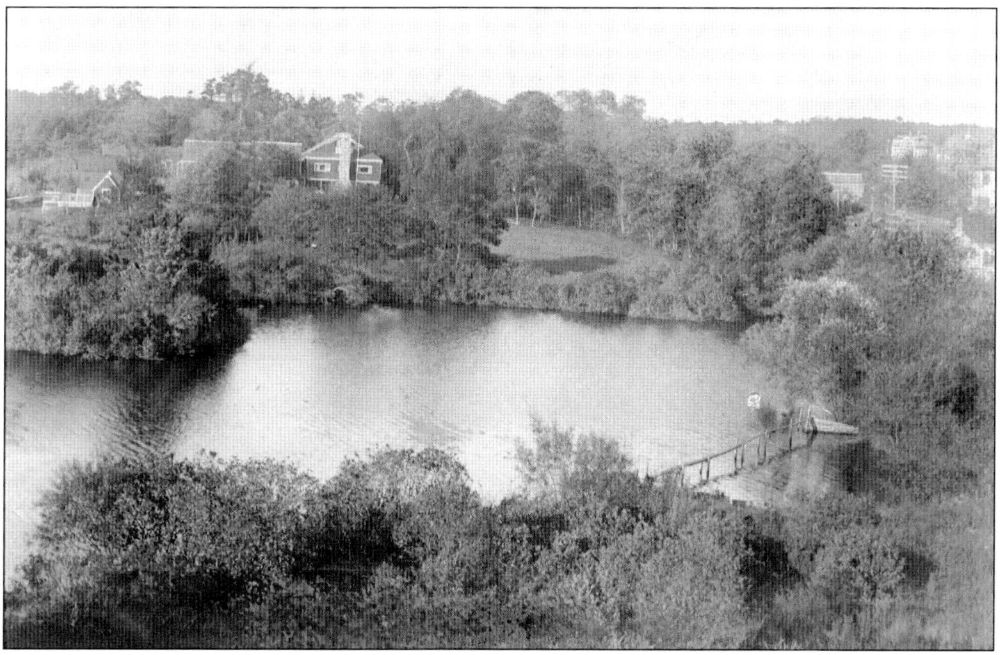

The east end of Mill Pond about 1910 had a structure across the outlet that may be a fish weir. The house is Dr. J. Haydn Higgins's Redwing, the former William Marston house. To the right is the house of blacksmith Revilo Benson, with newly installed telephone poles along the east-west highway.

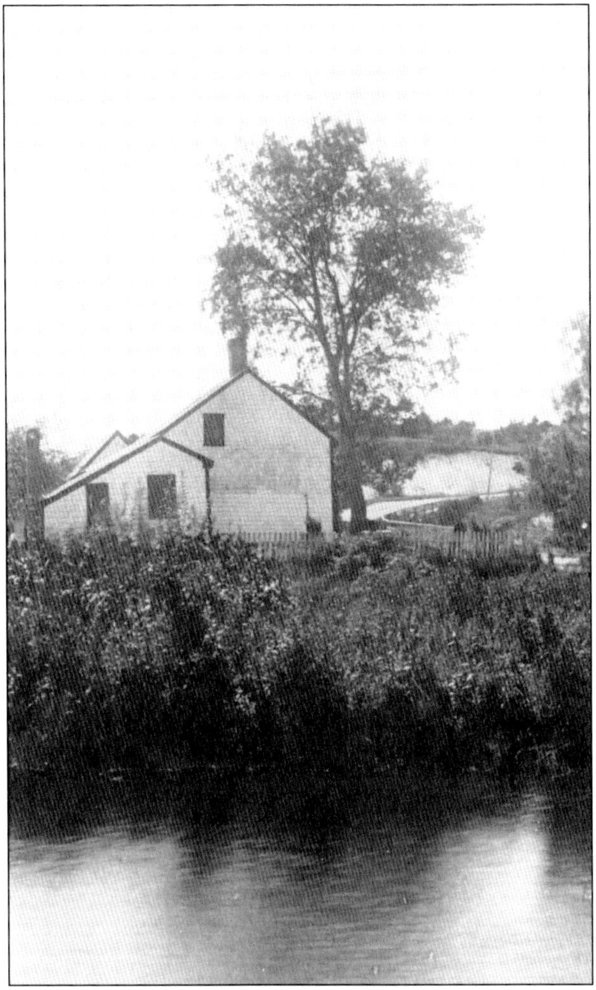

The Reuben Backus house was built after his marriage in 1810 to Patience Marston, daughter of Benjamin Marston Jr. Backus was a dyer, a skill important to the Marstons' business of fulling and carding woolen cloth. The dye ponds were probably near this home. The house lay on a marshy island between the gristmill's holding pond and the stone bridge and herring run. The residence burned down on the Fourth of July some year shortly after 1907.

Nathaniel Hinckley built this house next to the mill for his miller Charles Bassett (1796–1873), who moved the post office here in 1854. On the north side was a huge balm of Gilead, a balsam poplar whose buds produce a fragrant wax in the spring. In this view, taken about 1910, Revilo Benson's blacksmithy is on the hilltop behind the house. The house burned down and was replaced by the small cottage now at the site.

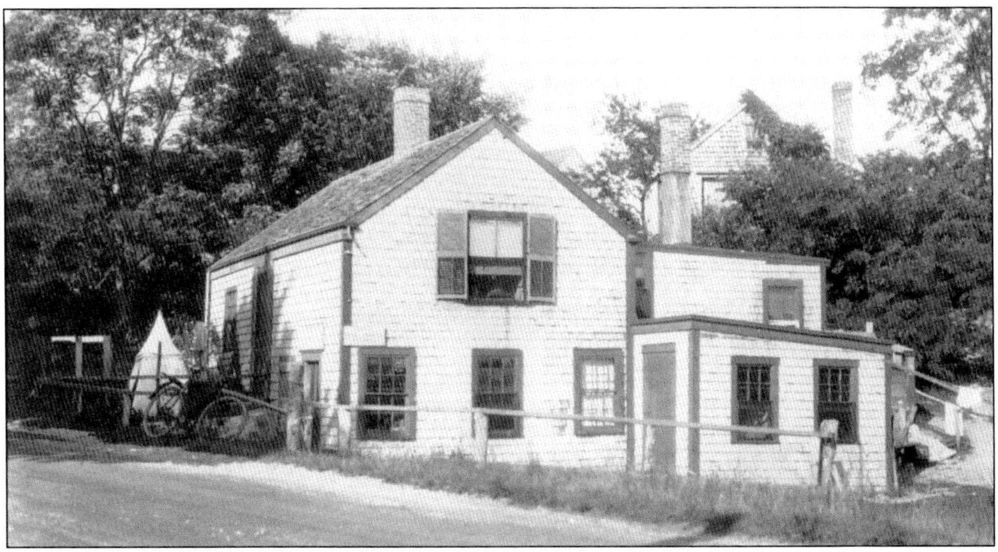

Two

THE VILLAGE CENTER

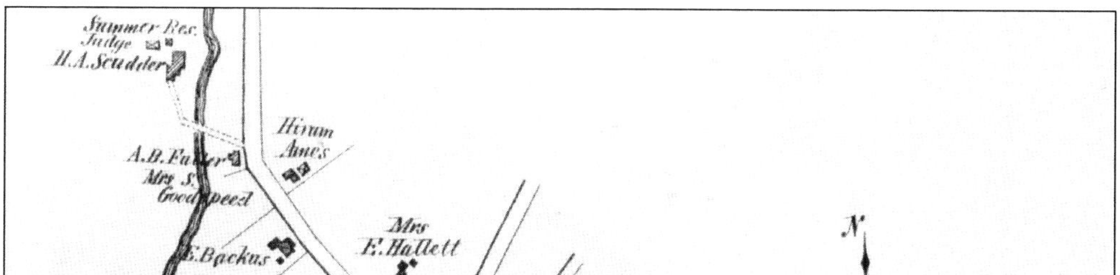

In the Walker Atlas of 1880, the three principal public buildings stand out. There are two blacksmith shops (B.S.Sh.). River Road began at the flume of the gristmill, running between the Marston and Hinckley houses. The road on the east side of the village hall has since disappeared. All trace of the fulling mill and its pond has gone. Instead, the first summer home, that of Judge Scudder, is shown.

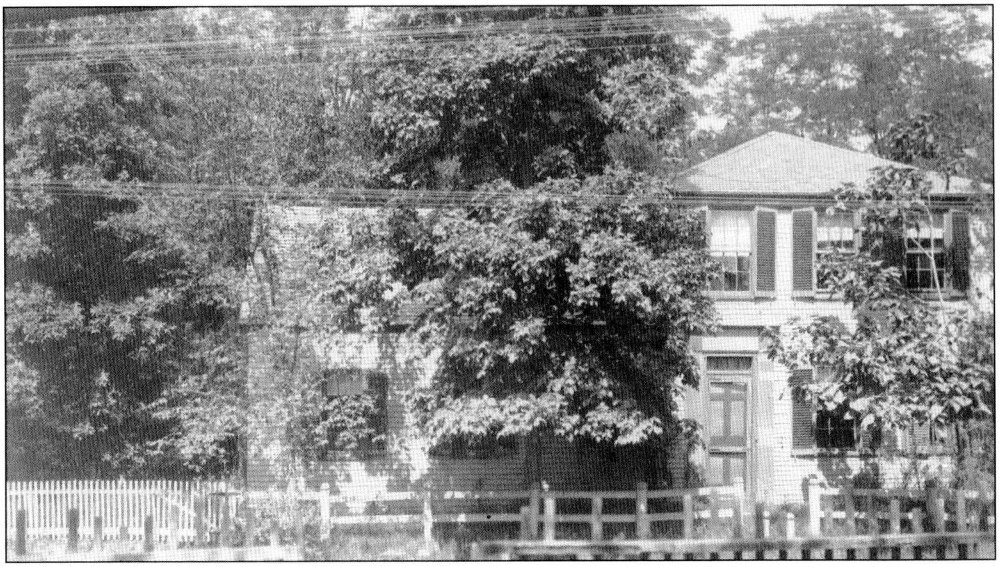

Coming into Marstons Mills from Cotuit was the Nathaniel Hinckley house. Hinckley opened a general store in 1826. In 1828, he added a wing where he ran the first village post office for 25 years. After his widow's death in 1910, the house was sold and moved up Cotuit Road; it was later demolished. Dr. James Haydn Higgins moved the post office wing to the front of his house for his office, and later it was moved up the hill, becoming the home of his daughter Priscilla.

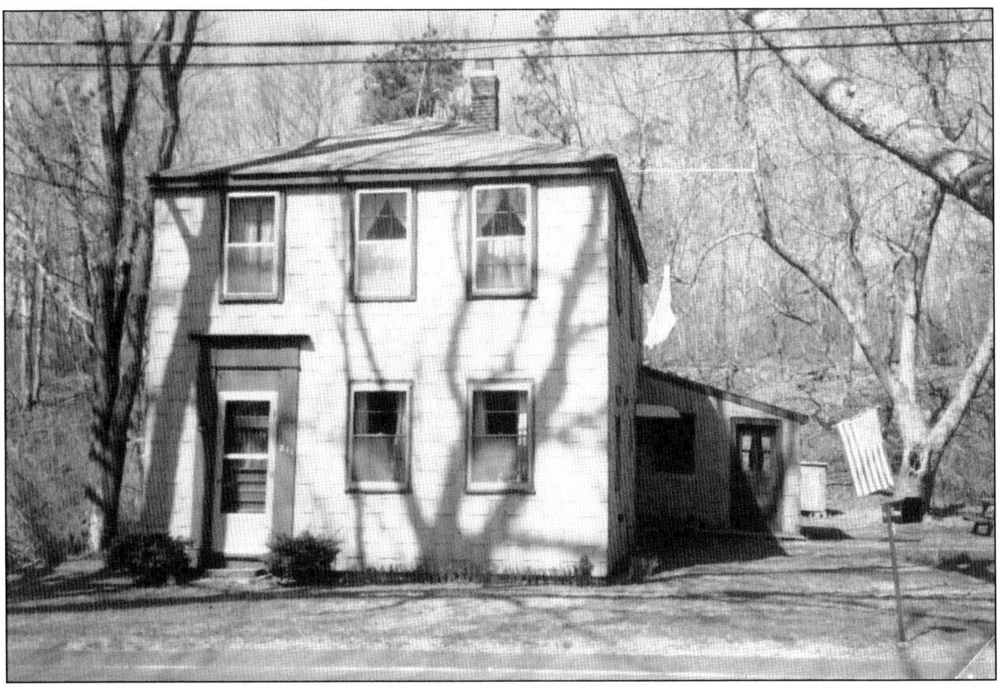

Nathaniel Hinckley dominated the village for most of the 19th century, holding most of the political offices, including that of the first postmaster. He owned the grocery, three gristmills, a third of the fulling mill, and the best farmland. As a politician, the *Barnstable Patriot* called him "the voice of the people." This is the Nathaniel Hinckley house as it appeared in 1986 after being moved about 200 yards up Cotuit Road (Route 149) before being demolished.

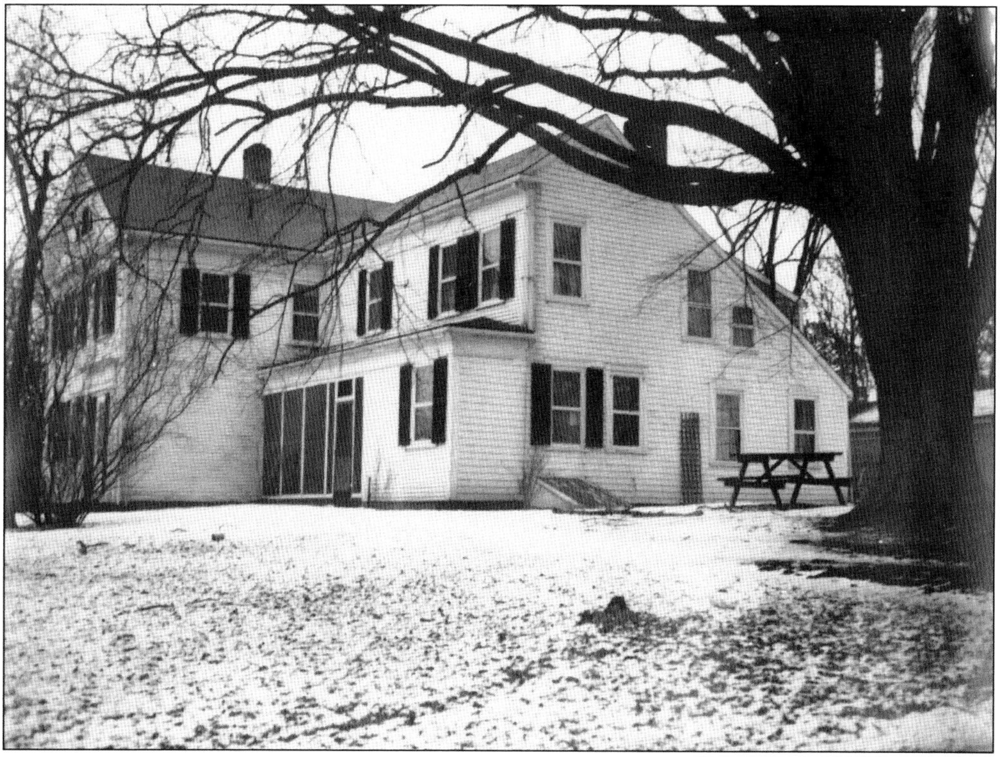

Next to the Nathaniel Hinckley house was the Capt. Josiah Hamblin house, built about 1842 in the Greek Revival style. Captain Hamblin (1811–1873) had made a successful whaling voyage to the Pacific in the Nantucket ship *Phenix,* and continued whaling until the Civil War. The house was inherited by his daughter Isadore, who married Revilo Benson, the last village blacksmith.

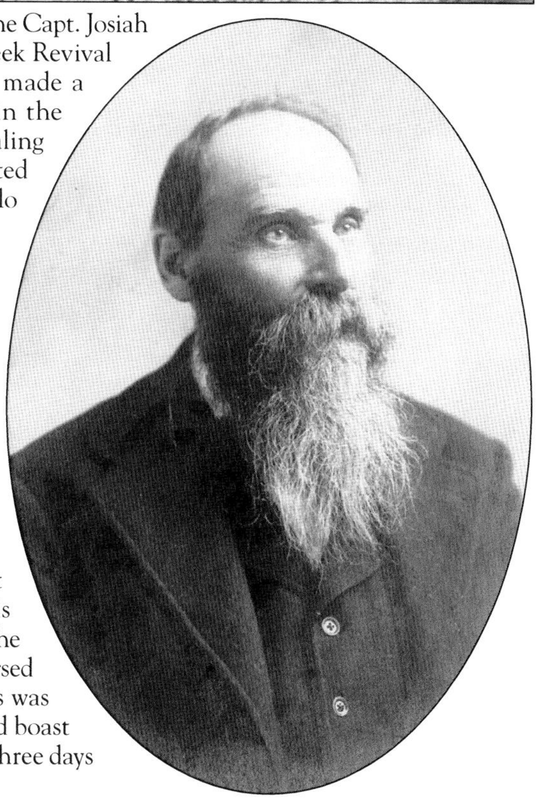

Revilo Benson (1845–1936) was the oldest blacksmith on Cape Cod at the time of his death at age 91. When he came to the village, he found too many men named Oliver, so he reversed his given name to Revilo. His main business was as a farrier, shoeing horses, of which he could boast "sharpening" 200 hooves against slipping in three days of an icy spell in 1891.

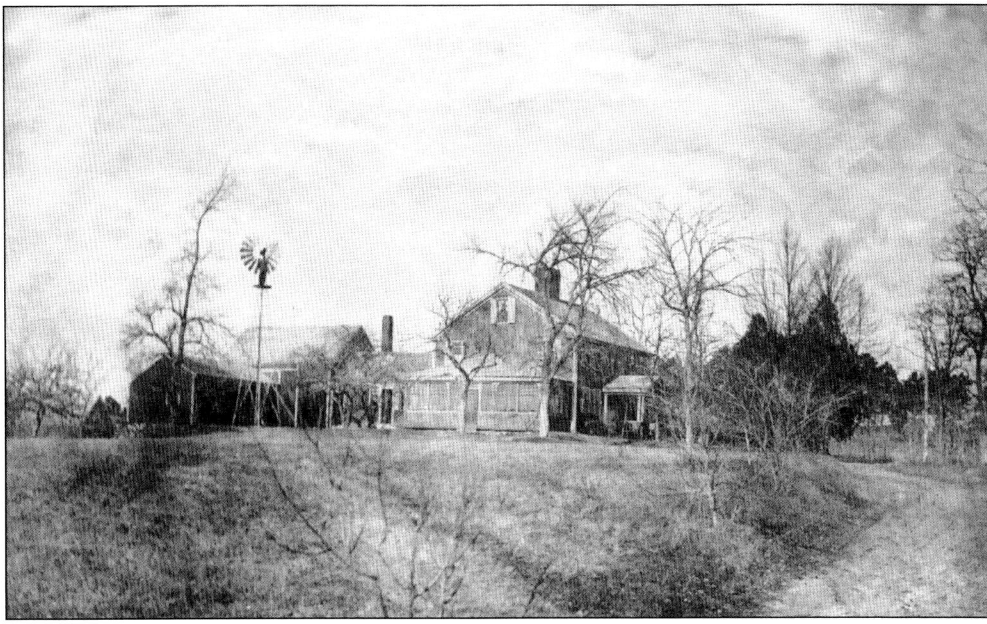

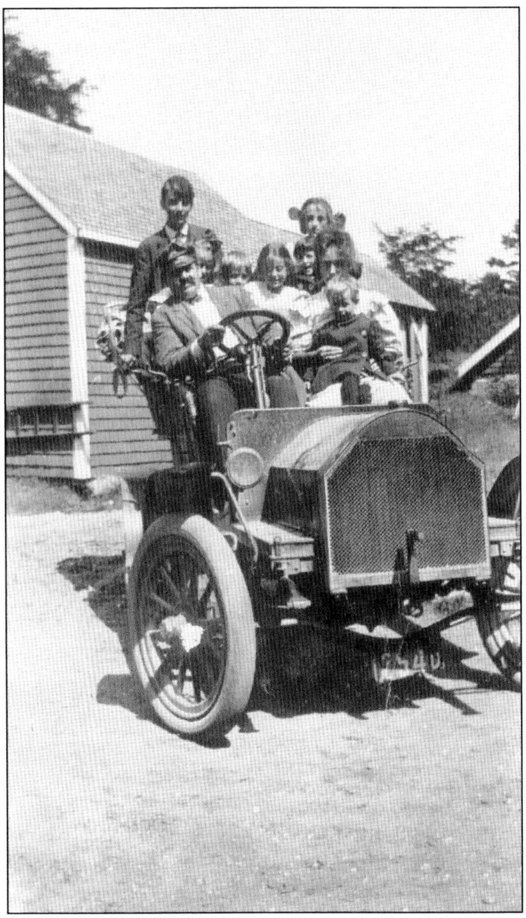

On the left above Mill Pond is the William Marston homestead. This fine Georgian house was built about 1780. Marston (1802–1882) took over Nathaniel Hinckley's grocery. The house is shown in 1910, with River Road on the right separating it from the Nathaniel Hinckley house. The former post office annex has been added onto the front as the doctor's office, with the nimble Dr. Higgins on top of the windmill.

Dr. James Haydn Higgins (1871–1942) was the physician for the local area for 35 years, with his office and home in the William Marston house, which he named Redwing after his childhood home in Minnesota. A technological pioneer, he installed an indoor flush toilet in 1895 and brought the first automobile to Cape Cod. His Stanley Steamer froze up in winter, so this was the gasoline-powered substitute into which he piled his wife, Grace, and their children.

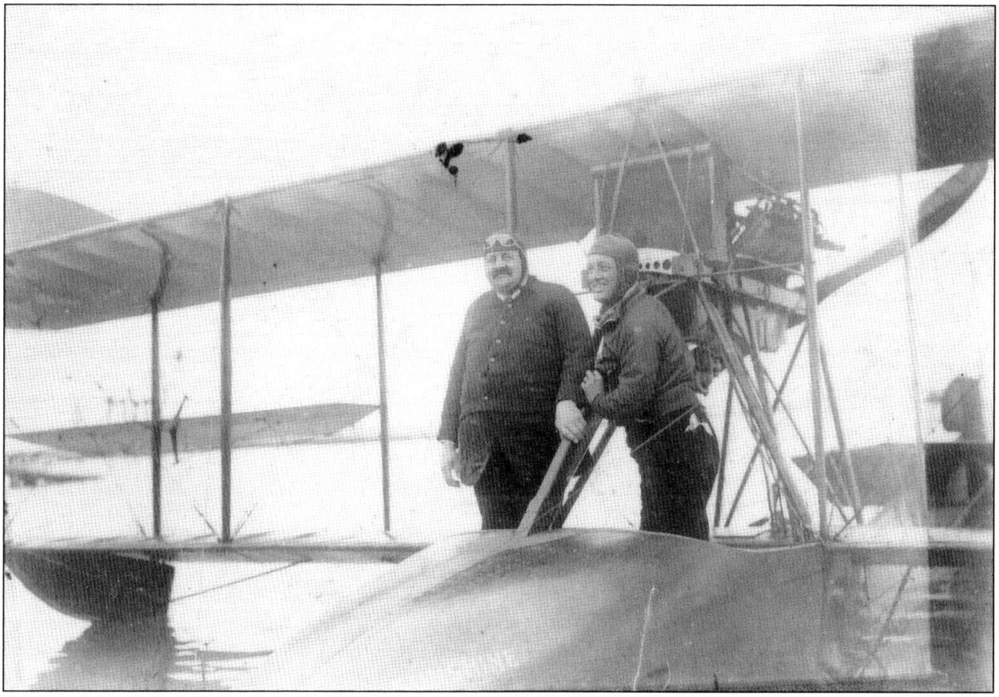

Dr. Higgins learned to fly a plane in 1919 in St. Petersburg, Florida. The Smithsonian National Air and Space Museum has identified this plane as a Benoist Type XIV flying boat, which was flown on the St. Petersburg-to-Tampa line before the war. The wings were 35 feet long, lifting 1,190 pounds at a speed of 64 miles per hour.

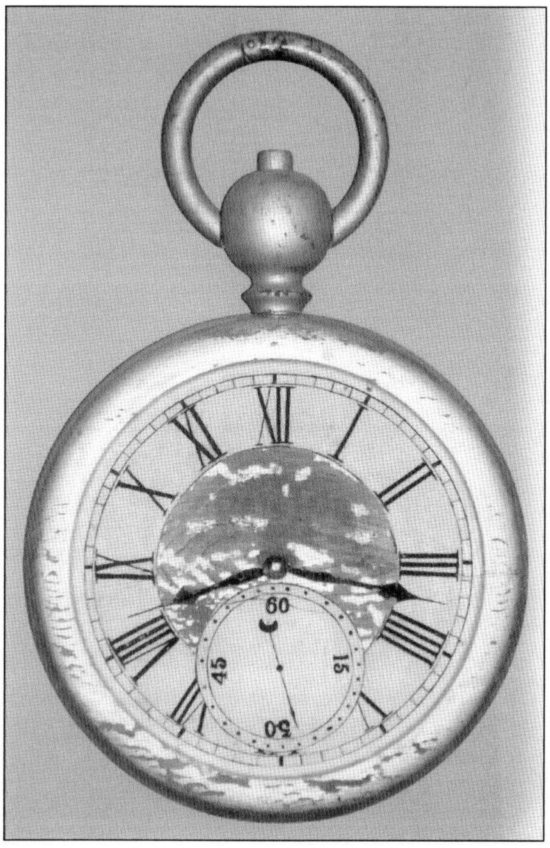

Dr. Higgins's father, David Higgins (1831–1911), joined his son's family in 1901 and set up a small watch repair shop on the street, with this great gold sign out front. He had been an itinerant watchmaker, born in Nova Scotia and trained at the Waltham Watch works, but went to sea with his father, the captain of a schooner to the West Indies. In the Civil War, he served in the 29th New York Volunteers. The shop is now the core of the house where River Road joins Lovell's Lane.

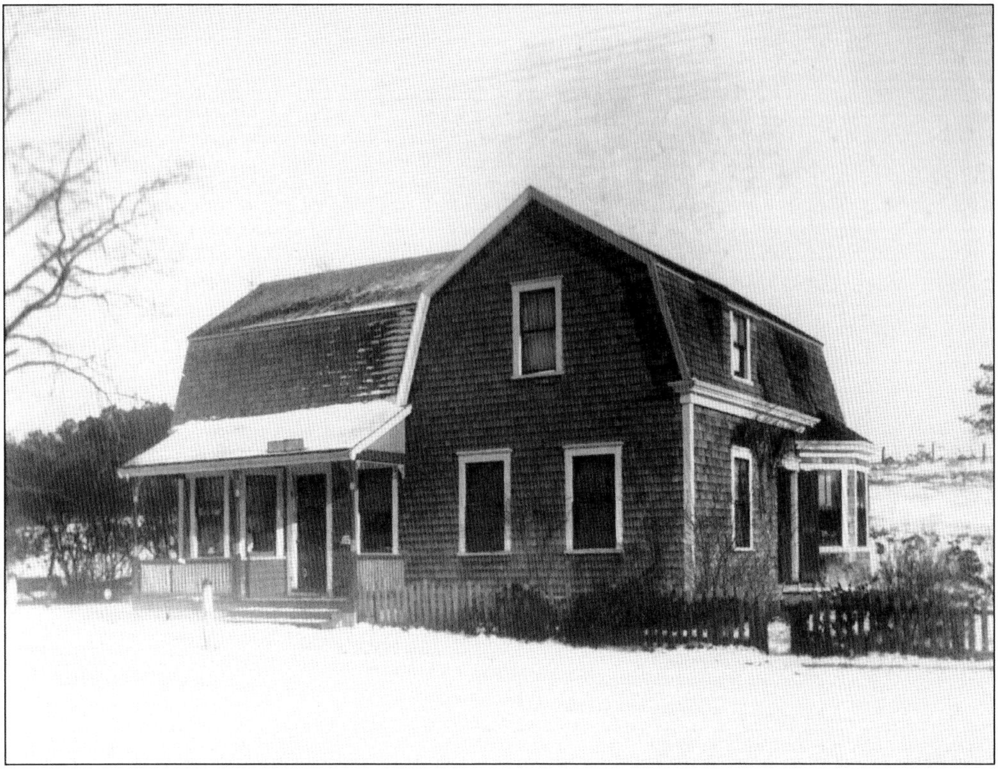

The Old Post House was built in 1897 by Hattie Mecarta (1859–1949), who became the first female local postmistress after her husband, Dennis, died of tuberculosis in 1885. Her term was also the longest—35 years, until 1920. In addition to the post office, this was her home where she ran a variety store selling notions like sewing supplies, postcards, and souvenirs.

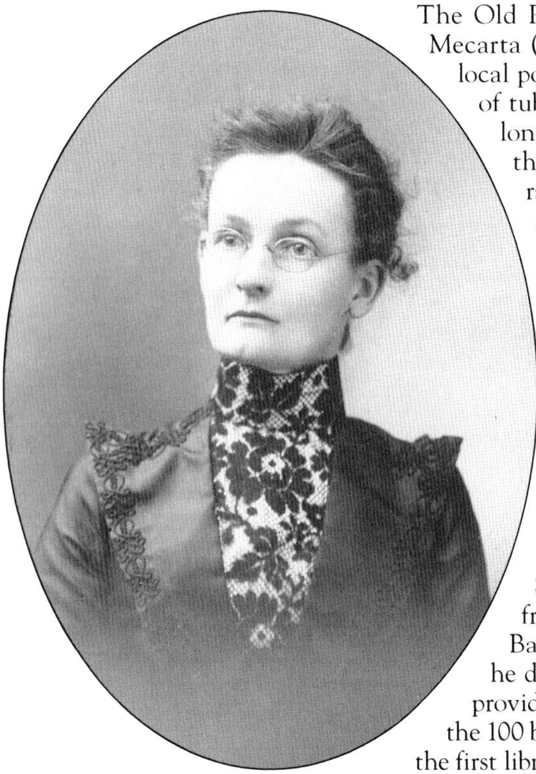

Postmistress Hattie Mecarta was born Harriet Augusta Crocker in Pondsville. She was the daughter of Capt. Joseph Crocker. She married harness-maker Dennis Mecarta from Harwich, who set up shop in the former Bassett house next to the gristmill. When he died, his wife took over the post office. She provided a glass bookcase with seven shelves for the 100 books of the revived library, of which she was the first librarian.

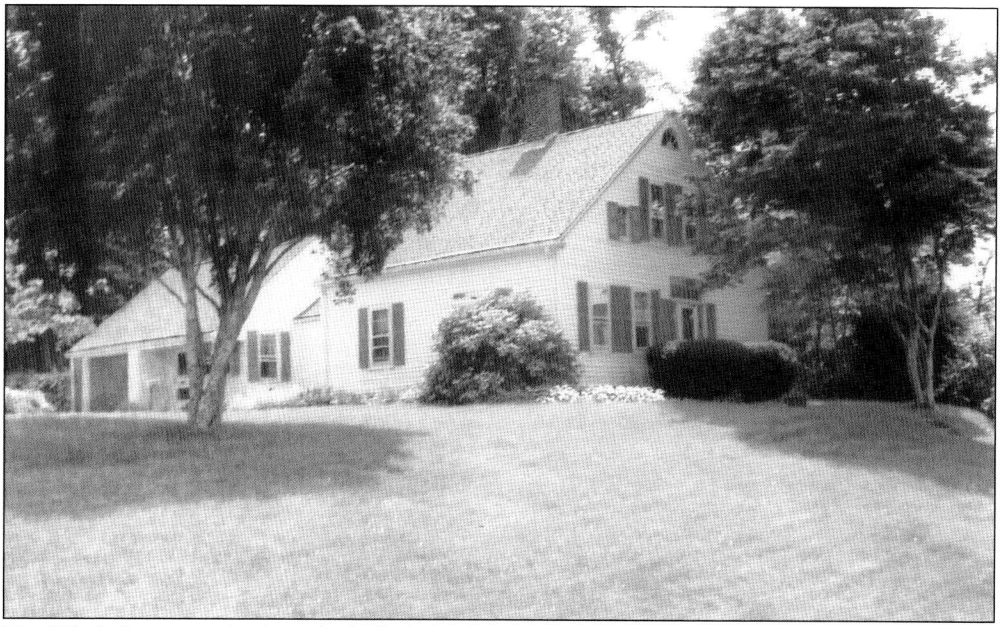

The Weeks house was built on the hillside by shipwright Capt. Evander White in 1838. In 1843, the blacksmith Robinson Weeks (1816–1904) paid $750 for the house and built his blacksmith shop nearer the road. He joined the forty-niners and spent eight years in California as a blacksmith. His son Rev. William Marston Weeks was a minister in Wisconsin Territory. Robinson's grandson William R. Weeks inherited the house and was a village character who sported a silver-tipped cane.

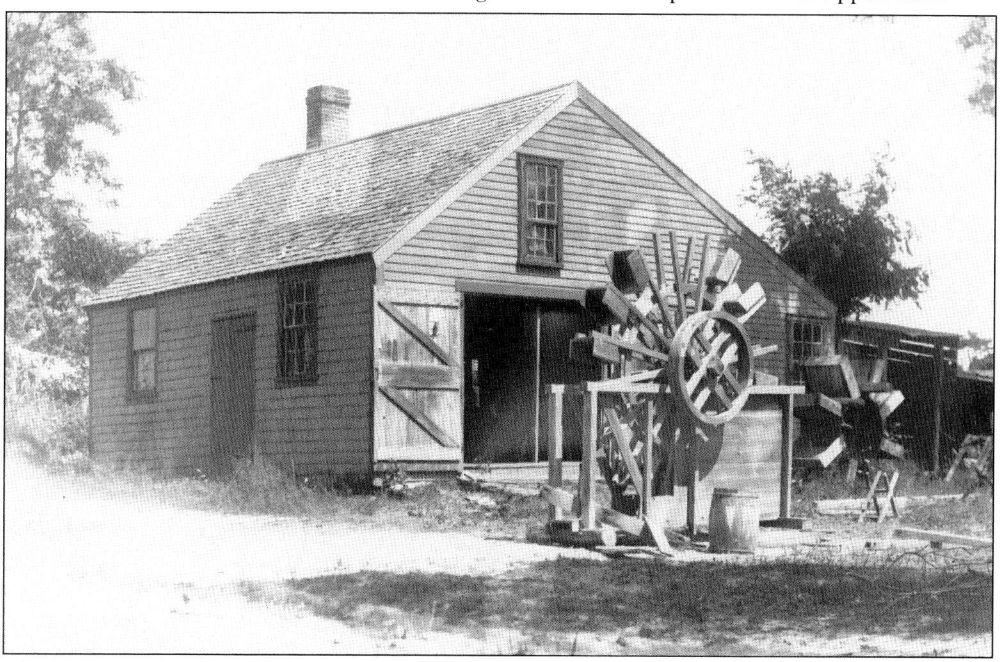

The blacksmith shop of Robinson Weeks not only shoed horses, but also repaired wagons, buggies, farm equipment and tools, and gristmill and fulling mill machinery. Here, the waterwheel is under repair. Weeks's forge was on Main Street below his home on Hilltop Drive in 1843 for 40 years. A singing blacksmith, he took Cape Cod choirs to the Peace Jubilees in Boston in 1869 and 1872.

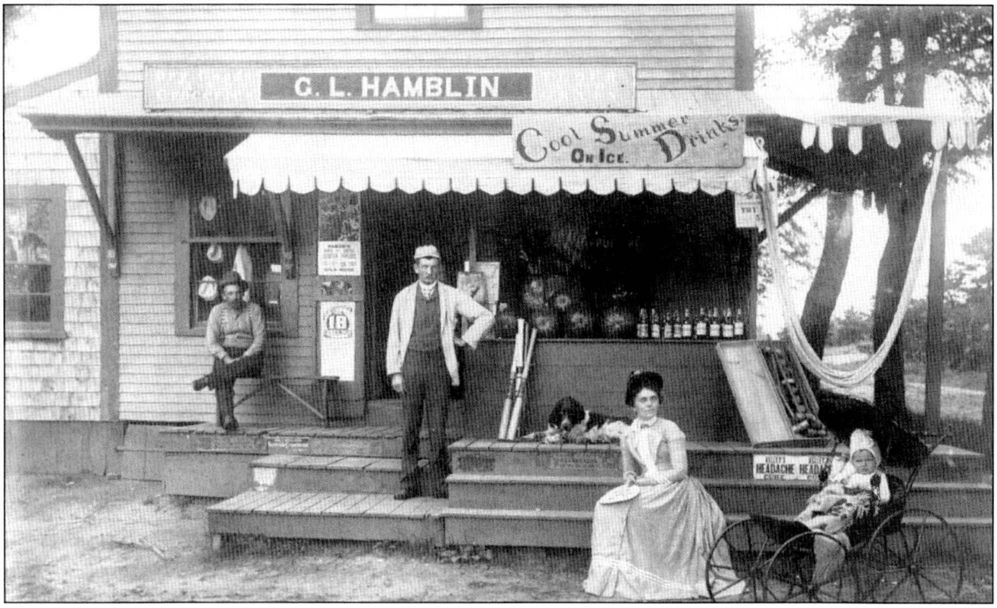

In 1881, Lewis Nelson Hamblin (1849–1932) moved an old store belonging to Capt. Dennis Sturgis from Centerville to the center of this village, and bought the stock of William Marston's grocery. He sold half interest to his nephew George Lewis Hamblin (1860–1934), shown here with his wife, Nancy "Nannie" Crocker, and an infant child.

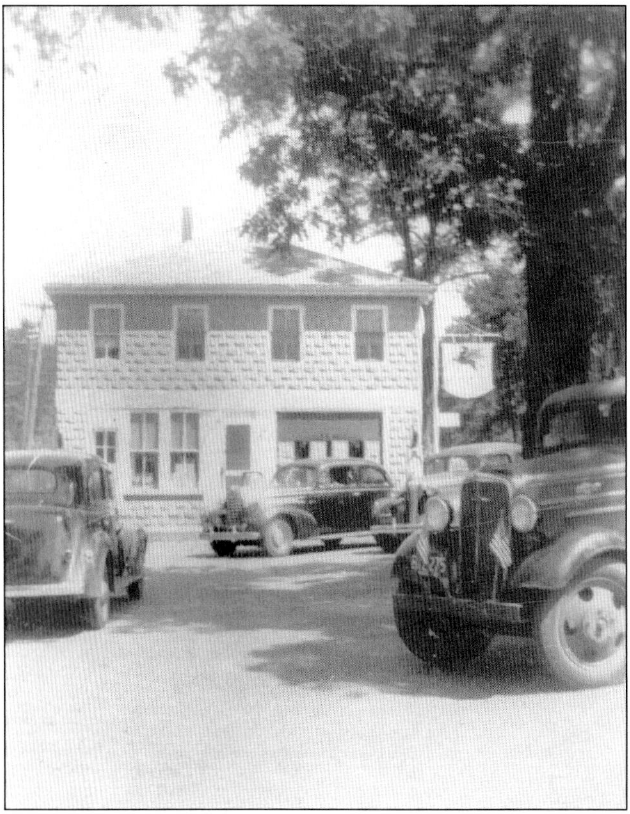

In 1914, Loring Goodspeed Jones Sr. (1894–1974) demolished the old vermin-infested Hamblin store and built the present Cash Market of concrete blocks made nearby by George Hamblin's son Leonard. In 1915, Jones put in the first gas pump, which even fueled airplanes. In 1925, he began selling cars, displayed behind big glass windows. In 1926, the grocery was revived with a soda fountain and ice cream parlor.

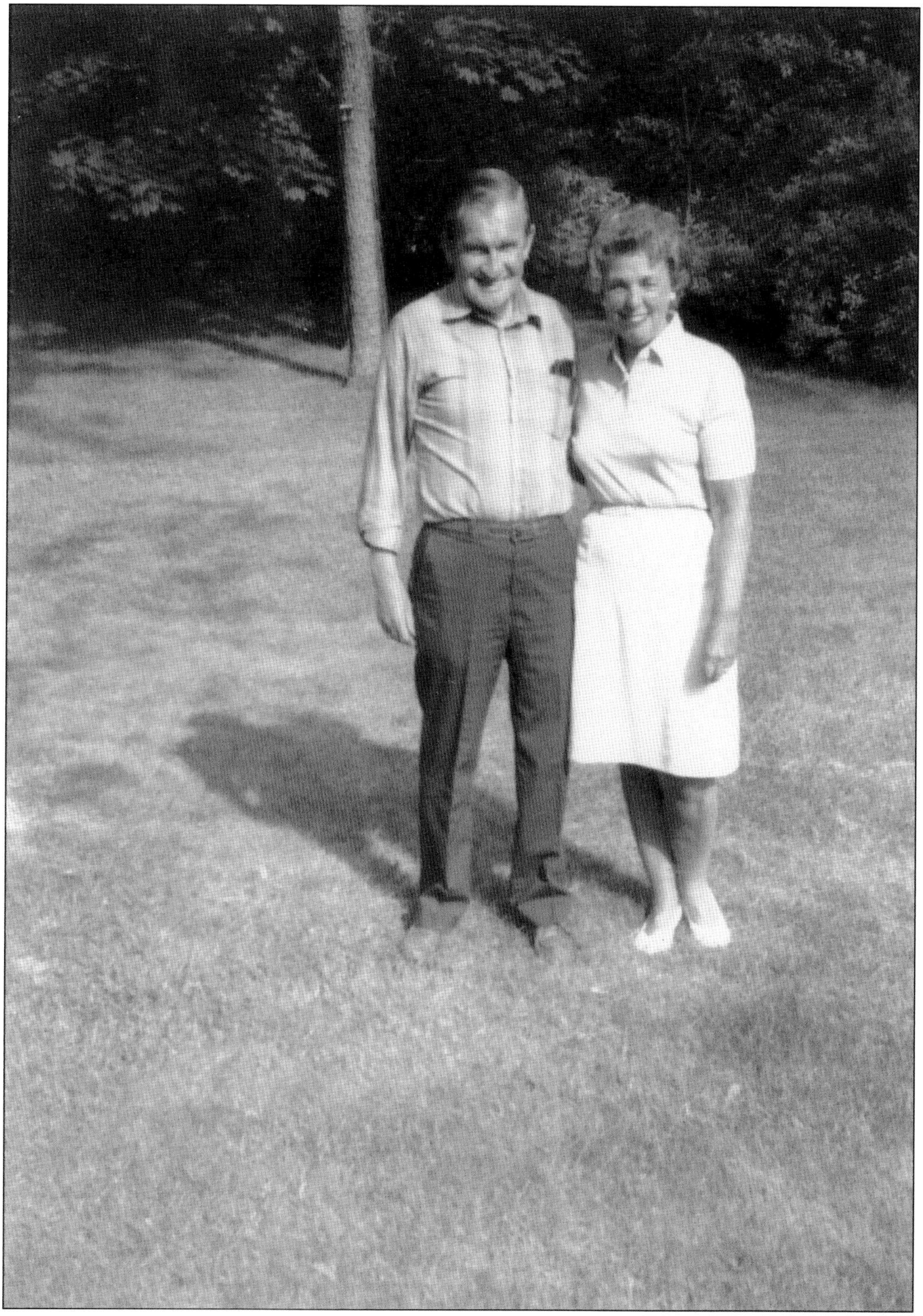

Loring Goodspeed Jones Jr. (1918–2005), known as "Junior," and his wife, Adele Pond Jones (born 1923), ran the store and post office. As a girl, Adele rode beside her father, the rural mailman. She was clerk at the post office for many years. The couple was very active in village activities and in the Methodist church.

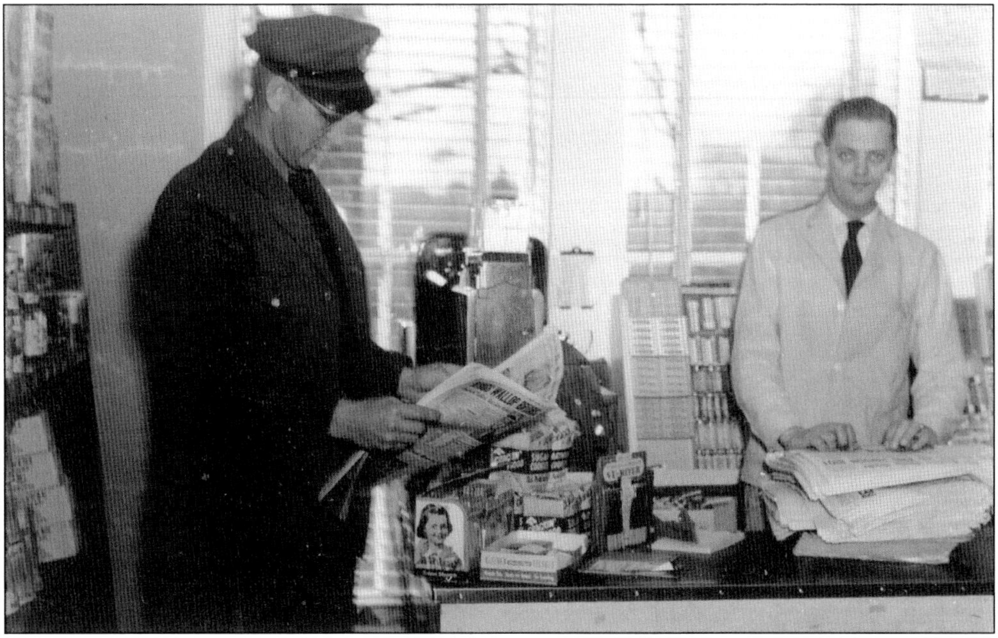

In 1949, Loring Jones Jr. took in a partner, Frank McClusky (1917–1982). He came home from service in the Army in World War II with the ambition of being a grocer, and found it in 30 years at the Cash Market, where he trained himself to be a butcher. Here, the local policeman checks the latest tabloid news.

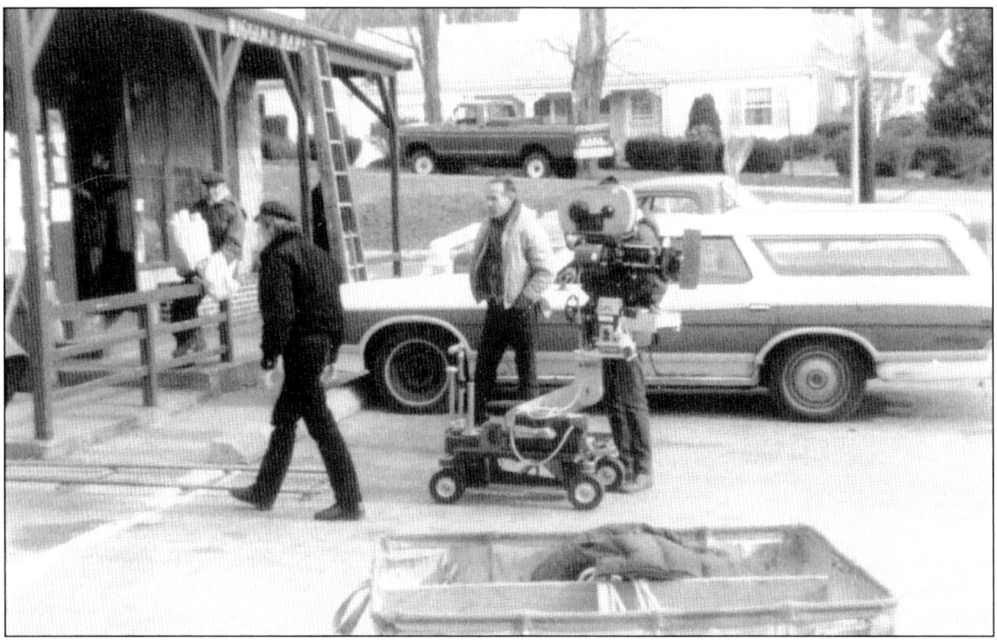

The Cash Market starred as "Wiggins Market" in the 1986 movie *Where Are the Children?*, in which Jill Clayburgh plays a Cape Cod mother whose two children are kidnapped, reviving the terror of her previous conviction of murder of two earlier children, for which she had been acquitted. The movie was directed by Bruce Malamuth and based on the novel by Mary Higgins Clark. The man in black is the actor Frederic Forrest.

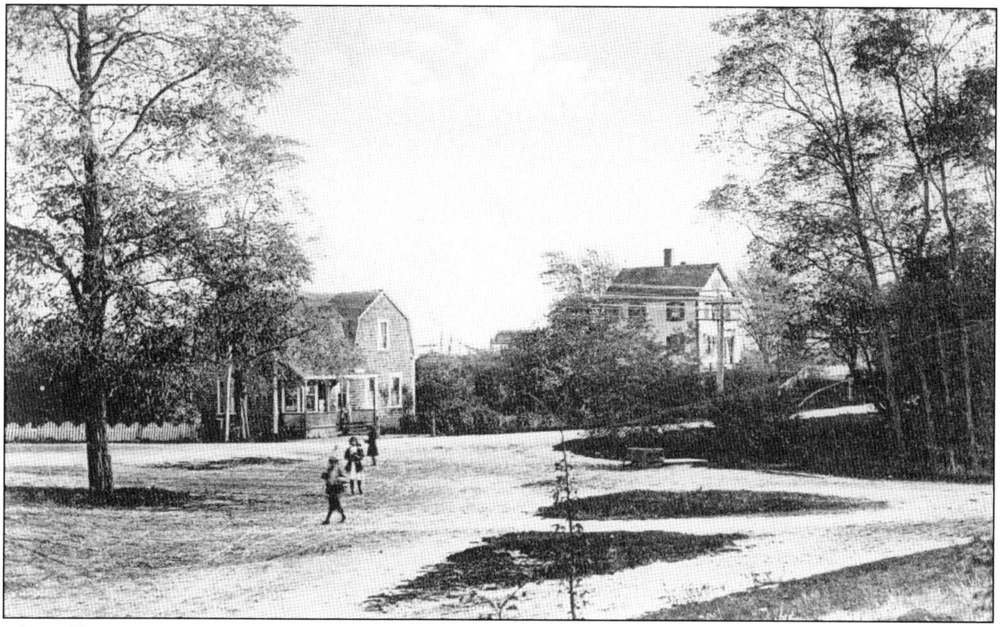

The village center is seen from Foster Crocker's store before 1914. In the center is Hattie Mecarta's post office and store; at the right is Revilo Benson's home (formerly whaling Capt. Josiah Hamblin's), with Benson's blacksmith shop behind; in the middle ground are the horse trough and pump; and at the far left, in front of the grocery store, is the great honey locust that died in 1989, at 154 years old.

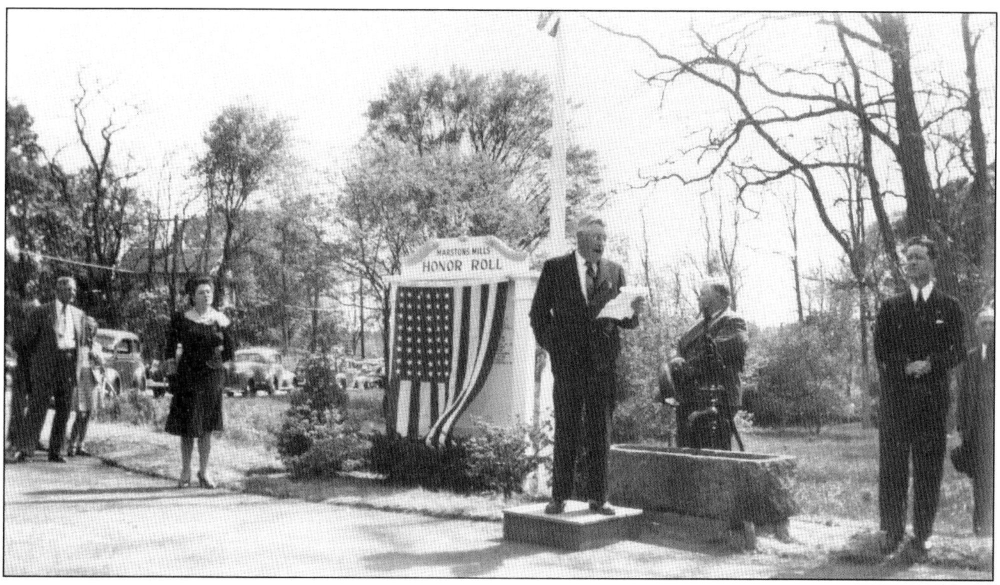

During World War II, the names of local men in service were posted on this board beside the pump and watering trough in the village center. The tribute was read by Chester Crocker (1881–1962) born in Newtown and a selectman from 1929 until 1950. To his right are Sheriff Lauchlan Crocker and Rev. Jackson Butler. At the left is Mary Carm Hamblin. (Courtesy of Charles E. Hamblin.)

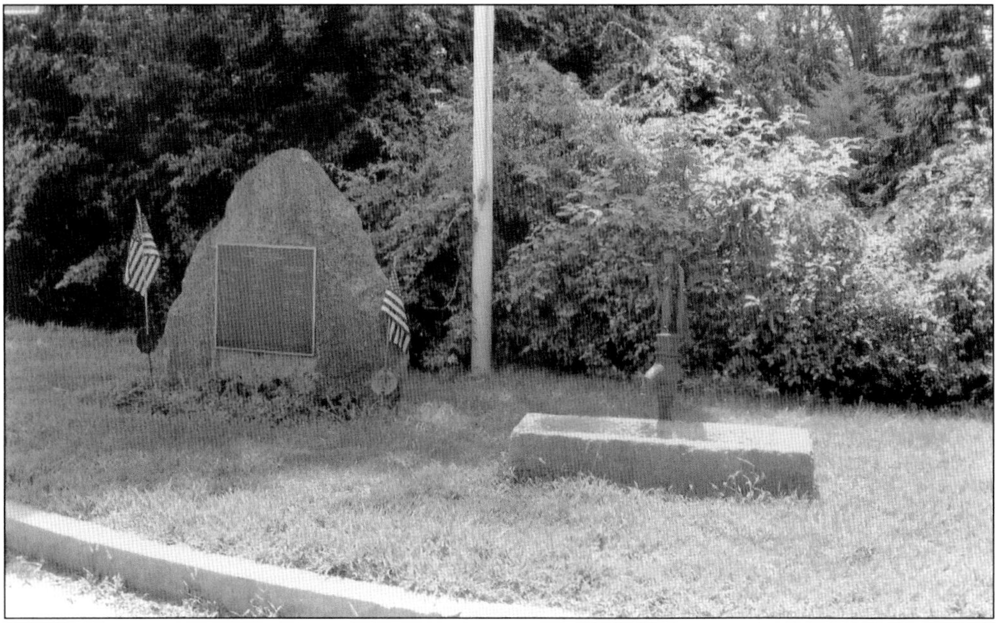

Following the war, in 1949, the servicemen's board was replaced by a brass plaque on a granite boulder honoring all the veterans of both wars. In 2002, a new plaque listed the names of all 86 veterans—10 from World War I, and 76 from World War II. The granite horse trough dates from the 1880s, when the town installed the pump on a public well.

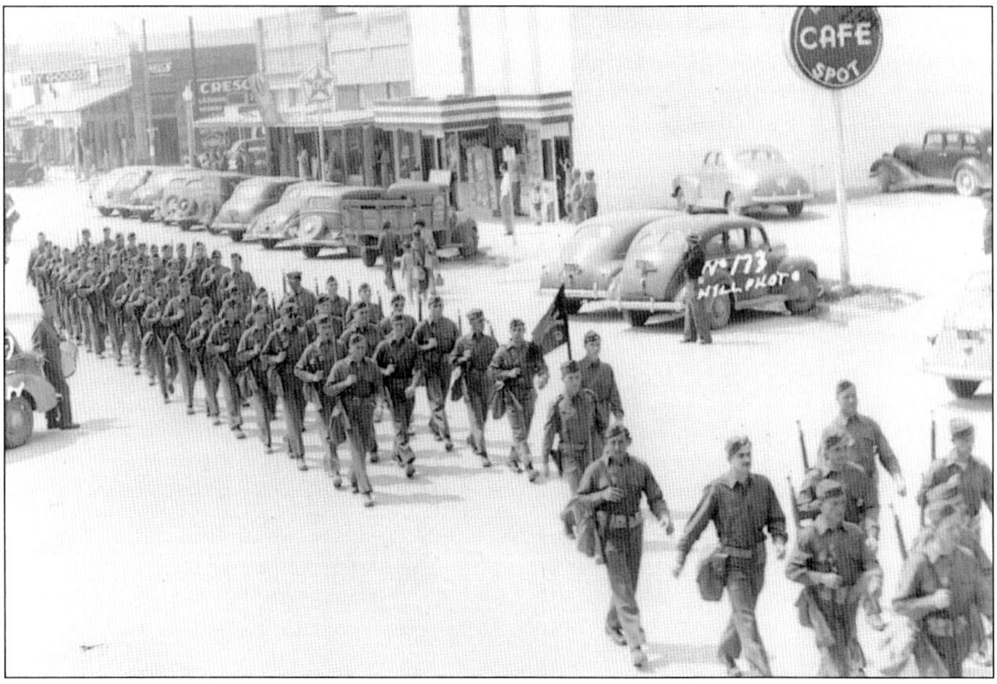

The first Marstons Mills men to serve in World War II were with the 211th Anti-aircraft Artillery of the Massachusetts National Guard. One of the earliest units mobilized in 1940, it was sent to Camp Hulen, Texas, for training, but dispersed to other units after Pearl Harbor. Here, Charles E. Hamblin carries the guidon of the 211th. (Courtesy of Charles E. Hamblin.)

Three of the first soldiers in World War II were Marstons Mills men, from left to right, Charles Hamblin, Braddock Childs, and Seth Hamblin. In the background are tents, probably at Camp Edwards, before Marstons Mills carpenters built barracks there. The soldiers went by train to Fort Hulen at Palacios, on the coast of Texas, then to California. (Courtesy of Charles E. Hamblin.)

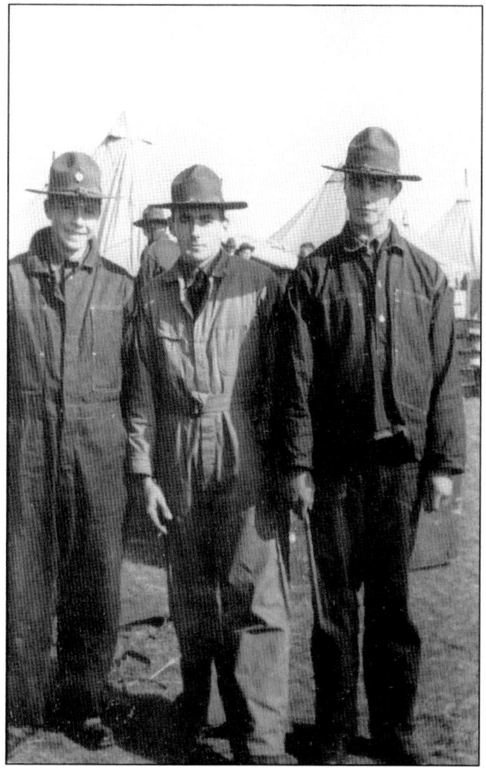

Women made their contributions to the war effort, too. The daughter of storekeeper Loring Jones Sr., Lena Frances Jones (born 1922, later Childs) drove a freight conveyor called a mule at Camp Edwards in 1943–1944. The Signal Corps photograph is captioned "There is nothing harder to drive than a mule, but perhaps all that is needed is a feminine touch." (Courtesy of Lena Jones Childs.)

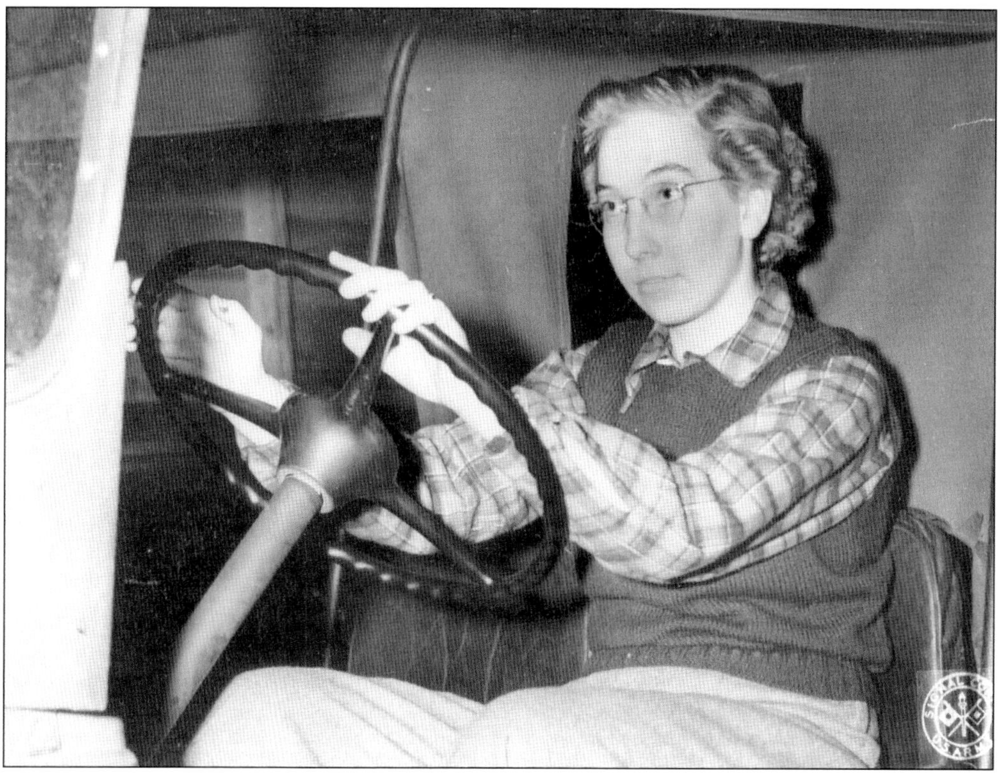

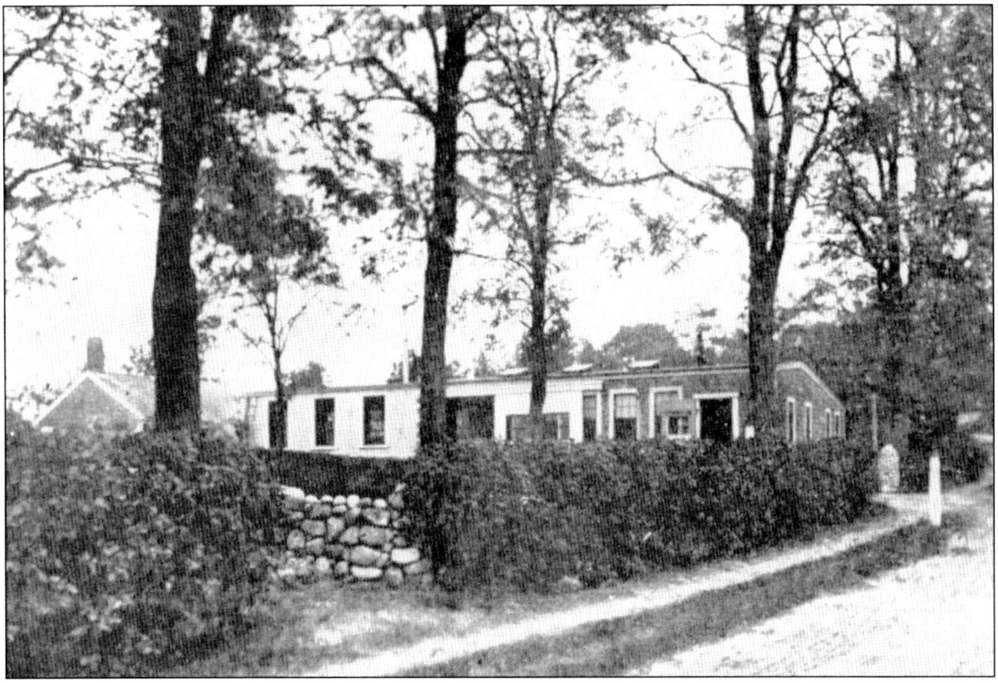

In 1891, Isaac J. Greene built this paint shop between River Road and Mill Pond, where he did a busy business painting signs and carriages—as many as 50 horse-drawn vehicles in the spring of that year. On the right is the shop he built for G. Webster Hallett to carry on his business as a tinsmith and selling stoves. Greene was an ardent hunter and a yacht master for wealthy clients.

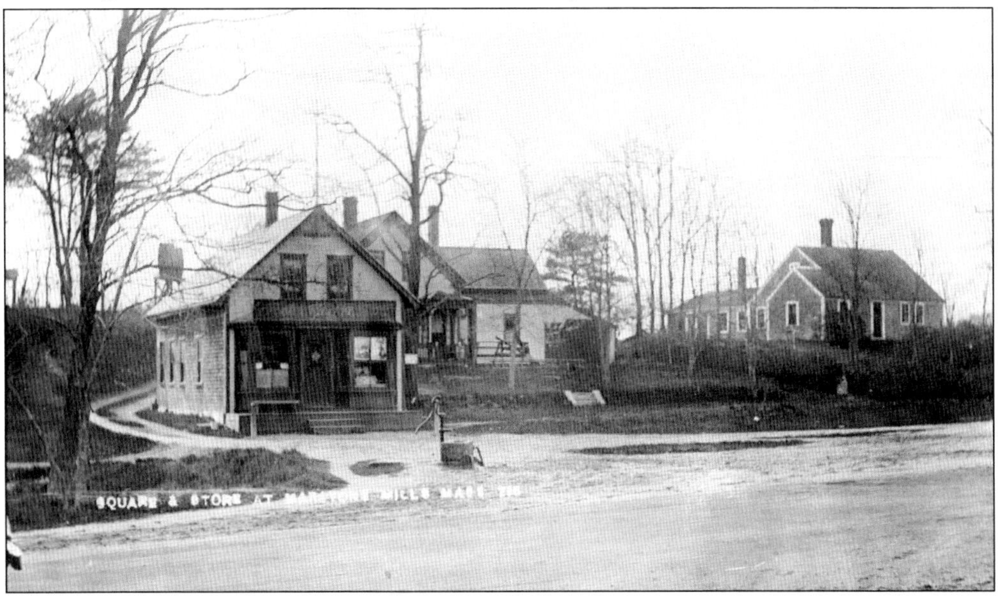

Foster Crocker's Hardware Store is shown about 1905. In 1885, Foster Crocker (1857–1923), son of whaling captain Oliver Crocker, in 1885, bought the house of the seaman Arthur F. Greene (at the rear), and built a mechanic shop facing River Road. This "celebrated machinist" sold and repaired Stanley Steamers, pumps for cranberry bogs, clay crushers for the brickworks, and Singer sewing machines. The Isaac Greene house is pictured on the right.

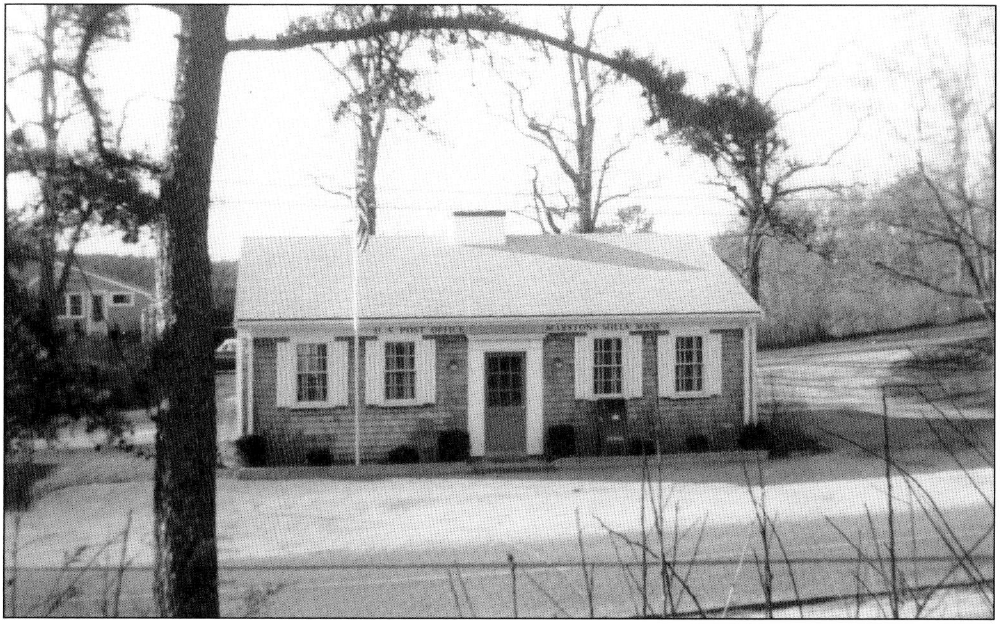

In 1941, storekeeper Loring Jones Jr. (1918–2005) became the youngest postmaster in the United States, at age 22. He moved service from the Gifford Farm to the back of the Cash Market, then to the old Arthur Marston house behind the store. In 1959, he built this Cape Cod style building. The village post office was here for 26 years—until 1985, when the present one was built on the hill beyond this.

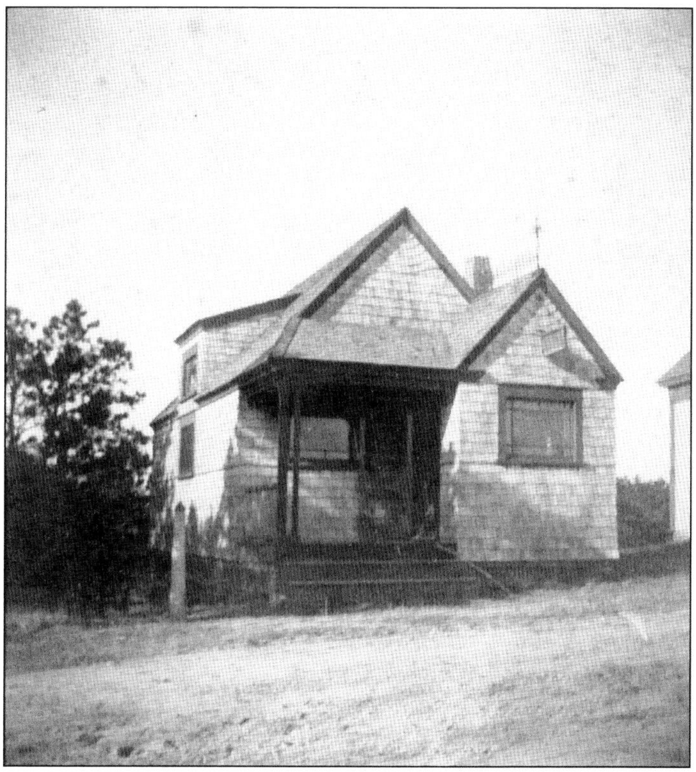

This shows the library shortly after it was constructed in 1893 for $425 by local builder Edward H. Fuller. On two earlier occasions, in 1797 and 1888, Marstons Mills shared library space with Cotuit, but it was not until 1891 that books were located in the village itself, in Hattie Mecarta's post office. Local physician Frank Pierce led a drive to build a permanent home. Blacksmith Weeks gave the land south of Liberty Hall.

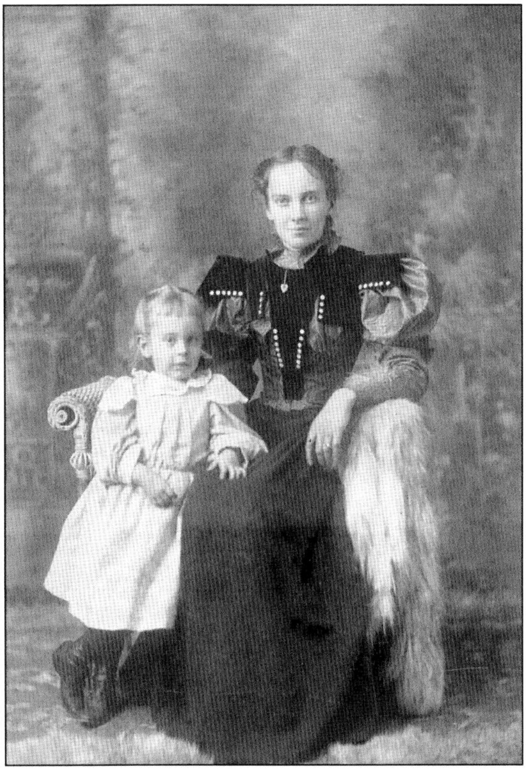

Longtime librarian Caroline "Carrie" Fuller Coleman (1865–1937) lived near the library. She served for a quarter of a century, from 1908 to 1936. She was first paid 50¢ a week for opening the building for one afternoon and one evening a week, including lighting a fire. After 11 years, her pay was raised to $1 a week. In this 1897 photograph, she is shown with her four-year-old daughter Alice, who later became librarian.

The first expansion of the tiny library came in 1981, under librarian Barbara Conathan, when mover Bob Hayden relocated the former Osterville Radio and TV store in two sections from Main Street in Osterville three miles to the south side of the original library. The added 1,500 square feet tripled the size of the library. Conathan was also librarian when the Living History Project began collecting oral histories of old residents.

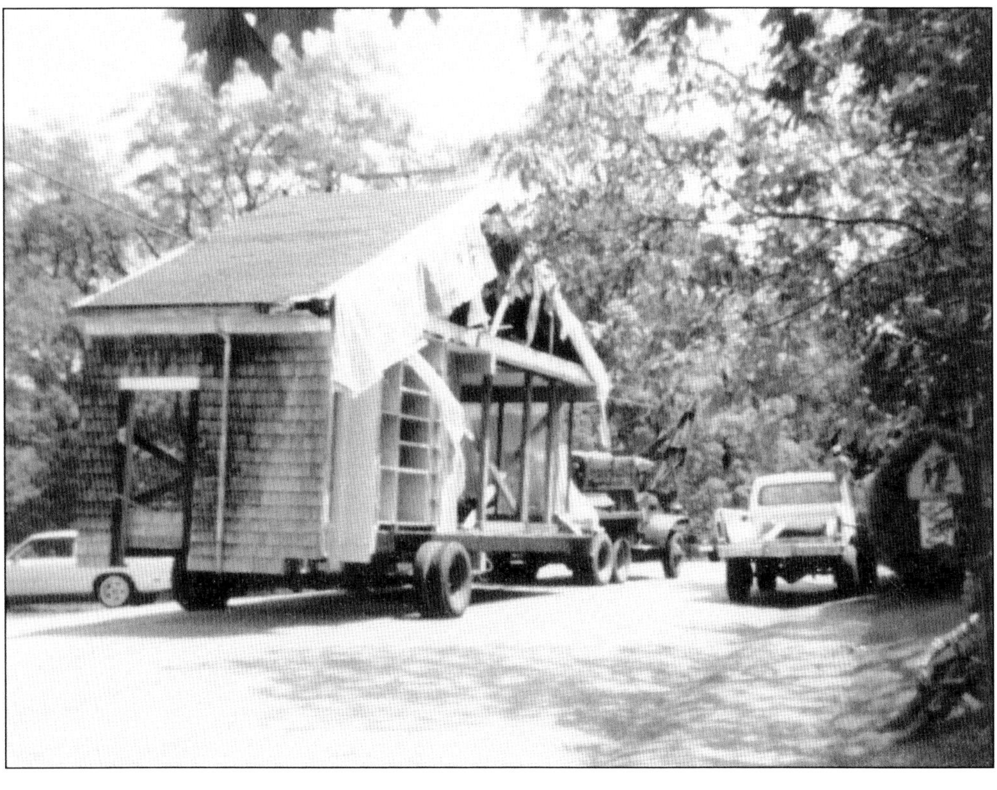

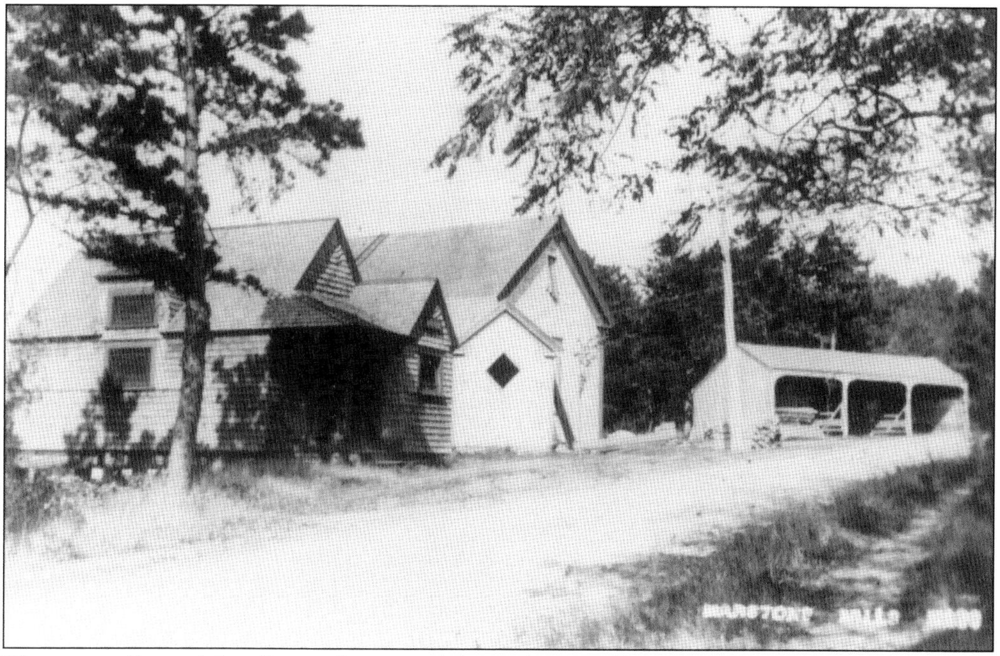

This view of lower Main Street about 1905 shows the 1893 library on the left, Liberty Hall (built in 1859) in the center, and long-demolished horse sheds on the right. The open-fronted stalls were shared by Liberty Hall and the church across the street when people came to church by horse and wagon.

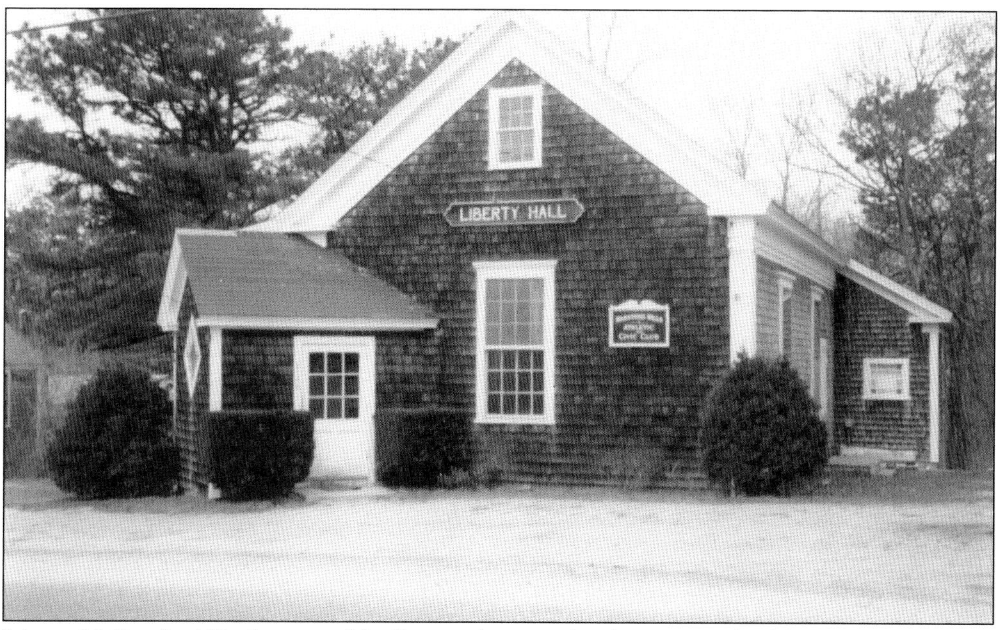

Liberty Hall is the 150-plus-year-old village auditorium for plays, musicals, debates, oyster suppers, baked bean suppers, clambakes, whist parties, dances, concerts, Christmas celebrations, voting, political rallies, fairs, fund-raisers, and even church services. It was built in 1859 by shareholders who donated their work, a tradition that continues today. Much of the initiative came from "liberal Christian" Universalists.

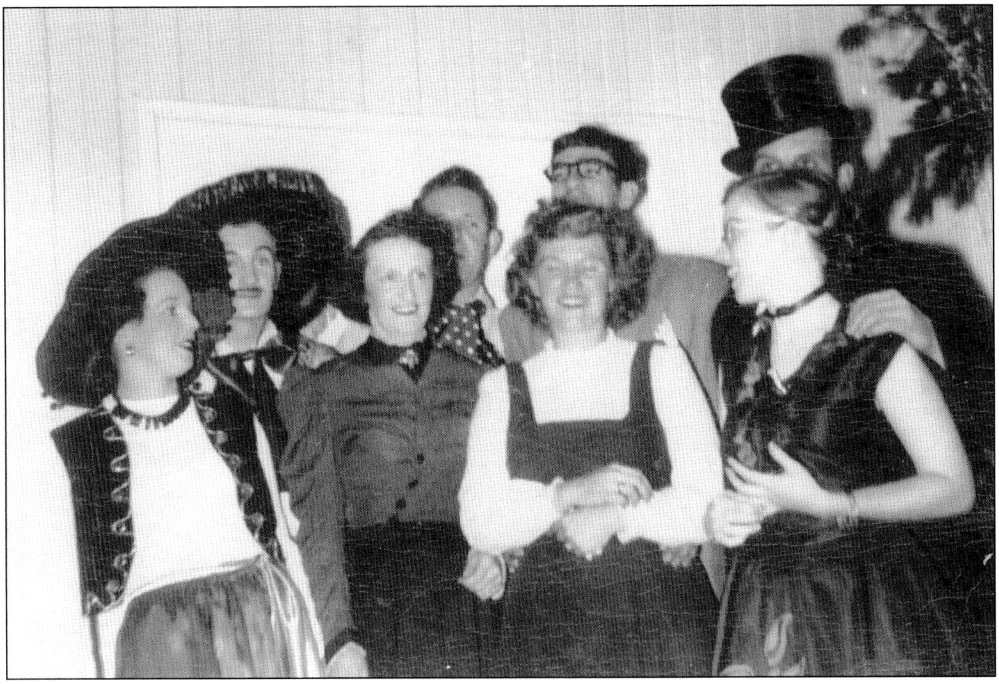

Fun at Liberty Hall about 1947 features, from left to right, Adele (Pond) and Loring Jones Jr., Olive (Gifford) and James Kearns, Helen (Barry) and Charles Hazelton, and Priscilla (Hinckley) and Dana Lapham. This was probably put on by the Marstons Mills Athletic Club, which played softball on the school ground and volleyball at the former USO building in Hyannis.

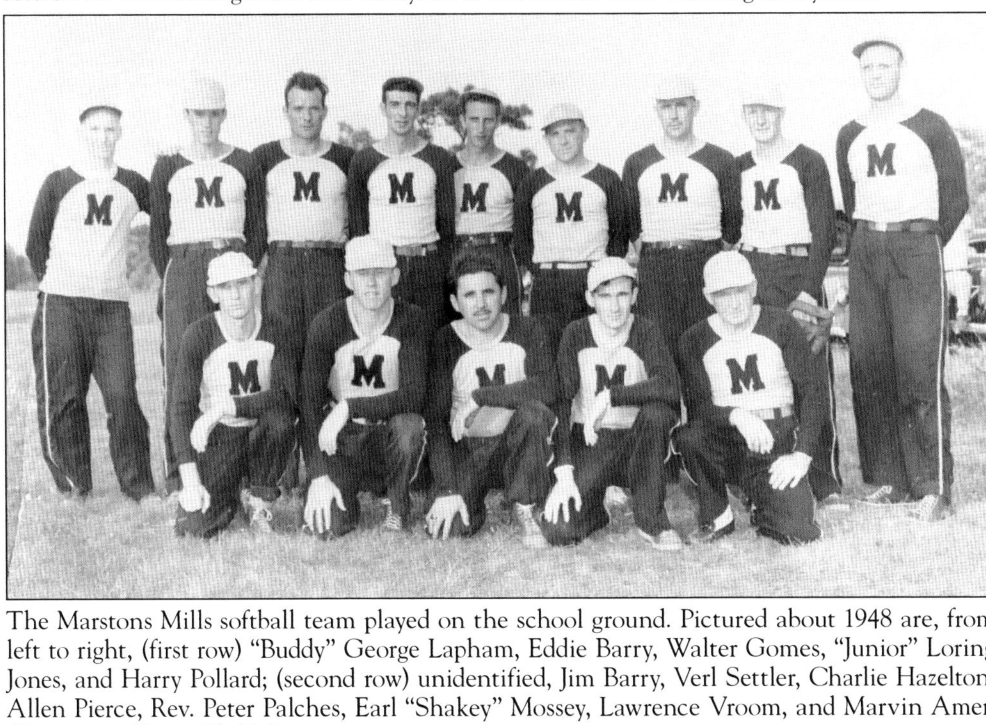

The Marstons Mills softball team played on the school ground. Pictured about 1948 are, from left to right, (first row) "Buddy" George Lapham, Eddie Barry, Walter Gomes, "Junior" Loring Jones, and Harry Pollard; (second row) unidentified, Jim Barry, Verl Settler, Charlie Hazelton, Allen Pierce, Rev. Peter Palches, Earl "Shakey" Mossey, Lawrence Vroom, and Marvin Amer. (Courtesy of Lena Childs.)

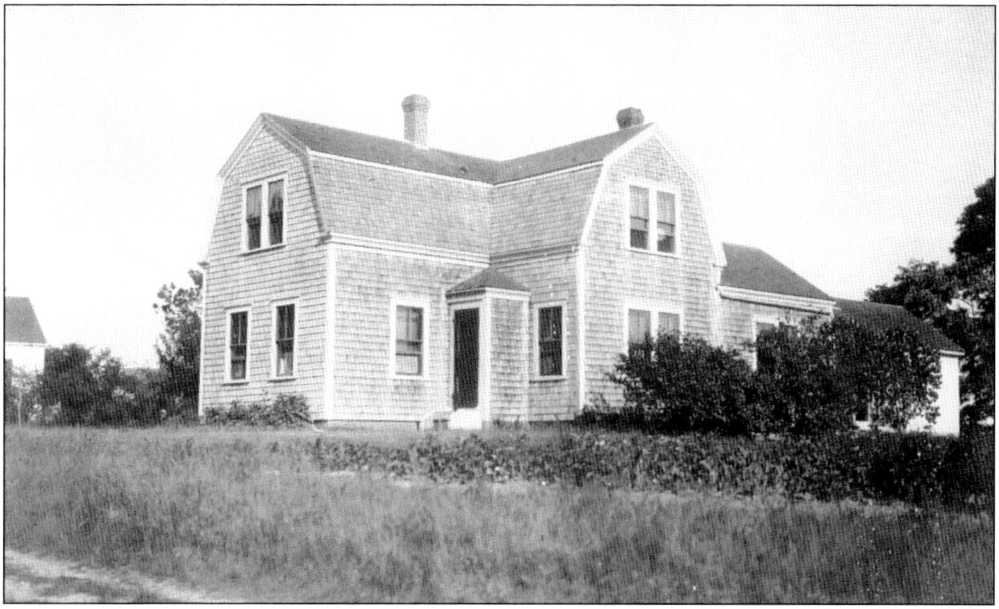

The favorite schoolteacher, Addie Gertrude Crosby (1853–1949), built this gambrel-roofed house on the west side of the church in 1897, after the death of her well-to-do husband, the coasting schooner captain Abner F. Crosby of Cotuit. Addie wrote poetry, and this house was later the home of Bea Lapham, who published two books of her poetry.

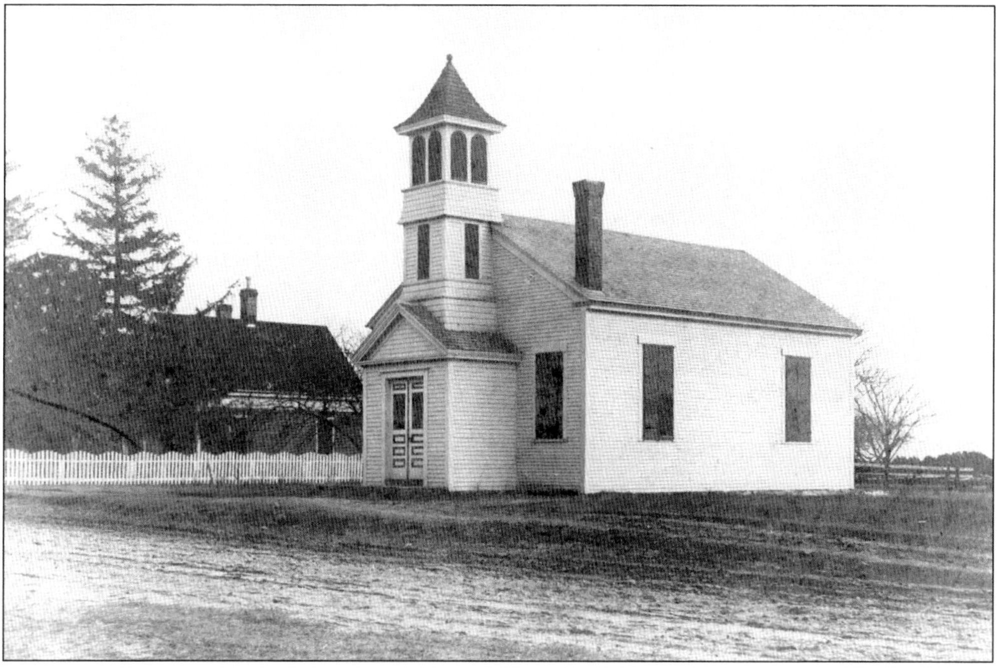

The Methodist Episcopal church was on the south side of Main Street. Since 1819, local Methodists had met in members' homes. In 1830, the Methodist Society bought an unused church in Yarmouthport for $200 and moved it, by oxteam, eight miles to this site. When the church merged with the Osterville United Methodist Church in 1968, this structure was sold. In 1980, Rev. Philip Sherman raised $55,000 to buy it for the nondenominational Community Church.

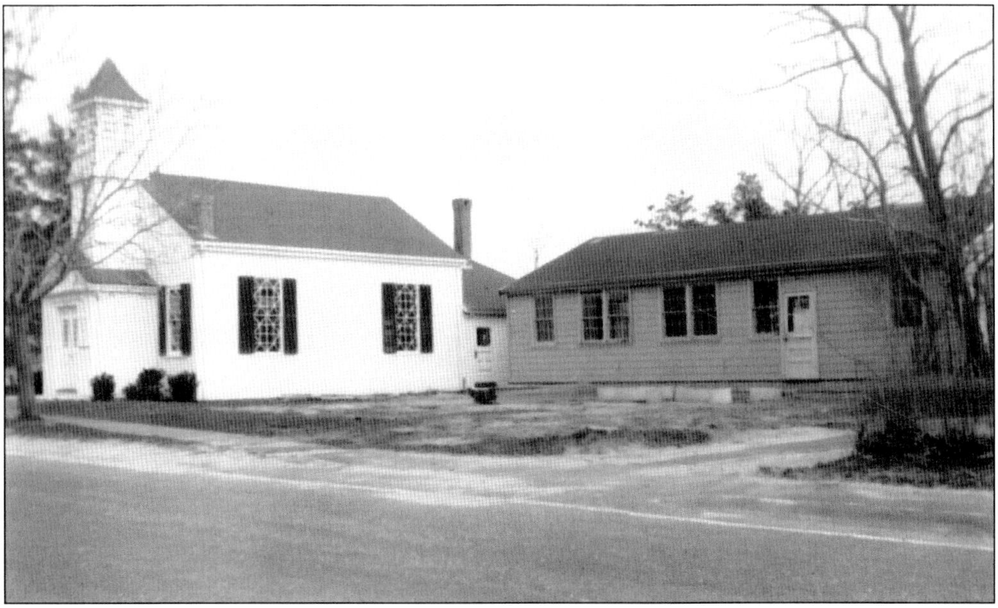

In 1960, the Methodists had Marstons Mills mover Bob Hayden relocate a surplus Army barracks from Camp Edwards to add to the west end for a large meeting hall, kitchen, and restrooms, with Sunday School rooms in the basement. After this became the Community Church, a 200-seat hall was built in 1993 on the south side for $105,000—or 50 times the cost of the original church.

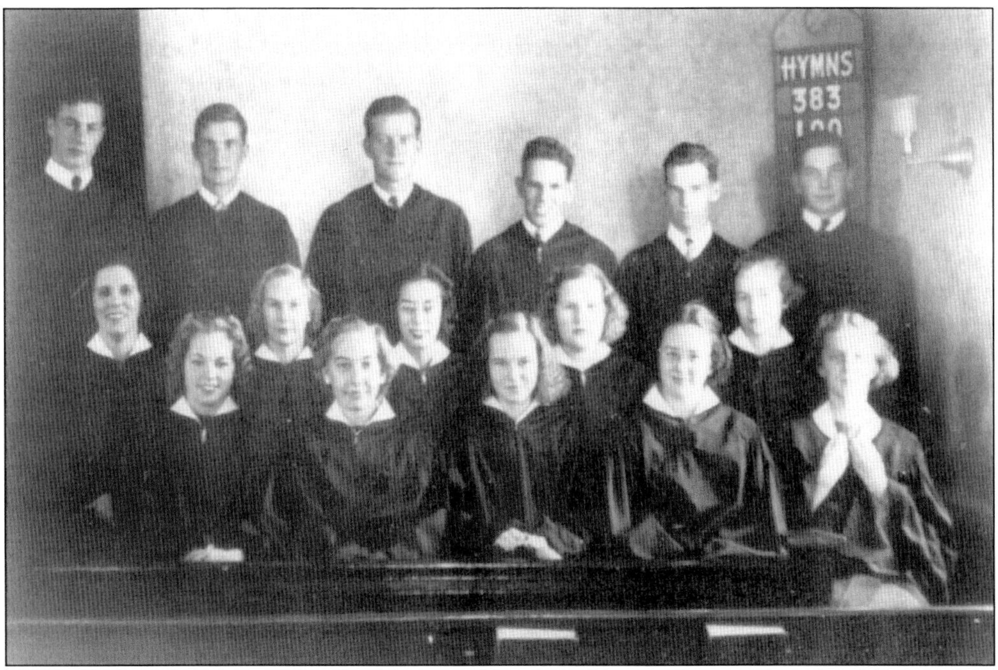

Methodist church choir members around 1938 are, from left to right, Seth and Roger Hamblin, Alfred Fuller, Dana and George Lapham, Curtis Jones; Myra (Rogers) Repose, Adele (Pond) Jones, Nancy (Jones) Amer, Lena (Jones) Childs, Kathleen (Lovell) Farrar, Janice (Lapham) Nickerson, Frances (Lapham) Hinckley, Dorothy (Pollard) Mossey, Persis (Jones) Childs, and Alice (Thifault) Elskamp. (Courtesy of Charles E. Hamblin.)

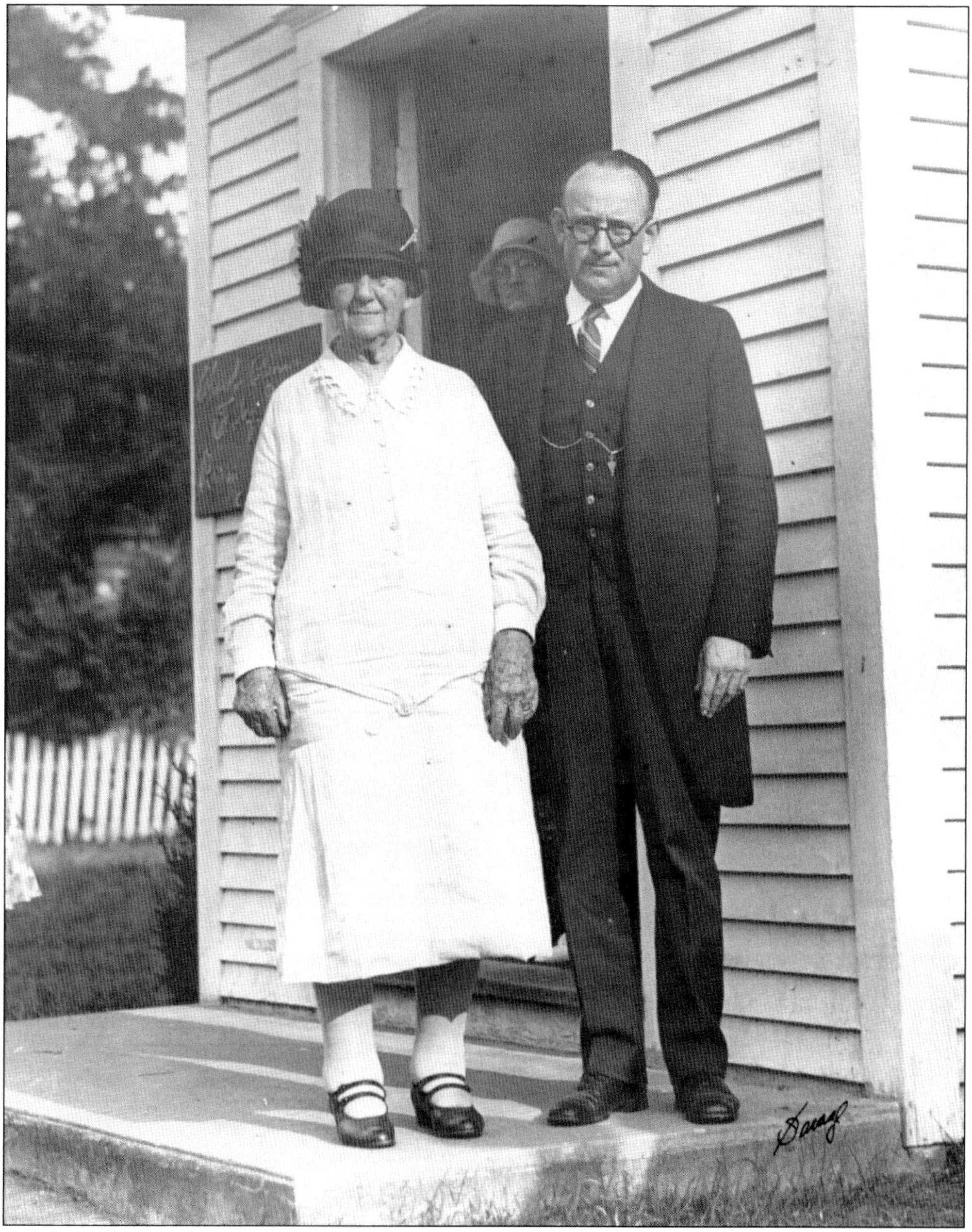

Aphia "Affie" Lucie Goodspeed Jones (1866–1953), widow of Ephraim Jones, was the last member of the founding family of Goodspeed in the village. Here, she is pictured about 1929 on the Methodist church steps with the Rev. Raymond W. Hibbard, who served as minister from 1929 to 1939.

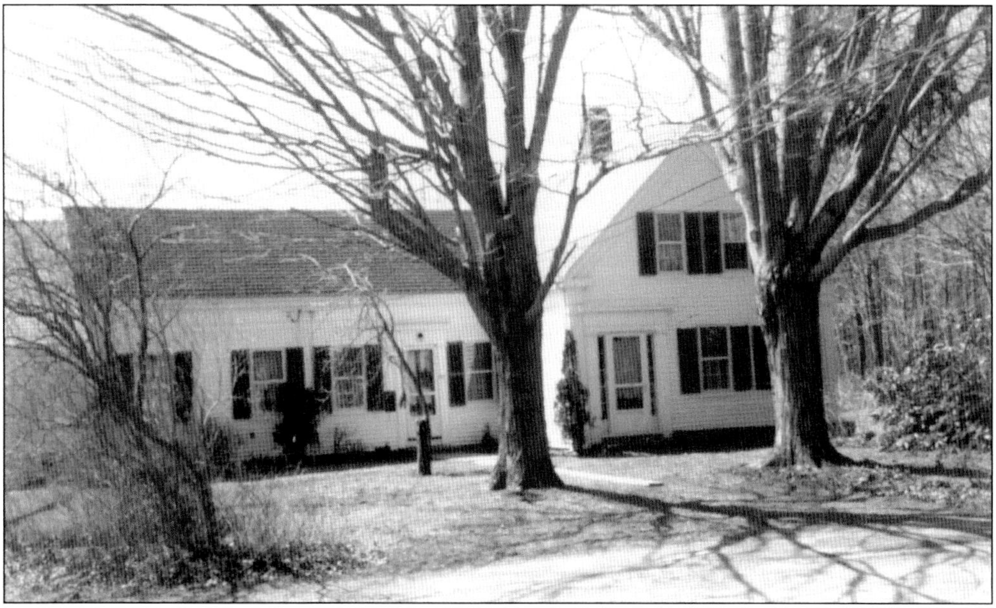

The home of whaling captain Oliver Alton Crocker (1825–1898) is on the east side of the church. In 1853, Capt. Crocker built this Greek Revival house, which has retained its original form. The property extended southward across the school ground all the way to saltwater, where Capt. Crocker had a dock and a Crosby catboat in which he took people for pleasure sails.

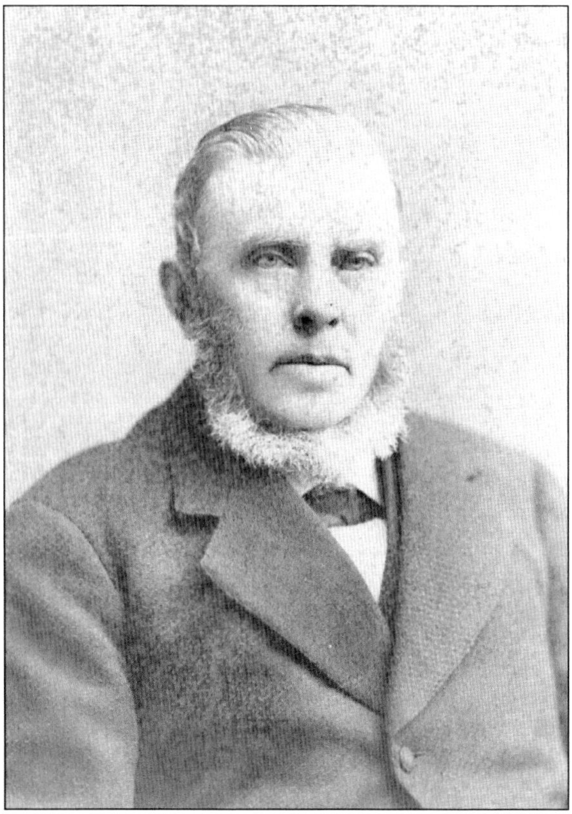

Capt. Oliver Alton Crocker was born in Newtown, went to sea at the age of 17, and became master of ships hunting whales in the Arctic, Pacific, and Indian Oceans. At age 24, he married Nancy Jones. They had four children: Foster, who became the village mechanic; Nannie, who became the wife of the grocer George Hamblin; Oliver Jr., who married three times; and Florence, who married Rev. Frank Hamblin.

Three

SALTWATER SEAPORT

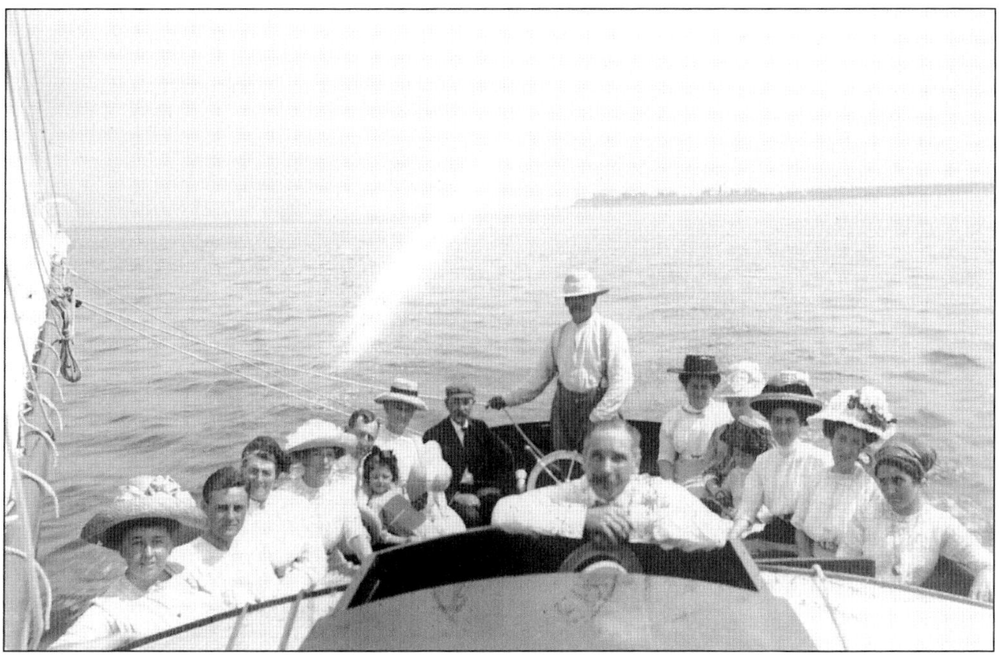

A favorite summer recreation was to hire a retired mariner to take a party out in a catboat to Nantucket or the Vineyard. Here, in 1911, is a party of 14 aboard the catboat *Storm King*, under sail to Falmouth. The man at the wheel is Oliver Alton Crocker Jr. (1854–1948), who had a dock in Warren's Cove.

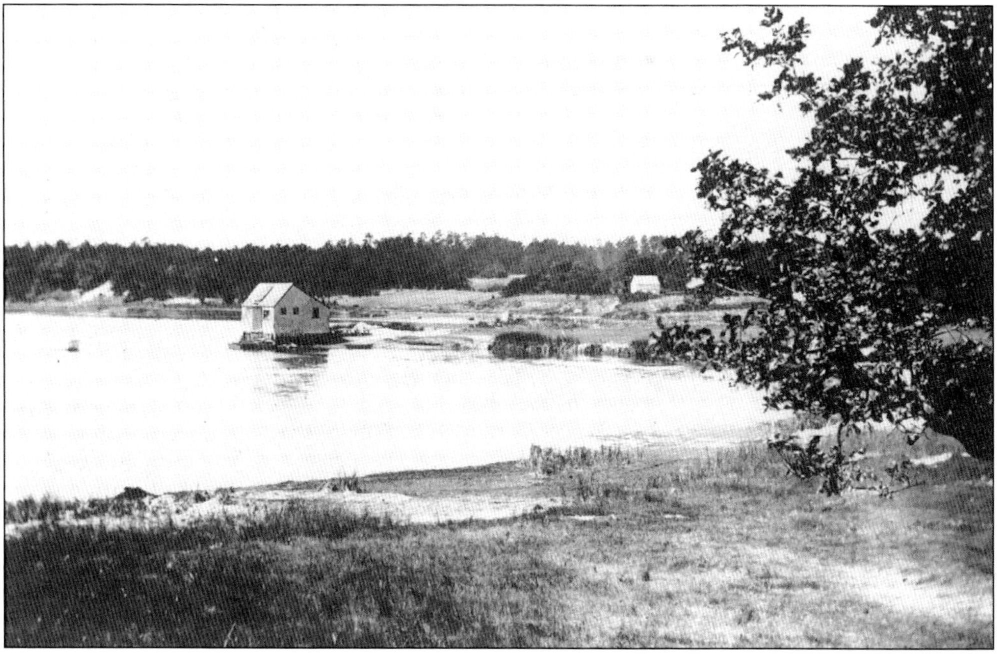

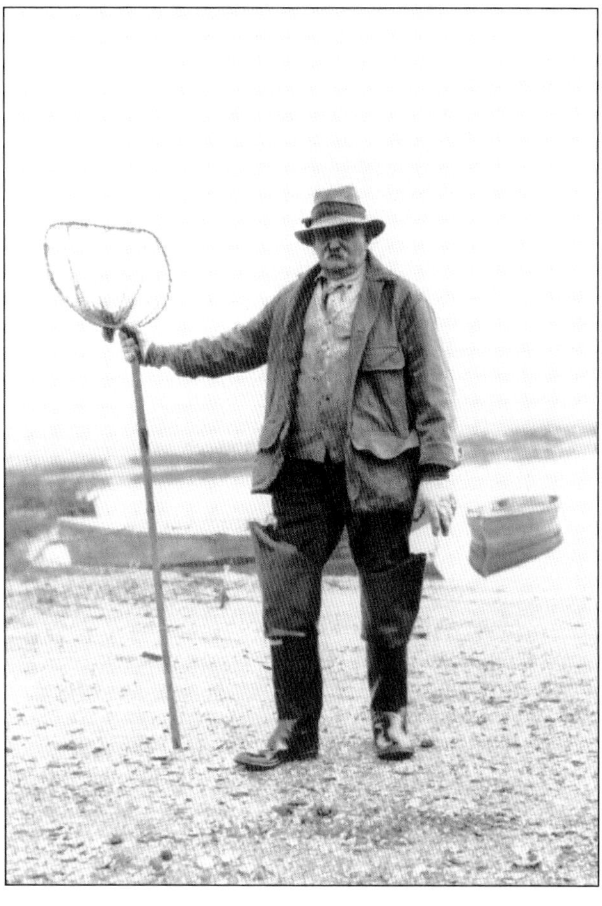

George Lewis Hamblin (1860–1934) built this oyster house about 1902 after he gave up the grocery business and dry goods sales. The location is near the entrance to Warren's Cove, named for his father, Warren Francis Hamblin (1834–1908). Warren moved here in 1893 after his family homestead in The Plains burned down. In the background is Snapwood Creek, named for the fragrant bush that was used for spicy flavoring.

George Hamblin, a 70-year-old oysterman, stands on the shore in 1930. He married Nancy "Nannie" Ella Crocker, daughter of the whaler Capt. Oliver Alton Crocker Sr. As a young man, Hamblin ran the village grocery with his uncle Lewis and alternated with his uncle traveling to sell dry goods. George was the father of Leonard and Forest Hamblin, builders, cranberry growers, and last owners of the gristmill.

Nancy "Nannie" Ella Crocker Hamblin (1861–1944) and her children are pictured in 1902. She lost her first child, George Franklin, at age 19 months to brain fever. Here, the eldest is Bertha, born in 1888 and later married to Gerald Chapman of Dennis. The older boy is Leonard, born in 1890, who later worked as a mason, and the baby is Forest.

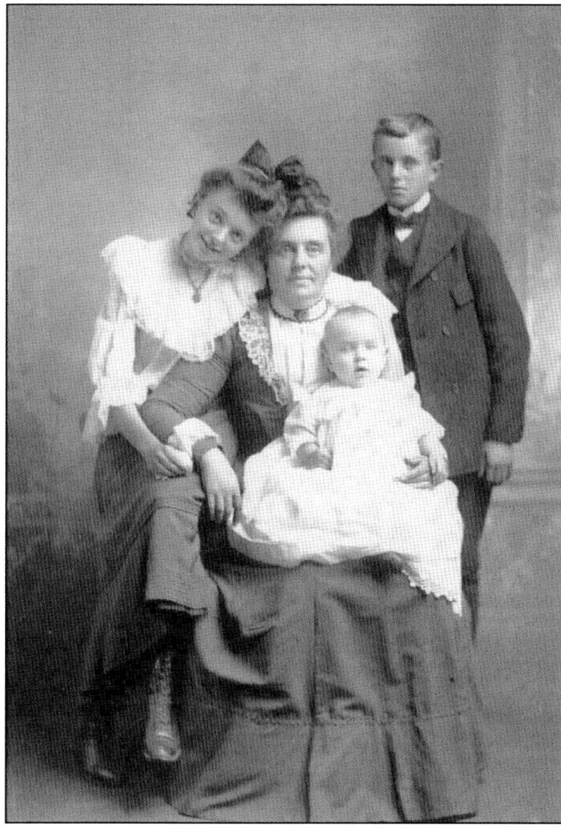

Cyrus B. Jones (1865–1934) ran an oyster business from this oyster shack on Turtle Island, seen in this view facing south toward North Bay. Born at the end of the Civil War, he was named for his uncle Cpl. Cyrus B. Fish, who died in a Confederate prison camp in Florence, South Carolina, where he is buried in an unmarked grave.

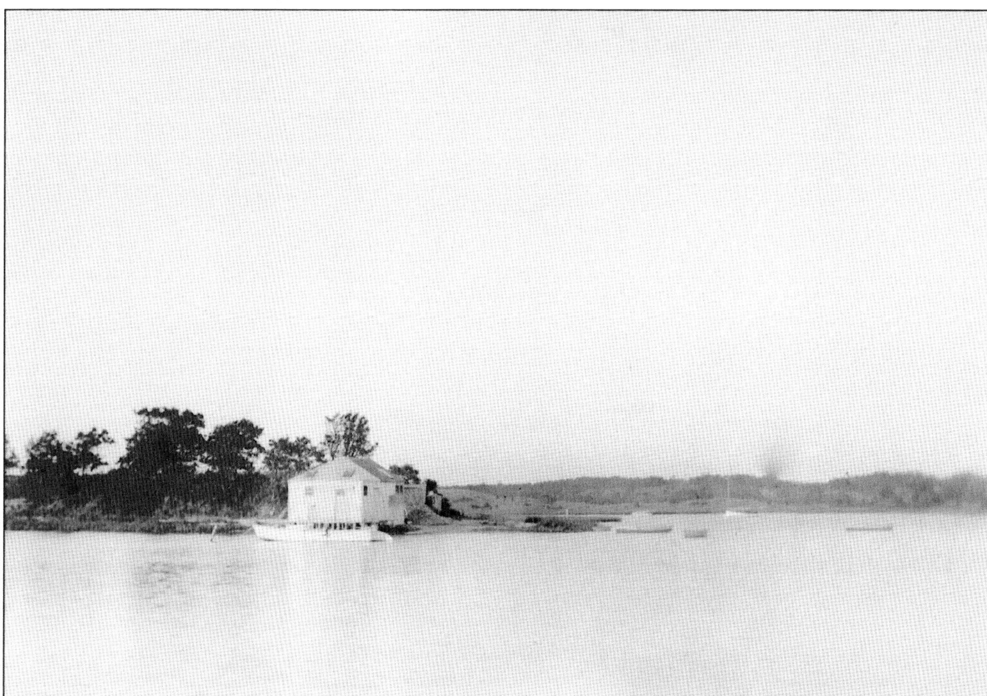

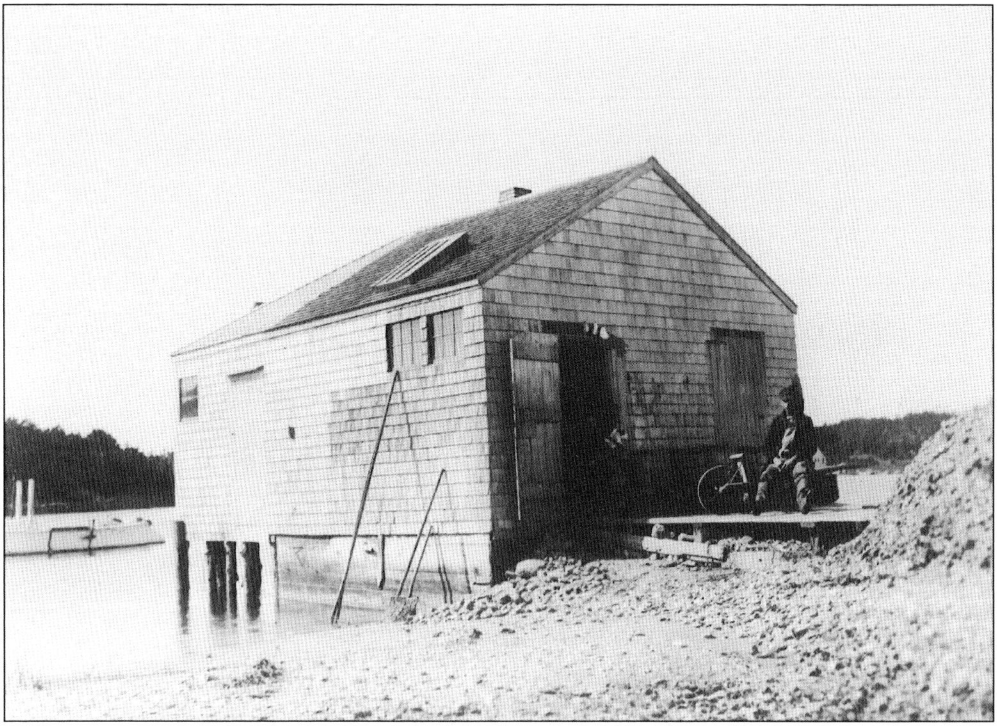

Cyrus B. Jones sits outside his oyster shack on Turtle Island, looking toward Prince's Cove about 1905, when he was 40. He could bike the short distance to his home on Prince Avenue (now the Prince House), which he inherited from his mother's Fish family. At the right is a mound of shucked oyster shells, later hauled off for surfacing roads.

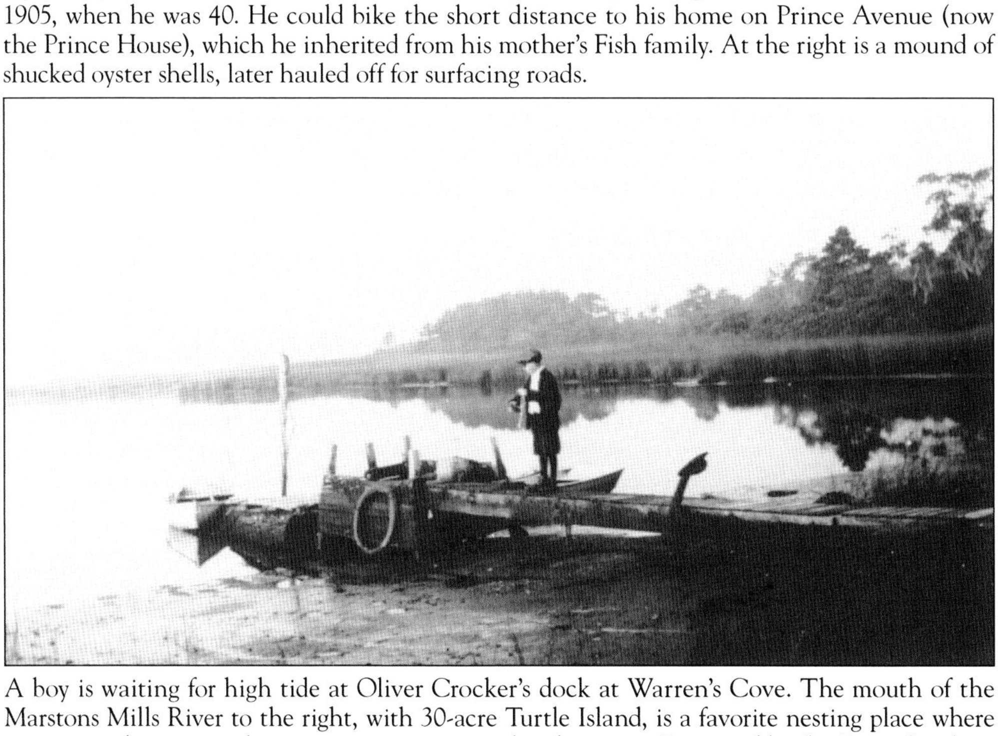

A boy is waiting for high tide at Oliver Crocker's dock at Warren's Cove. The mouth of the Marstons Mills River to the right, with 30-acre Turtle Island, is a favorite nesting place where various turtle species—box, snapping, terrapin—lay their eggs. Preserved by the Davis family, it is now protected by the Barnstable Land Trust.

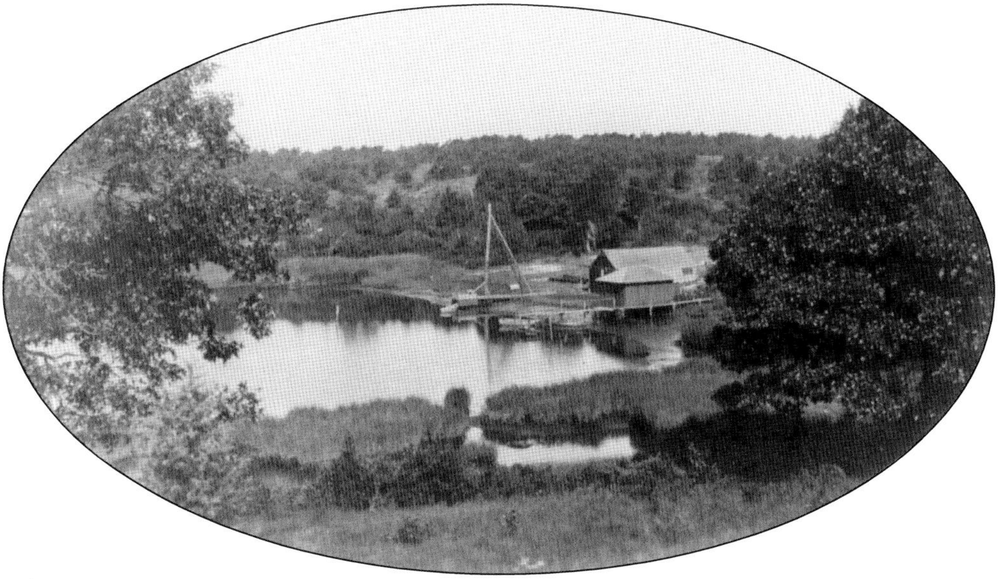

Felix Winternitz (1872–1948), concertmaster of Boston Symphony Orchestra, had a fine sailboat, *Sybil*, docked at Warren's Cove, where he had built this boathouse by 1906. Famed as "a musician's musician," this Austrian-born genius was a prodigy on the violin, playing in the Vienna Opera Orchestra at 13 and Boston Symphony at 17. He sold this house in 1929 to the wife of author J.P. Marquand.

A story is told that when Prentiss Barnard "Barney" Hinckley (1857–1932) took two ladies for a sail in his catboat, they offered to buy it. "I'd sell it for 1¢," he said. One paid him a penny, and he left the tiller. "It's your boat," he said. She appealed, "We don't know how to sail." Hinckley dryly replied, "It is your boat." She asked, "How much do you want to sail it back?" "That will cost you just $500."

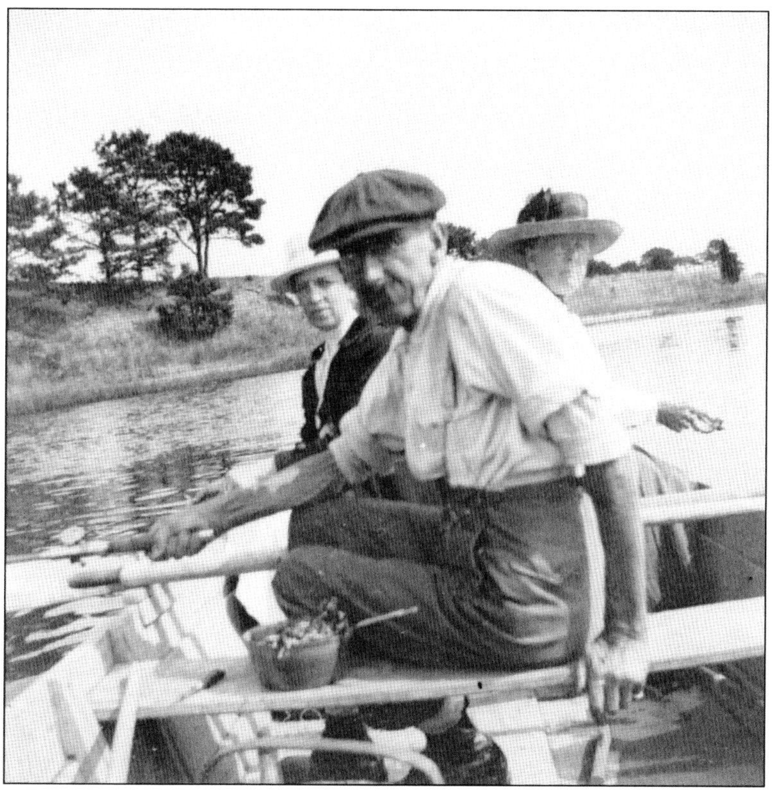

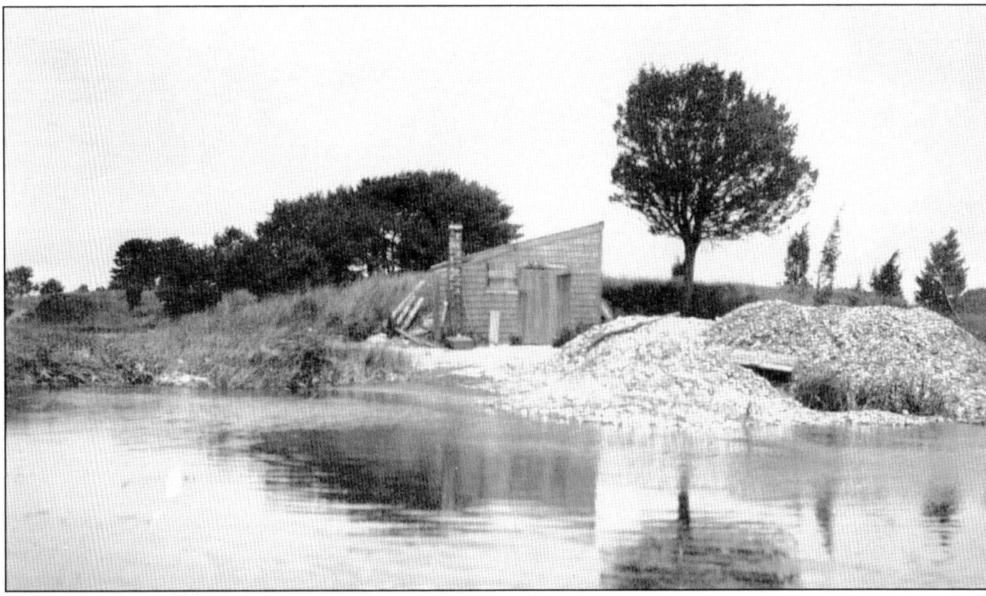

Barney Hinckley's oyster shanty at the third hole of the Seapuit Golf Course about 1913 was where he served fresh Marstons Mills oysters, washed down with a martini. The huge pile of shucked oyster shells was one of many, recalling thousands of years of Indian feasts on this shore. Barney had deeded rights down from his house to Cat Island. The shack was swept away in the Great New England Hurricane of 1938.

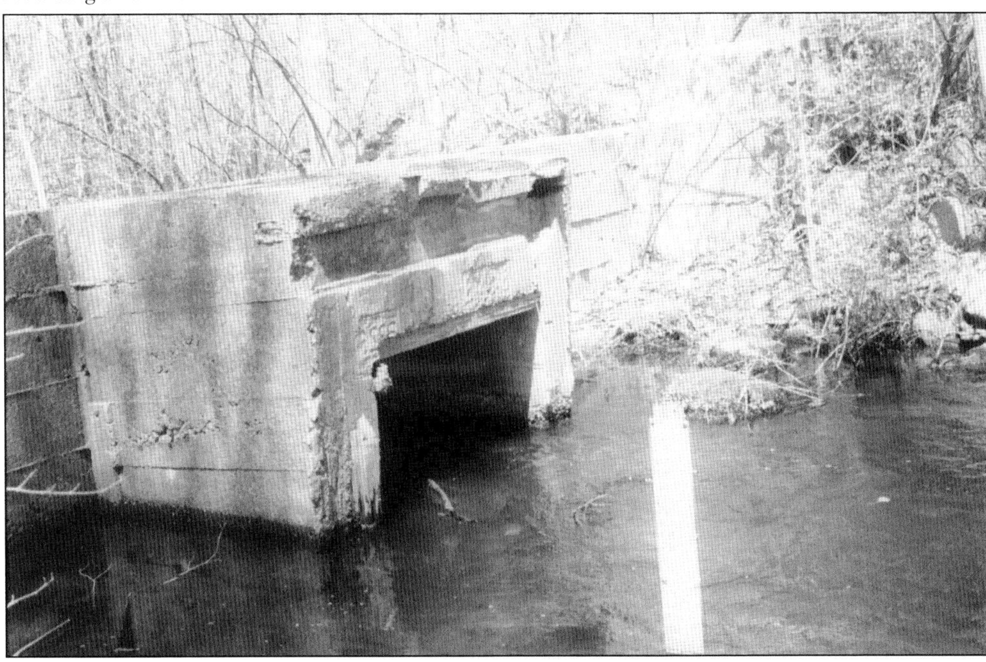

During World War II, there was an acute energy shortage, which steam engineer David Leland (1884–1959) met by building the first and only hydroelectric plant on Cape Cod. At the foot of the Marstons Mills River, he constructed huge concrete penstocks and turbine. On the Fourth of July in 1945, the only fireworks were the light of the lone lightbulb powered by the plant. After the war, most of the plant was wrecked.

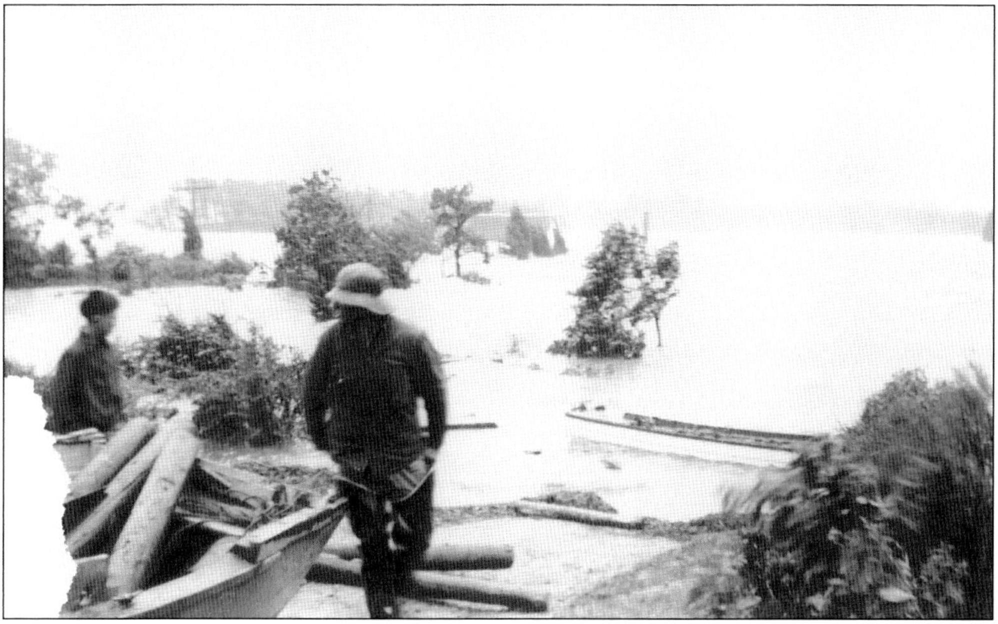

Hurricane Carol on August 31, 1954, struck Prince's Cove hard, with an extra-high tide. During the storm, Forest Hamblin put on foul-weather gear to check out the damage. His bait shack is still standing on the point, in the center of the photograph, as is Mrs. Ethel Houston's summerhouse. The shack washed away in a later hurricane, and the house was moved to Lovell's Lane.

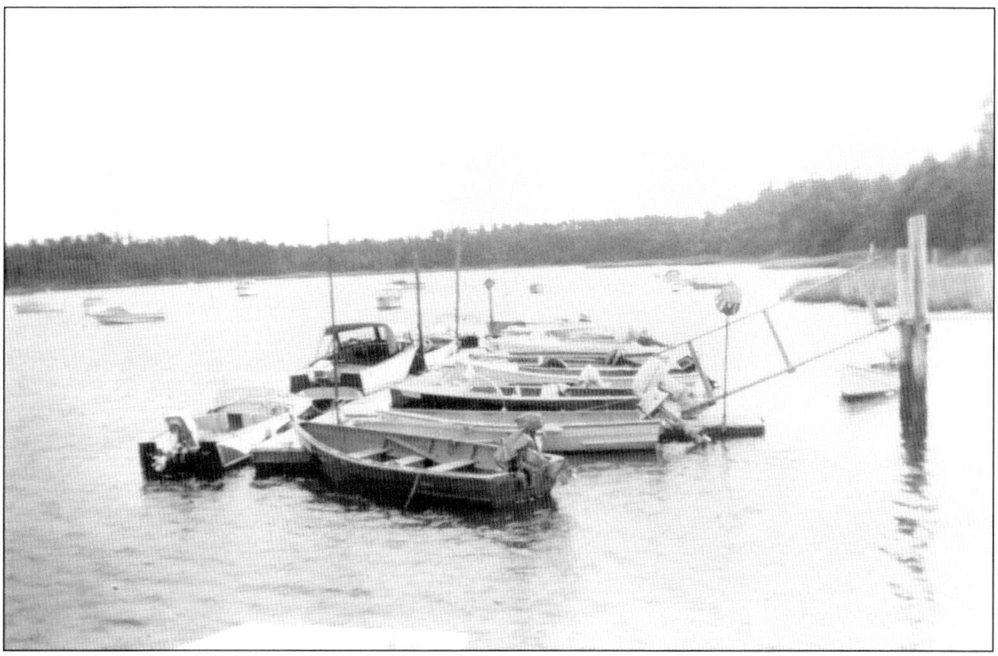

A pier was built in 1953 by Wilbur Cushing (1921–2009) on shore of the property of his stepfather, A.G. Griffin. Cushing salvaged poles and lumber from the former Clear Lake Duck Farm to build the first dock. Cushing repaired outboard motors and rented boats. His most memorable customer was retired Air Force general Jimmy Doolittle, whom Cushing took fishing in the summer of 1963.

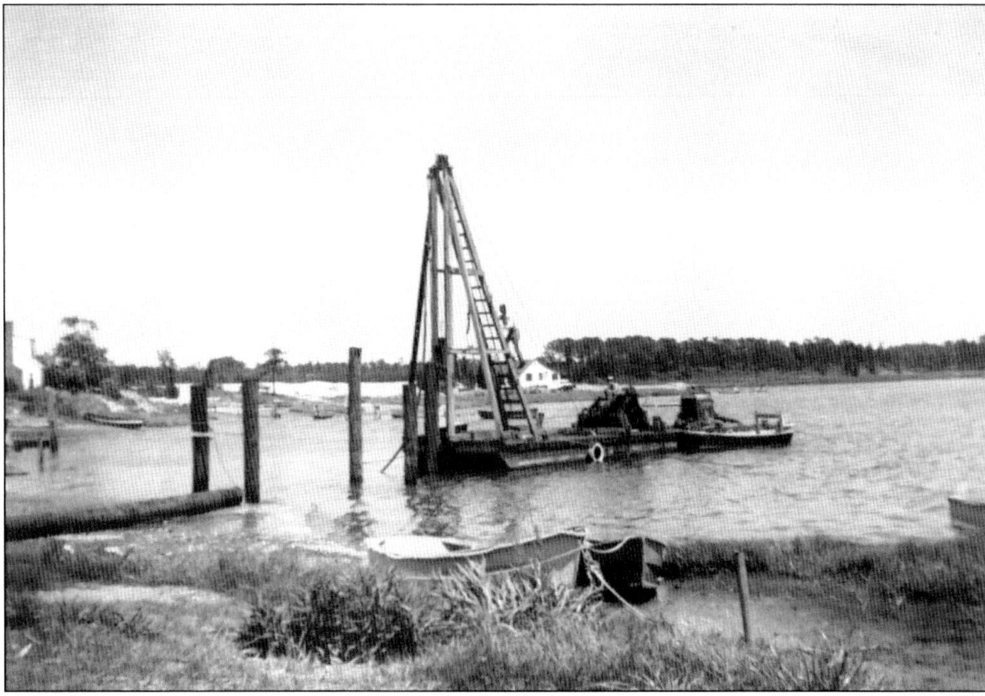

A pile driver drove pilings for a town dock at Prince's Cove in the spring of 1957. The town dredged the cove and brought in sand for a town beach. In 1964, the town paved the parking lot and created a "harbor of refuge" from hurricanes by dredging a depth that would accommodate large boats. The house at left center is that of summer resident Ethel Houston, who tied up her rowboat here.

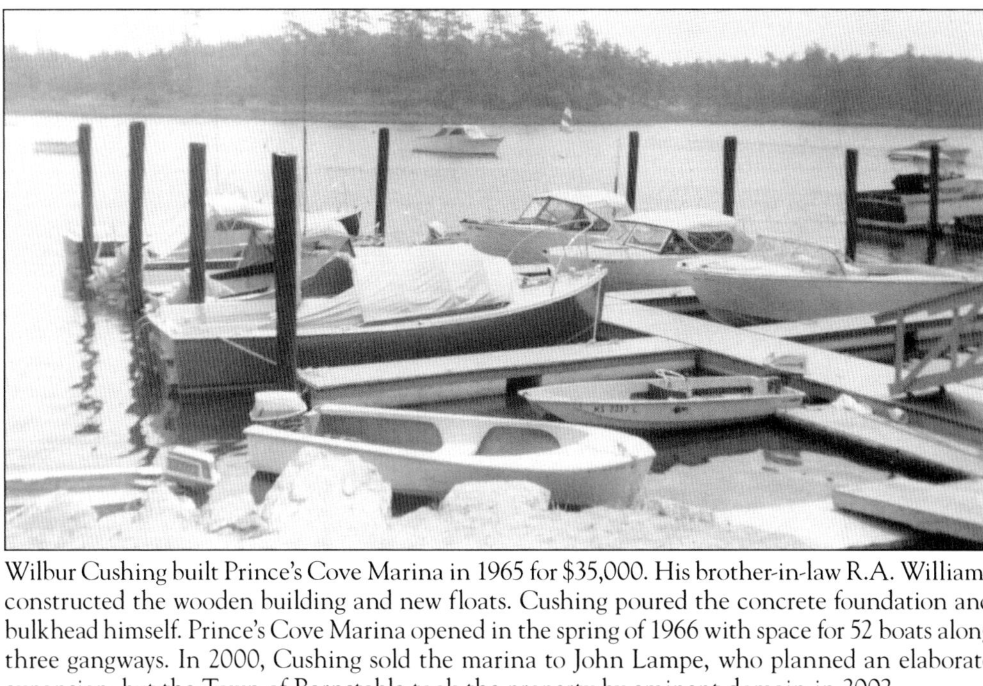

Wilbur Cushing built Prince's Cove Marina in 1965 for $35,000. His brother-in-law R.A. Williams constructed the wooden building and new floats. Cushing poured the concrete foundation and bulkhead himself. Prince's Cove Marina opened in the spring of 1966 with space for 52 boats along three gangways. In 2000, Cushing sold the marina to John Lampe, who planned an elaborate expansion, but the Town of Barnstable took the property by eminent domain in 2002.

Close neighbors of Prince's Cove were the prominent Perry family of boxing renown, who came here from Fogo in the Cape Verde Islands. The patriarch was six-foot-four Benjamin Perry (1863–1955), respected foreman of Makepeace's cranberry bogs and said to be afraid of no man. The pugnacious matriarch was tiny Mary Perry, who encouraged her seven boys to fight back when they were bullied for being black. (Courtesy of Perry family.)

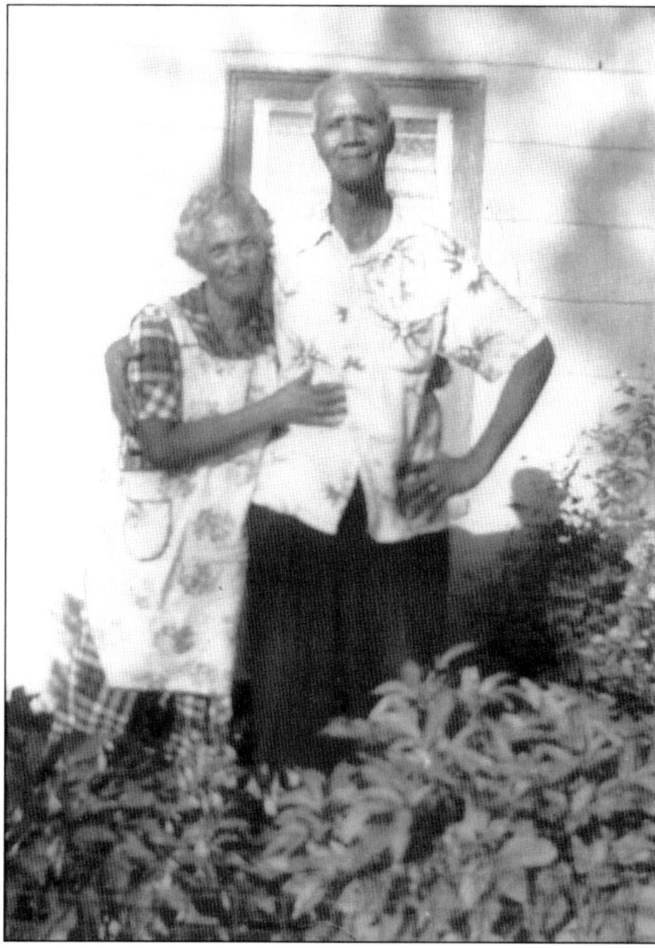

Ben Perry set up an outdoor boxing ring in front of the Charles Marston house on Route 28 and had the well-known policeman boxer Jack Dempsey train local youth. Here, in 1949, are the Perry boys with friends, including Wampanoags from neighboring Mashpee. (Courtesy of Perry family.)

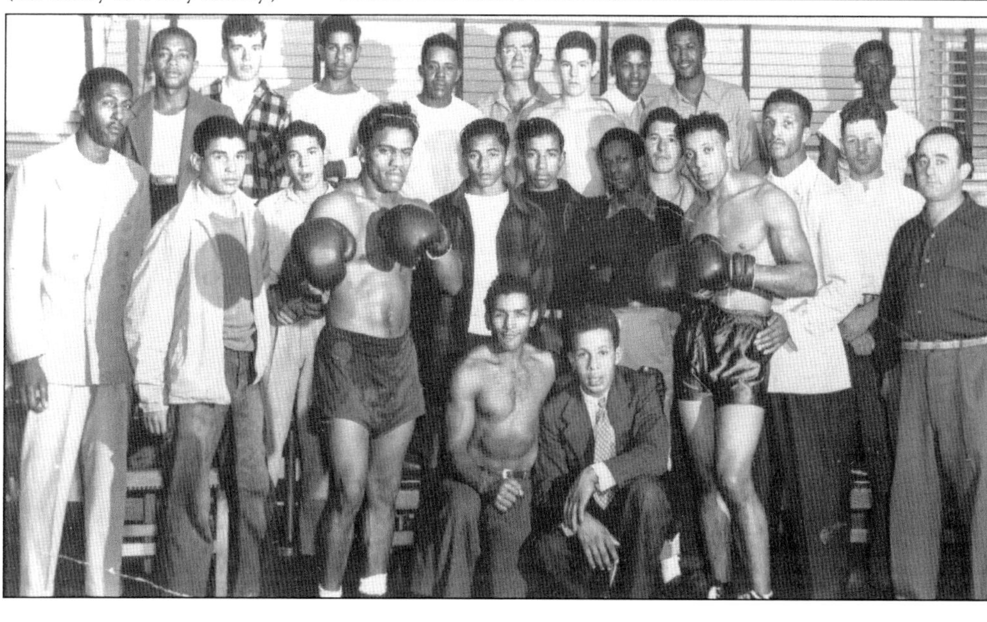

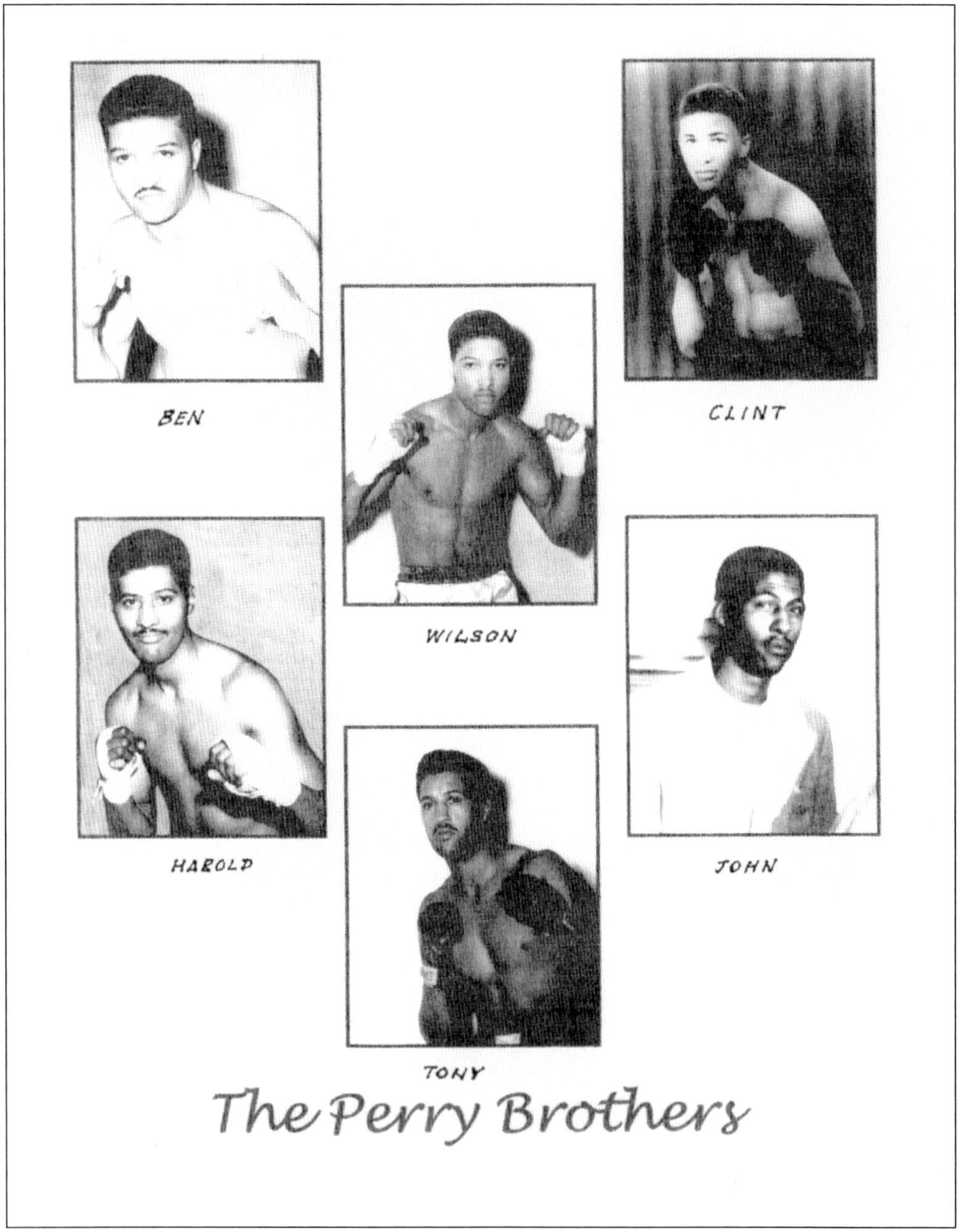

Joe Perry, the eldest (not shown), preferred fishing and wrestling to boxing. "The Brown Bomber" Ben and his brother Clint both fought in the 1937 Golden Gloves, and after wartime service in the Army came home to train their brothers Chico (or Tony) and John, who fought in postwar amateur competitions, and the two youngest, Harold and Wilson, who won the Golden Gloves together in 1949. (Courtesy of Perry family.)

This ancient five-bay Cape Cod cottage was built on Prince Avenue by the David Fish family by 1830. Lauchlan Crocker (1895–1945), son of Zenas Crocker IV, of an old Barnstable family, bought the former Fish home after service as a noncom in World War I. He was born in a sod hut on the North Dakota prairie where his father ran a grocery before returning to Marstons Mills. (Courtesy of Jacqi Easter.)

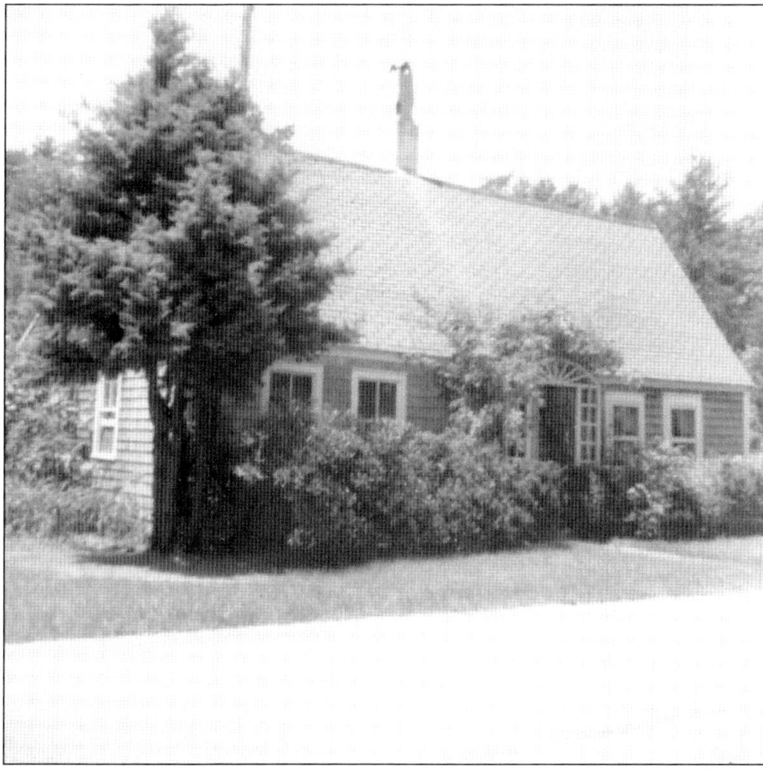

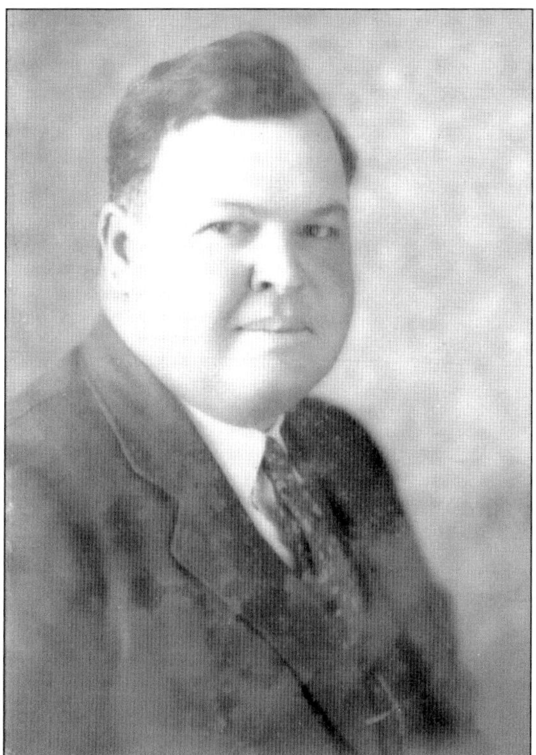

Lauchlan Crocker was appointed sheriff of Barnstable County in 1933. He opened the prison farm, installed the first radio system and fingerprinting, and campaigned for prison reform, maintaining that jailing a man for nonsupport only made the problem worse. (Courtesy of Jacqi Easter.)

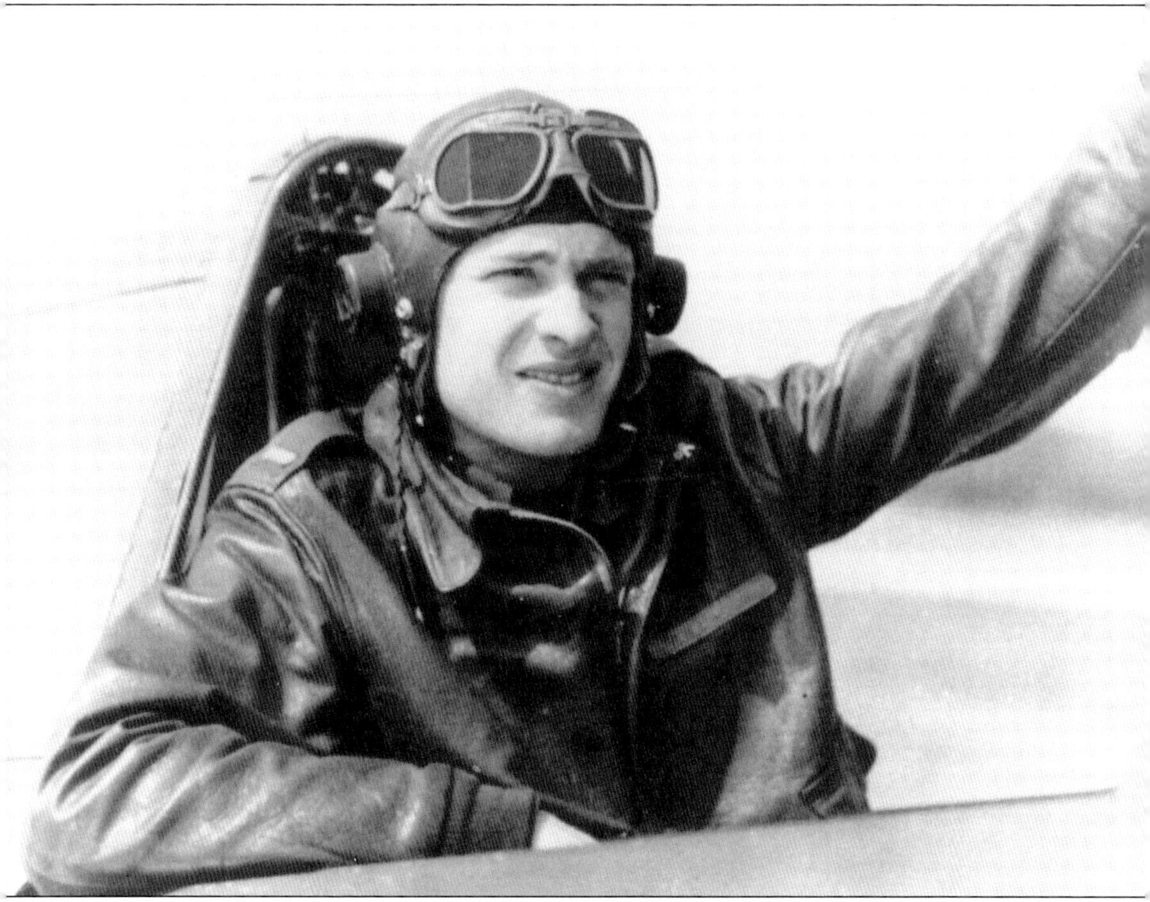

At the intersection of Routes 149 and 28 is a boulder in memory of Air Force captain Sherman Crocker (1920–1945), who was born and grew up on Prince Avenue nearby and was the son of Sheriff Lauchlan Crocker. The younger Crocker died in February 1945 when his P-47 fighter-bomber *Harriet* (named for his fiancée) was shot down by an 88-mm antiaircraft gun near the Rhine River. (Courtesy of Jacqi Easter.)

Four

SCHOOLHOUSES

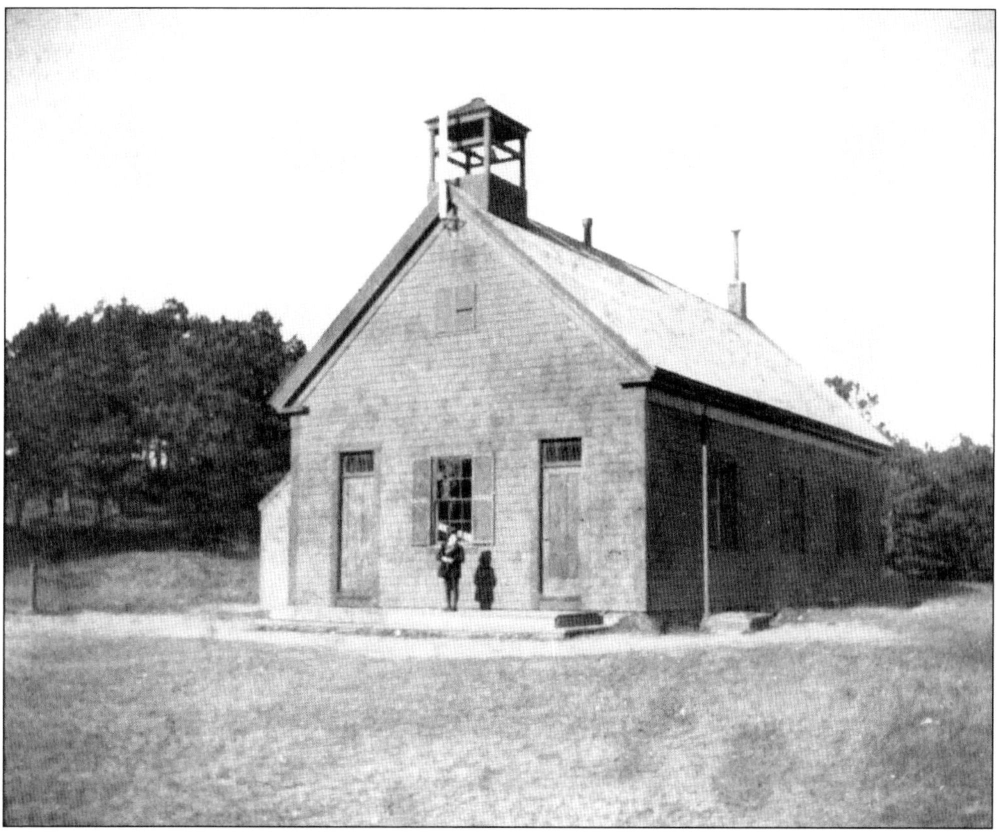

In 1848, the town declared the old school one of several that were "little better than caves or dog kennels, unfit for anything save habitations for cattle and swine." A new one-room Marstons Mills Schoolhouse was built about where the Mills Restaurant now stands, on land bought from Chipman Hinckley. Finished in October 1851 by builder C.E. King, the school was officially called "one of the best in town."

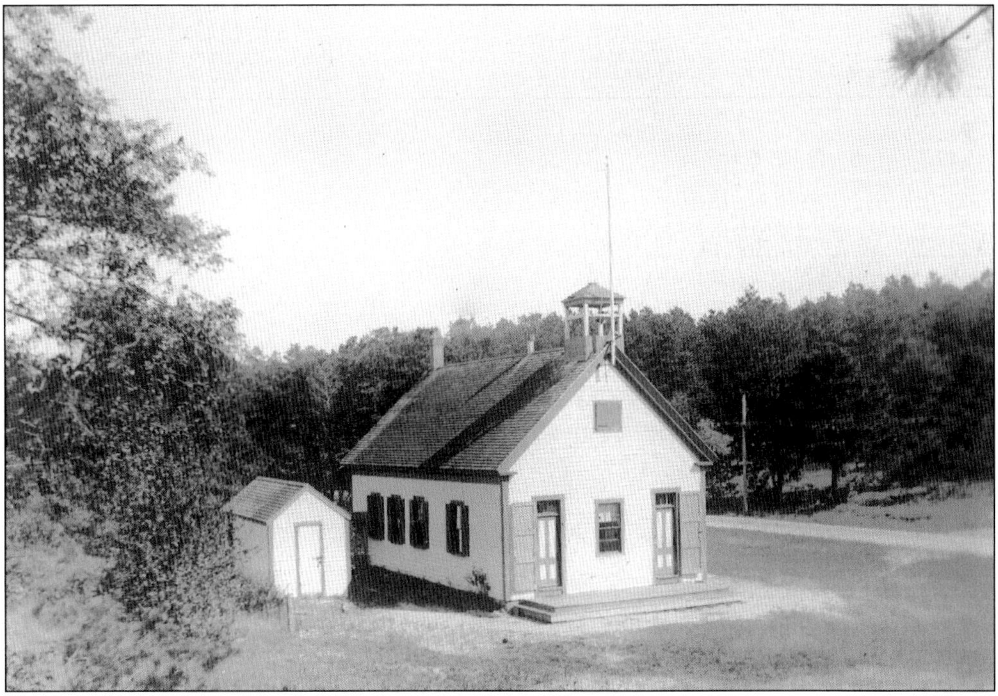

This one-room building faced south on the road to West Barnstable, with separate boys' and girls' entrances. On the gable peak were a flagpole and a cupola with a big brass bell. Outside, there was a pump with a metal "community" dipper and girls' and boys' toilets.

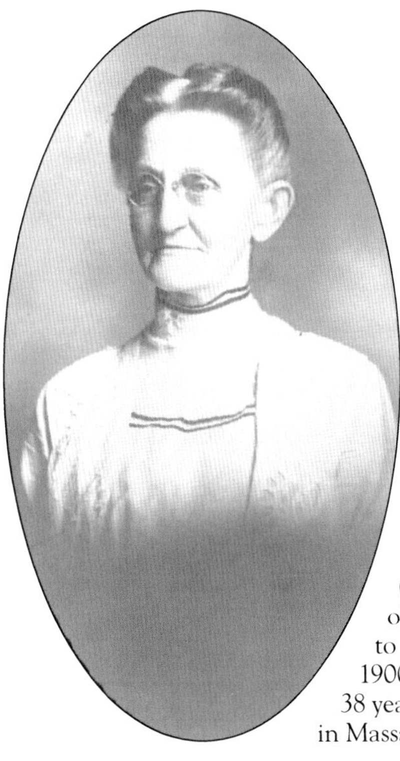

A favorite teacher was Addie Gertrude (Crocker) Crosby (1853–1949), whom one student remembered fondly as "an old-time teacher [who] demanded attention. There, you began to learn your three R's and no fooling." She taught here until 1900, when she transferred to Osterville. On retirement after 38 years of teaching, she was lauded as "one of the best teachers in Massachusetts."

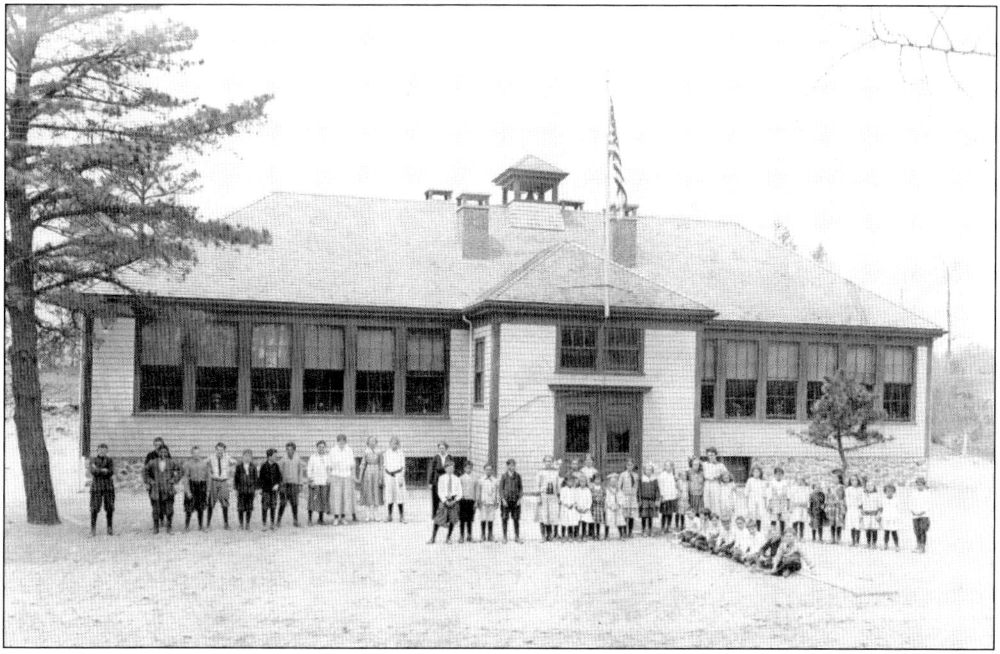

In 1915, some $5,250 was spent to have H.E. Fish expand the old schoolhouse (on the right) by adding a second room and indoor toilets, with a new entrance facing Cotuit Road. Students came from the former Newtown and Plains schools to make a total of 48 pupils in the lower grades.

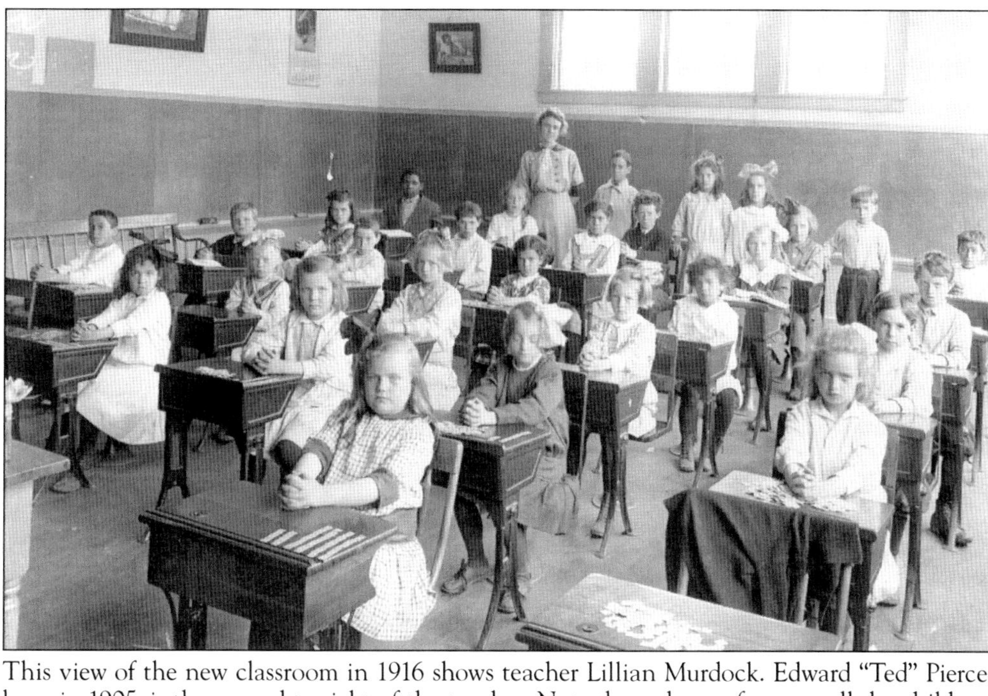

This view of the new classroom in 1916 shows teacher Lillian Murdock. Edward "Ted" Pierce, born in 1905, is the second to right of the teacher. Note the unhappy faces on all the children. One of the old desks has been preserved by the historical society.

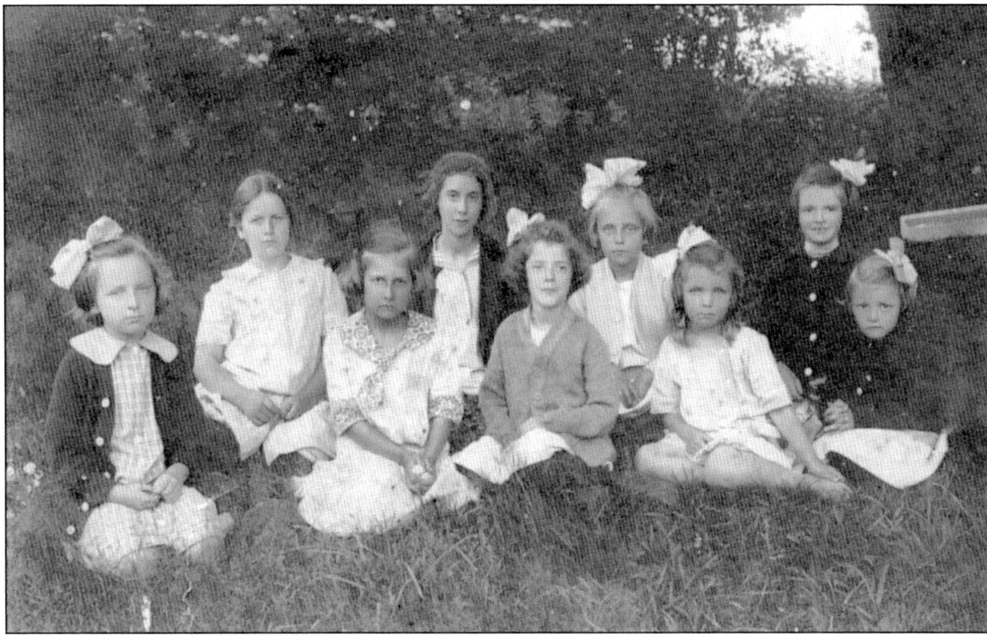

Marstons Mills schoolgirls' party about 1915 includes, from left to right, Halcyon Goodspeed, Katherine Taber, Marion Jones, Mildred Greene (1901–1967, married Orville Burrows), Violet Pierce (1908–1915, died shortly after this photograph), Miriam Goodspeed (married Carroll Fuller), Marion Lovell (born 1908, married William Oldham), Natalie Crocker (1905–1988, married Leonard Fish), and her sister Zilphia Crocker (1909–1958, married Fred Gordon).

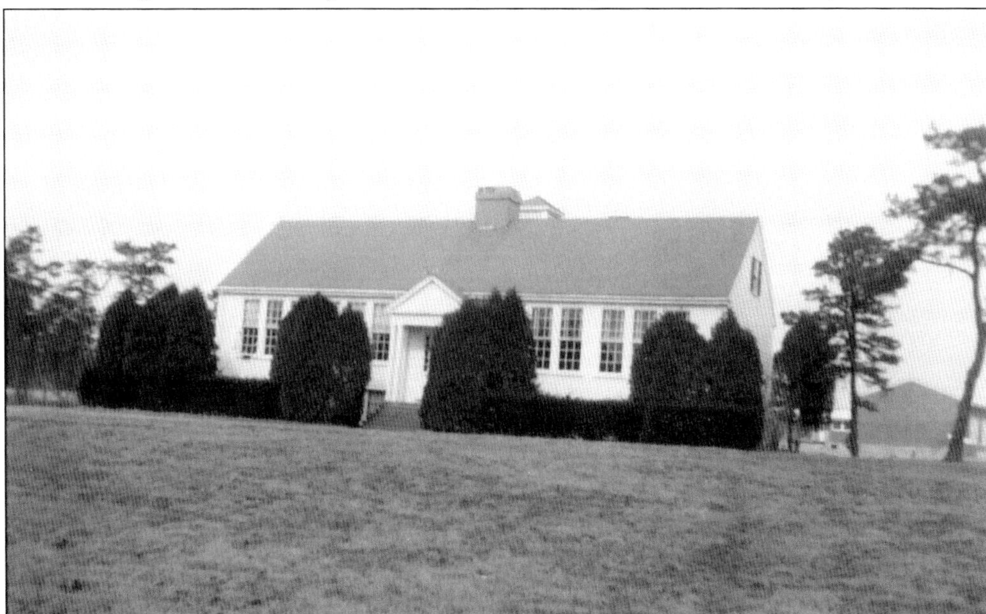

The two-room school was moved in 1936 from the village center to the hilltop facing the new Highway 28. At a cost of $27,000, the Marstons Mills Elementary School was enlarged at the back to four rooms, with a basement for a kitchen, toilets, and cafeteria with a stage for plays and graduation ceremonies.

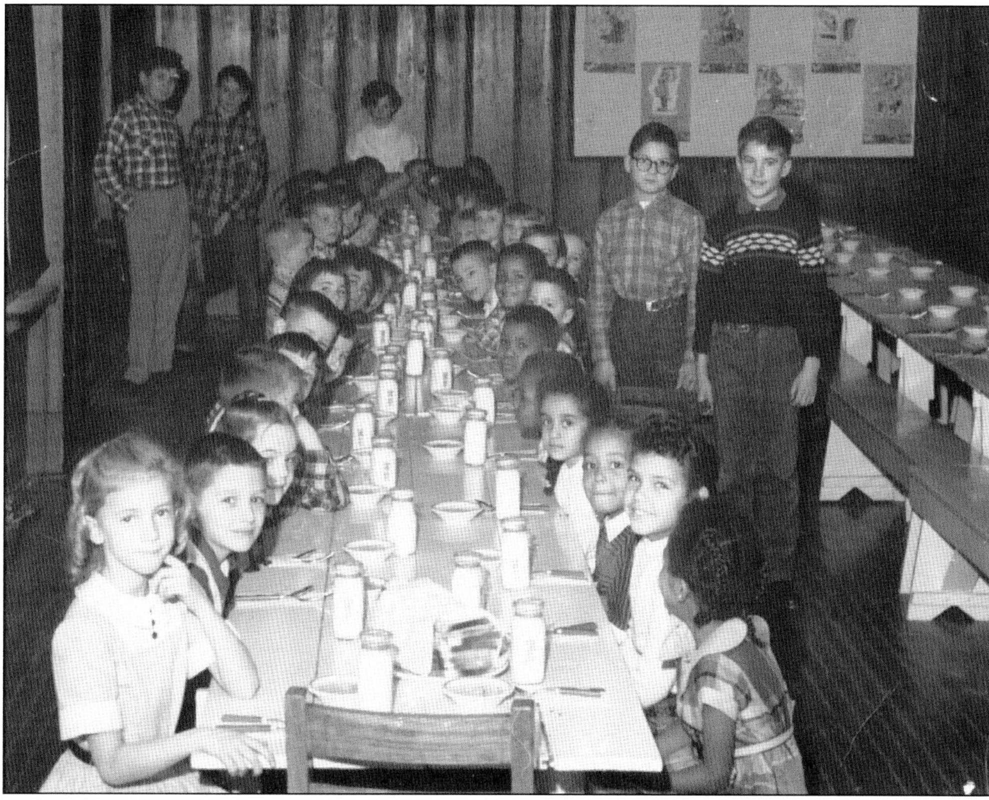

At lunch in the school cafeteria, students of all races got along and did not have problems. The hot-lunch program that began during the war was free, and all students had to eat here or go home for lunch. Oscar Kearney and his wife were cooks. Some meals were very good, but some soups, like peanut butter or spinach soups, were not well liked.

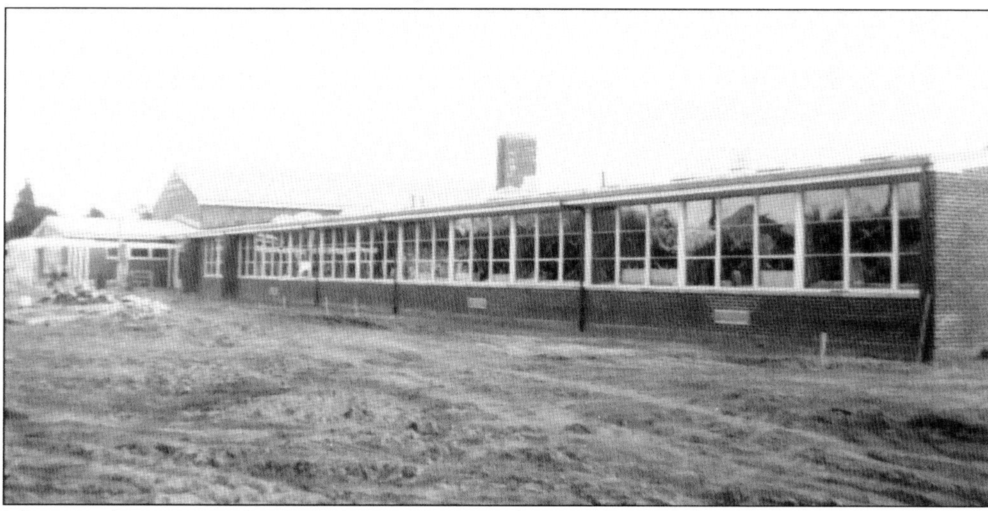

The new elementary school was built in 1958 for $420,000, with six classrooms for 200 students, the first kindergarten, and a multipurpose hall for cafeteria, gym, and assemblies. This was used until 1988, when population growth required a new building for 450 students on Osterville–West Barnstable Road.

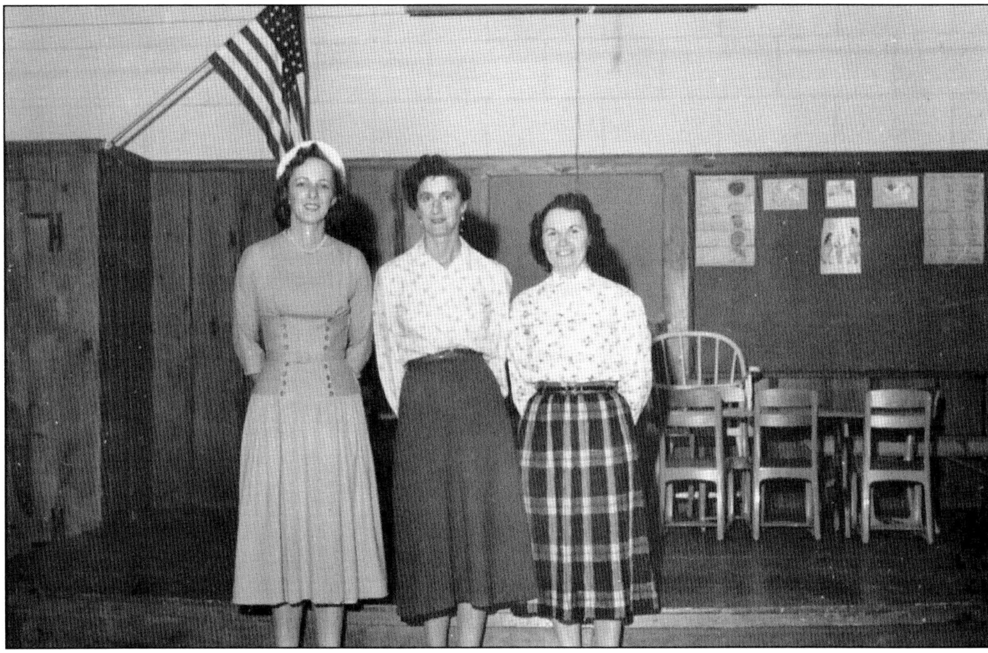

Lacking a Parent-Teacher Association, the principal suggested setting up a mother's group, the Go-Getters Club, in 1950. Its officers about 1953 were, pictured from left to right, Alice Elskamp, Marion Macomber, and Betty Souza Ranta. Club fundraisers gave the school its first film projector, freezer, and television as well as money for field trips, records, and films.

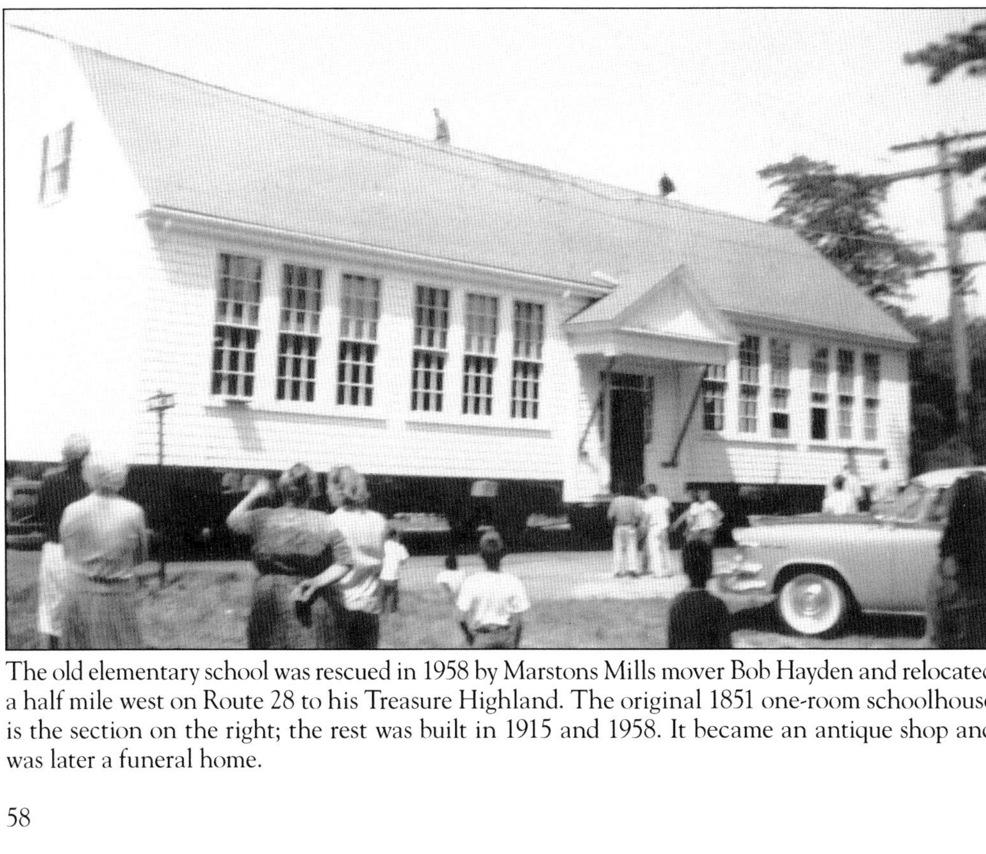

The old elementary school was rescued in 1958 by Marstons Mills mover Bob Hayden and relocated a half mile west on Route 28 to his Treasure Highland. The original 1851 one-room schoolhouse is the section on the right; the rest was built in 1915 and 1958. It became an antique shop and was later a funeral home.

Five

Main Street and Seaput

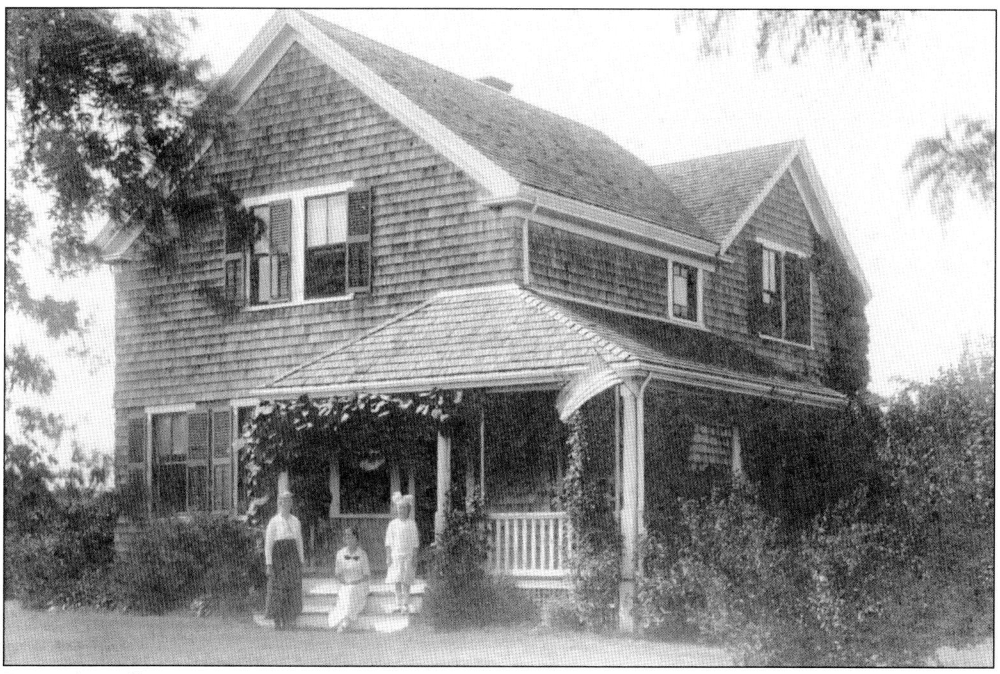

From the village center, Main Street continues east toward Osterville and Hyannis. Just past Lovell's Lane was the home of George Mecarta (1856–1941), longtime county sanitary inspector. The house was built after the Civil War by Capt. Joseph W. Scudder (1843–1888), who inherited part of the large Ebenezer Scudder farm here.

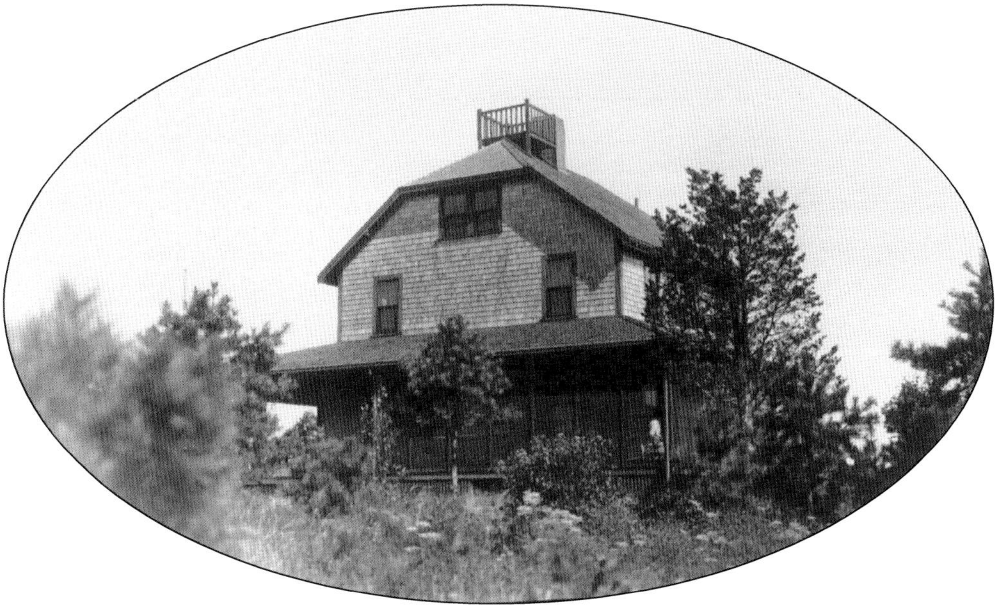

Opposite the Mecarta house was the summer home of the famous musician Felix Winternitz, built in 1906, with a boathouse on Warren's Cove. In 1929, it was bought by the wife of the famous writer J.P. Marquand (1893–1960), who wrote the Mr. Moto stories about the Japanese spy and began his satire about Boston Brahmins while here. The house burned down on Halloween 1971.

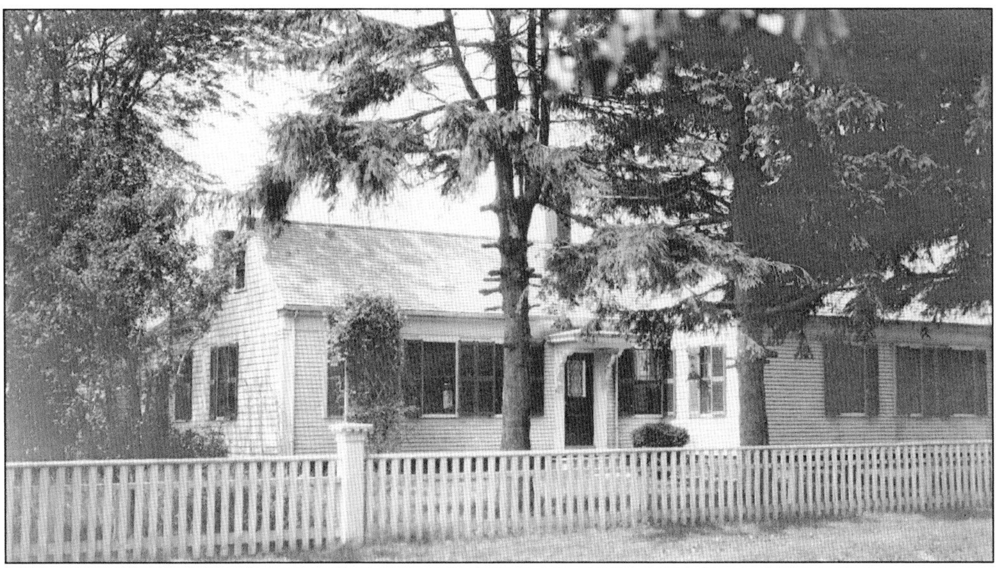

The housewright Andrew Phinney built this fine Greek Revival house in 1845. It remained in the family until 1923, when it was sold to Joseph Barry (1889–1972). At one time, it was a tearoom, a popular summer attraction for motoring tourists in the interwar period. In 1928, the new state highway cut through the back. From here on, Main Street becomes South County Road.

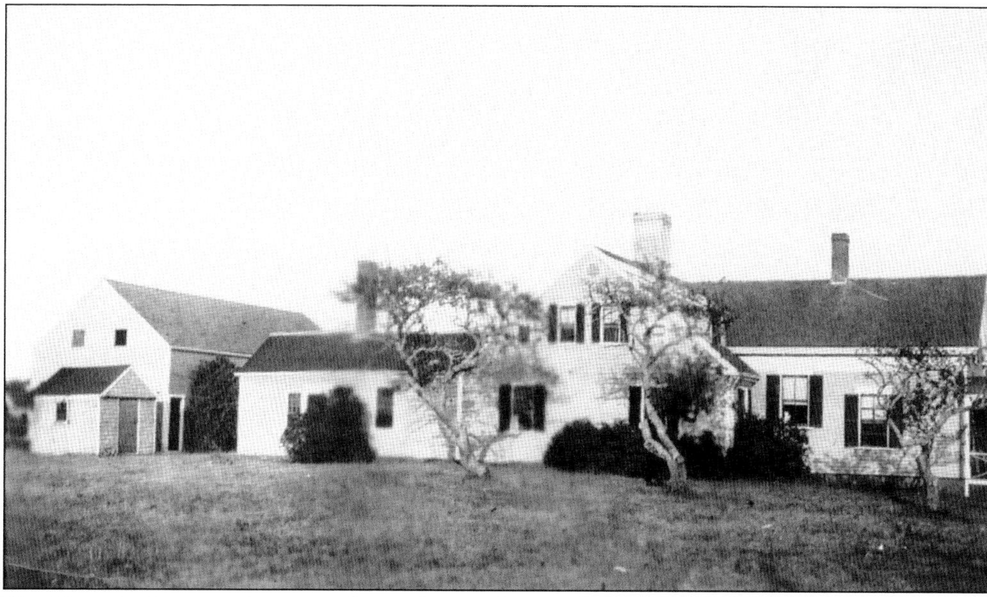

The Cape Cod cottage homestead on a 50-acre farm of Capt. Theophilus S. Adams (1786–1863) dates back to the early 19th century. From 1859 to 1889, it was owned by Elizabeth Gifford, wife of Christopher Gifford of Boston, and thereafter by the Merrill family of Melrose. In 1928, the state highway cut through the property, leaving it on the southeast corner of South County Road.

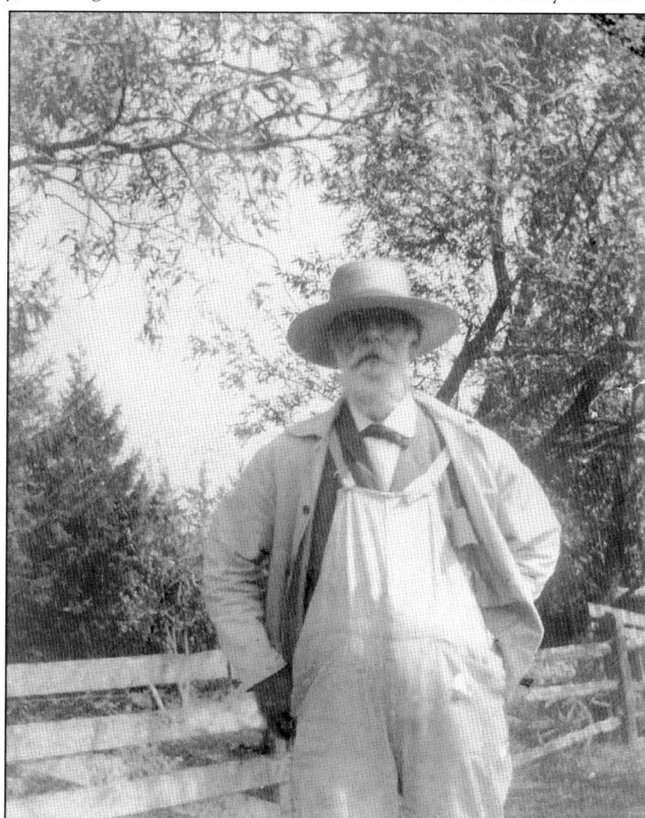

Capt. Samuel Sidney Baxter (1828–1907) went to sea at 11 on coasting ships and grew up to command luxurious steamships between New Orleans and Panama. In the Civil War, he was master of a steamer in the battles of Vicksburg and Port Royal. He retired after the war to grow oysters and prize strawberries here. (Courtesy of Osterville Historical Society.)

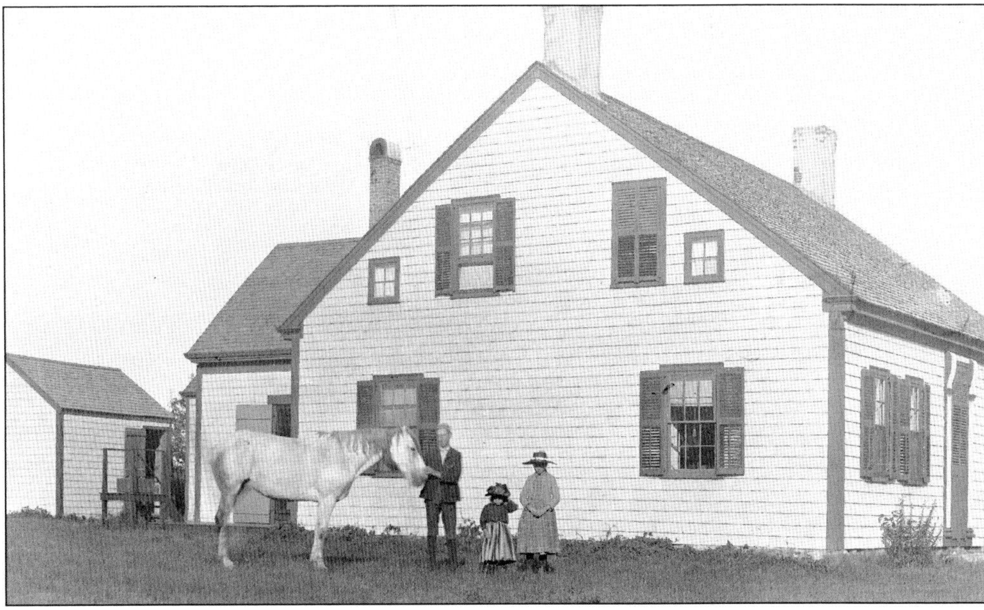

The Luther Hinckley homestead may date to the early 1700s. Here, Prentiss Barnard "Barney" Hinckley is seen with his niece Ann and an unidentified child. Thespian, debater, and civic leader, Barney ran an oyster business on the river below this house, serving martinis to golfers on Seapuit golf course next to his oyster shack. (Courtesy of Gretchen Perry.)

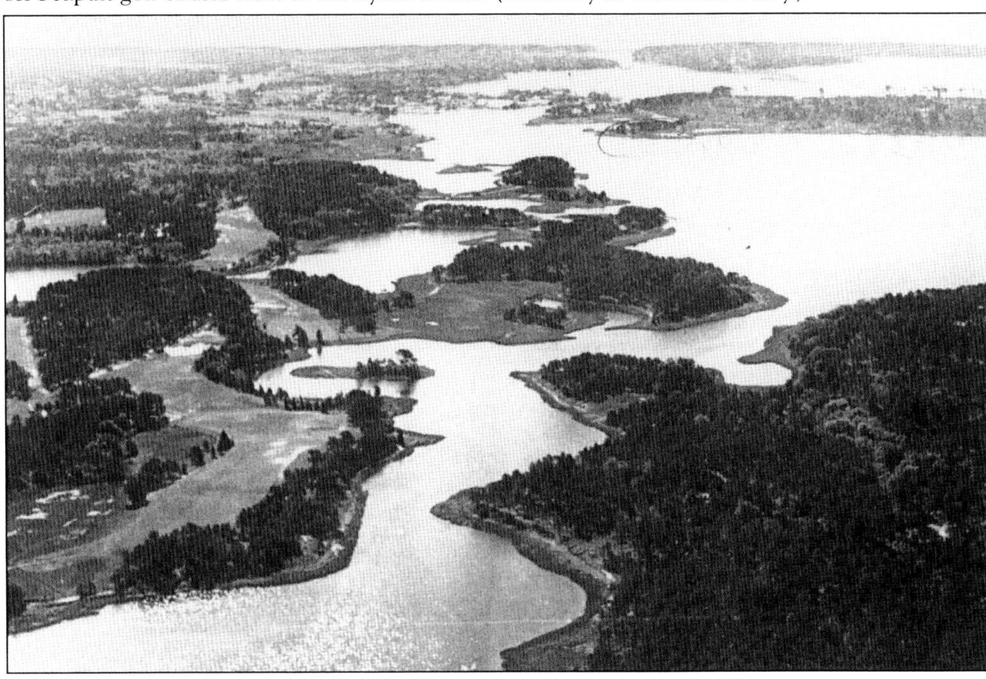

Seapuit Golf Course, one of the first in America, was laid out mostly in Marstons Mills in 1892 by Francis "Daddy" Parsons. Parsons named it for a supposed Indian chief, but the name Seapuit in Wampanoag means "Little River," appropriate for the first four fairways along the lower Marstons Mills River. At hole five, Wigwam Hill (at the left), Indians are said to have camped. (Courtesy of Joel Davis.)

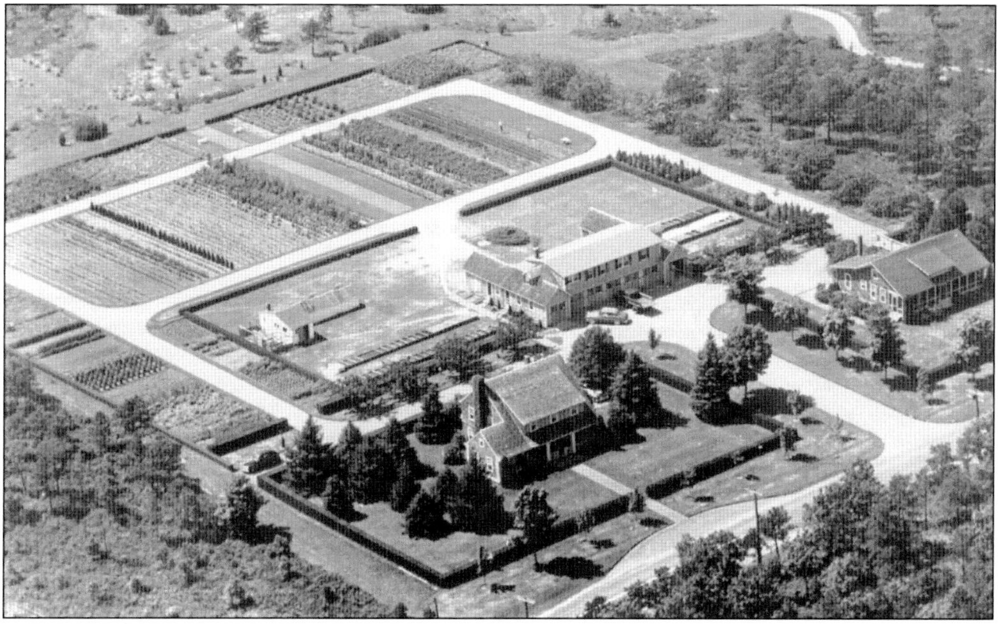

Seapuit Golf Course went bankrupt in the Depression and was bought by "Aluminum King" E.K. Davis, who abandoned the course after the 1944 hurricane felled most of its trees. Here, the extensive gardens of the Davis estate are shown, with the offices of Davis's Seapuit, Inc. and a chauffeur's cottage facing South County Road (at bottom right).

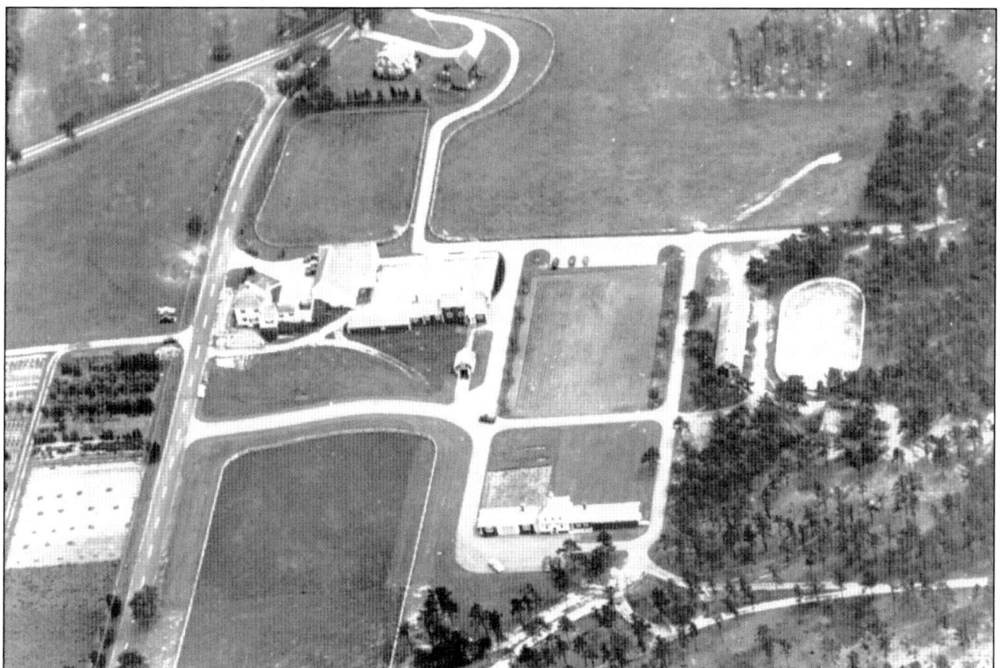

In this aerial view of Davis's Seapuit farm, at the left and facing South County Road is the Goodspeed farmhouse with barn and outbuildings. Stable and track are at the right. At the top is the junction of West Barnstable Road, just inside Osterville. The rest is Marstons Mills. In 1984, the barn was moved north to the Phinney house, where it collapsed.

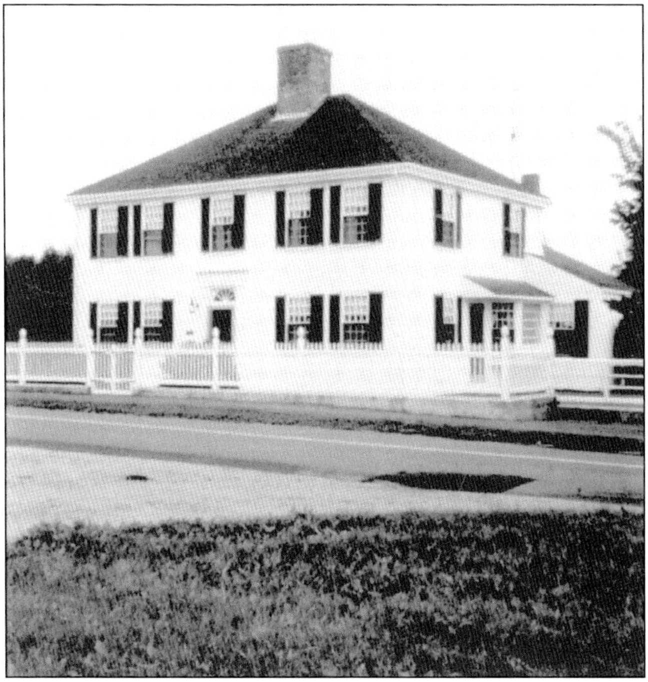

The Goodspeed homestead was built in classic Federal style about 1792, and once welcomed travelers as an inn. The last farmer, Henry Goodspeed (1834–1876) was a sergeant in the Civil War and a state representative. Later, the home was the centerpiece of gentleman farms including the last, belonging to E.K. Davis. In 1984, the house was moved about 300 yards south into Osterville. (Courtesy of Osterville Historical Society.)

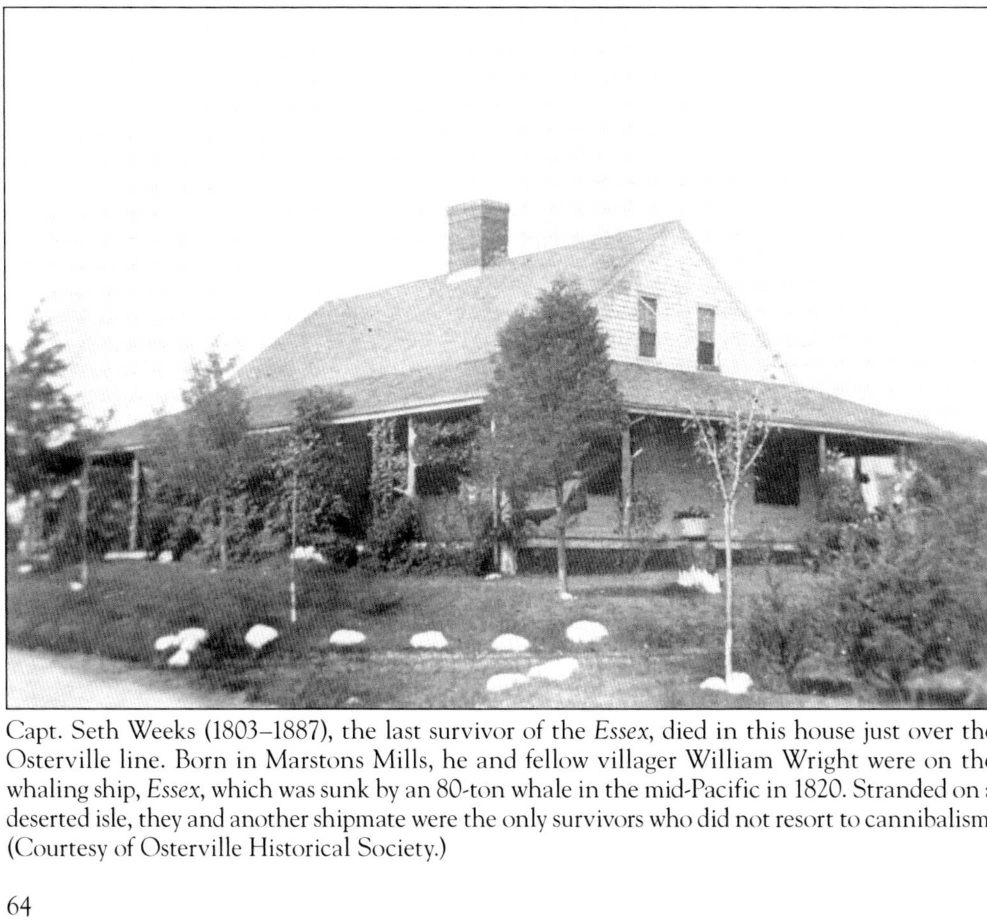

Capt. Seth Weeks (1803–1887), the last survivor of the *Essex*, died in this house just over the Osterville line. Born in Marstons Mills, he and fellow villager William Wright were on the whaling ship, *Essex*, which was sunk by an 80-ton whale in the mid-Pacific in 1820. Stranded on a deserted isle, they and another shipmate were the only survivors who did not resort to cannibalism. (Courtesy of Osterville Historical Society.)

Six

Hamblin's Pond Area

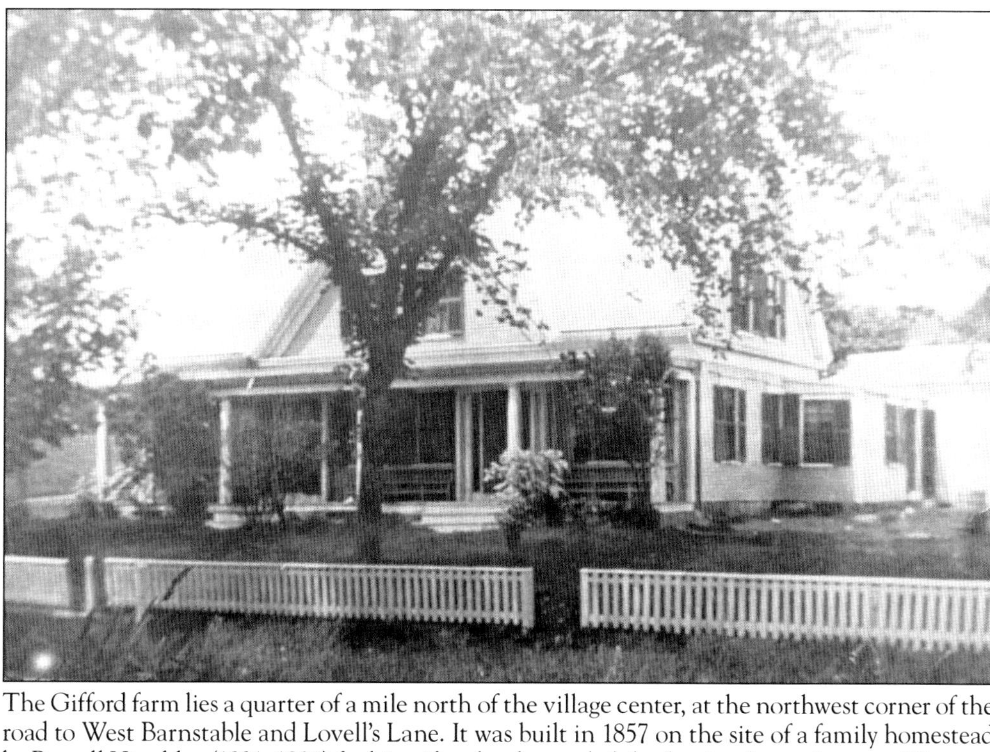

The Gifford farm lies a quarter of a mile north of the village center, at the northwest corner of the road to West Barnstable and Lovell's Lane. It was built in 1857 on the site of a family homestead by Russell Hinckley (1821–1891) for his wife, who demanded the fanciest house in town. The post office moved here in 1873. Later, this was the Bourne farm, then the Bodge farm, the Kleinschmidt dairy farm, and finally Gifford's.

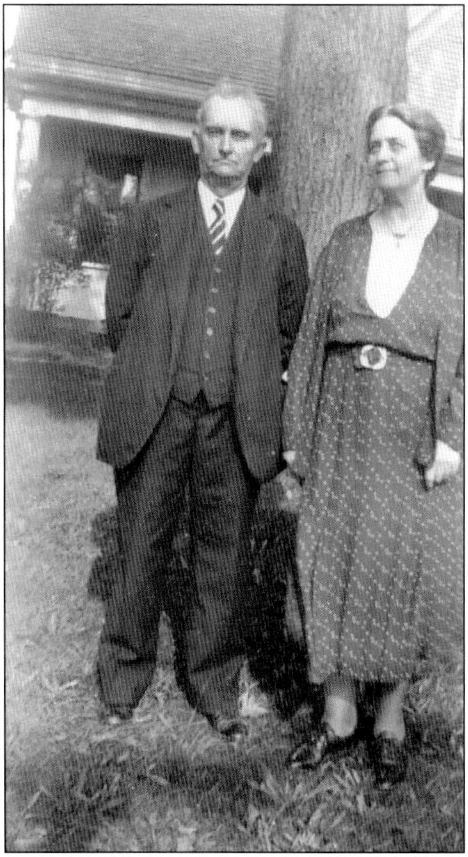

The Gifford farm was run by Lorenzo Gifford (1870–1952) and his wife, Nora (Pierce) (1879–1973), who bought the Kleinschmidt dairy in 1919, continuing the dairy with a local milk delivery route. The farm continued until 1957 as one of the last working farms in the area. Lorenzo's brother was Charles L. Gifford, a longtime congressman from Cape Cod. (Courtesy of Vercille Johnson.)

Lorenzo Gifford and his sons built a slaughterhouse and equipped it with an overhead wheel with hooks to hang carcasses. Lorenzo was a licensed butcher and provided meat for the county jail. In the fall, he slaughtered pigs he raised on "Hog Alley," as Lovell's Lane was called. Cows that no longer produced milk were brought here, fattened up, killed, and sold as beef at 10¢ a pound.

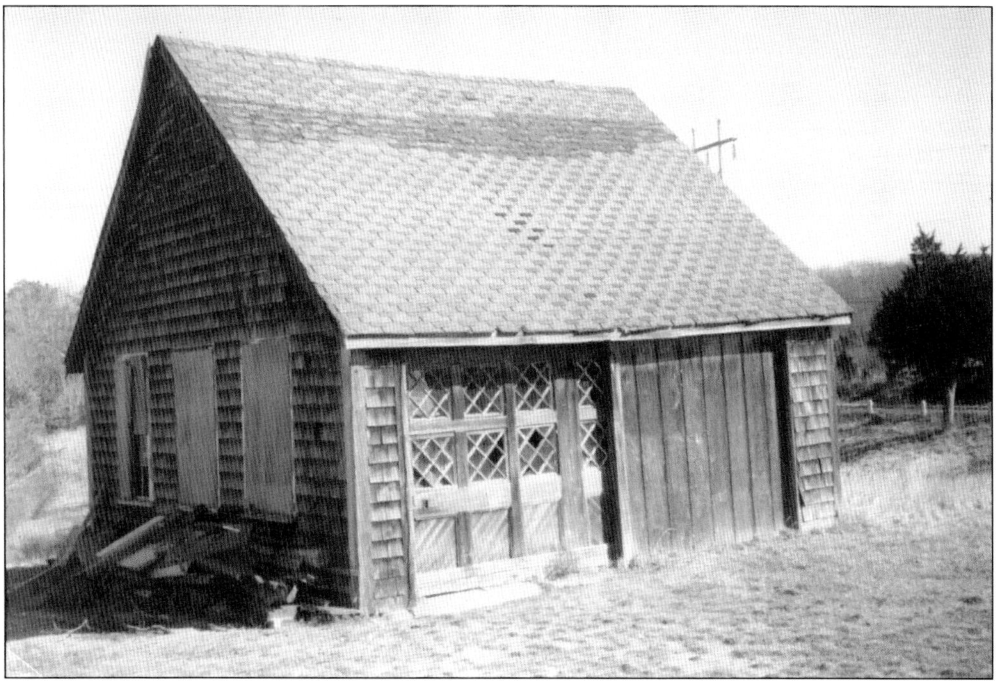

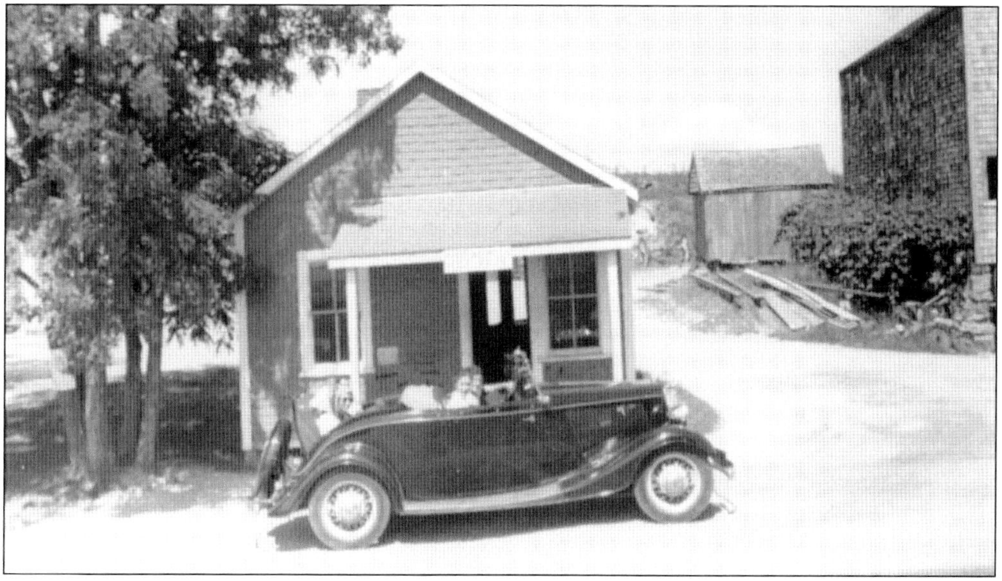

From 1926 to 1941, Nora Gifford was postmistress, with a small building in front of the house for her office. During the Depression, this became the center for the distribution of food under President Roosevelt's Public Assistance Program, where villagers lined up to get free canned goods and bags of sugar and flour. The Gifford children later remembered the huge hanks of bananas hanging in the post office.

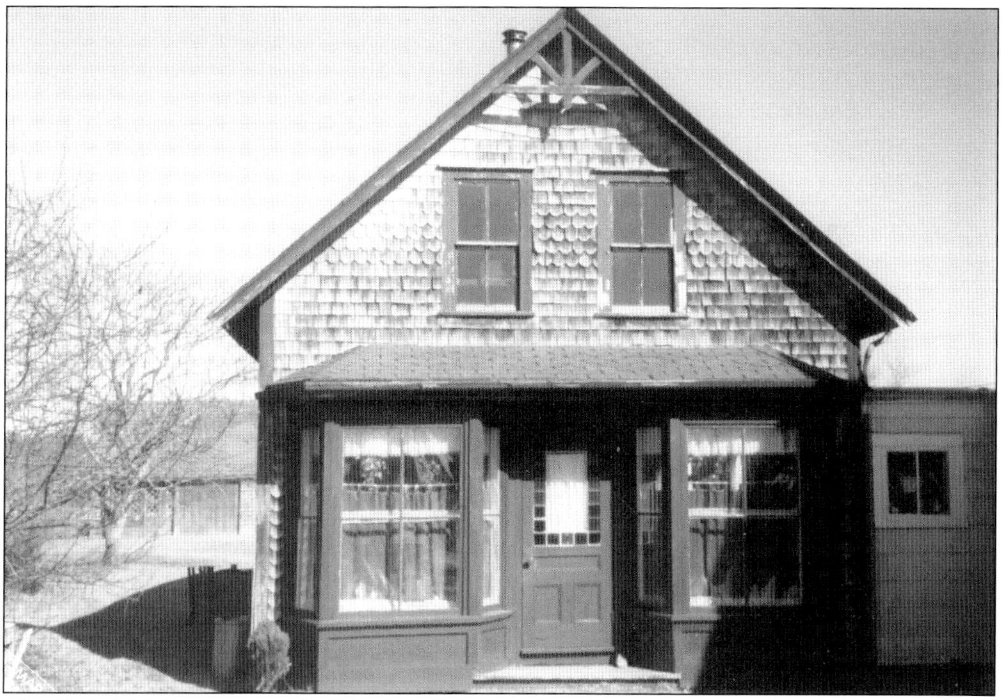

The abandoned Foster Crocker store in the village center was moved in 1927 by Lorenzo and attached to the back of the Gifford farmhouse. Here, Nora sterilized the dairy milk bottles and hung the year's crop of vegetables to dry. There was room for a quilting frame, where village women gathered to make quilts. The floor was cleared for family gatherings and dances.

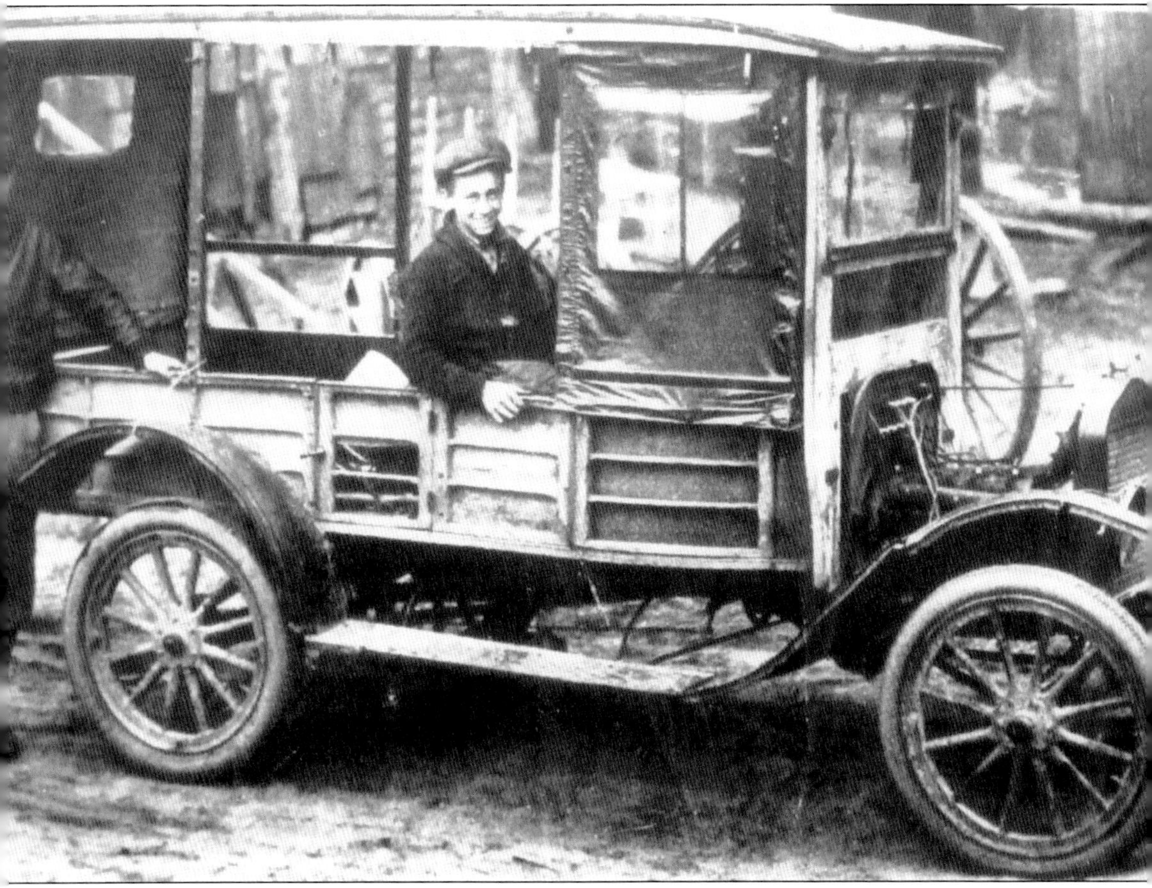

Nora Gifford raised 11 children—6 boys and 5 girls—and married off several from the front porch. The eighth child was Merrill Coleman Gifford (1915–1968), shown here in 1929 at age 15 driving a car he built from scratch for only $1. As a boy, he worked on the farm and in the family's slaughterhouse. After the war, he became a finish carpenter and married the widow of his brother Harold.

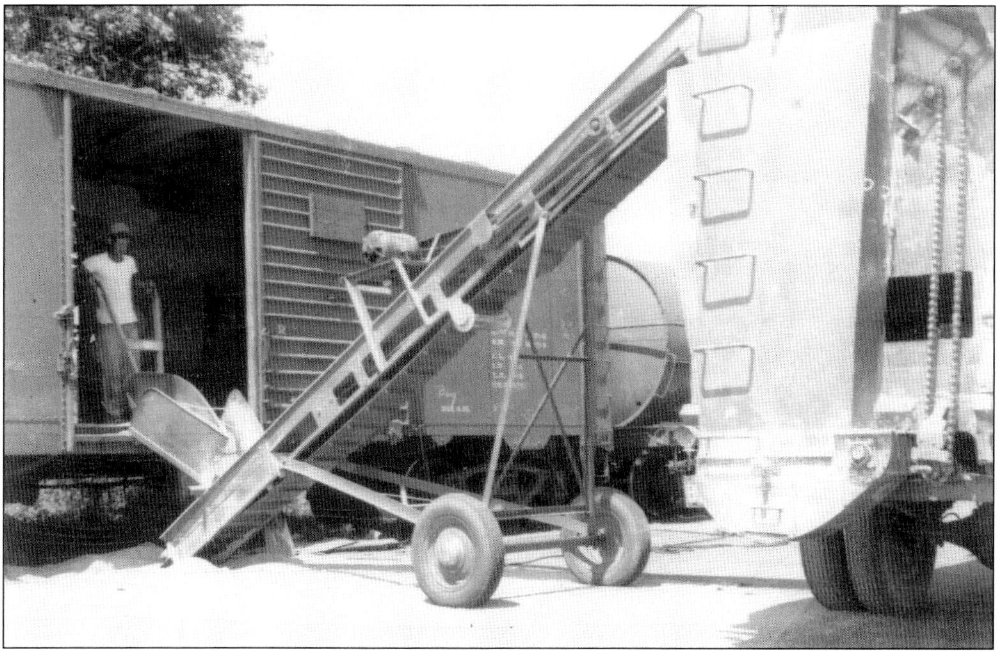

Thousands of ducks and turkeys required huge quantities of feed, which came by railcar to West Barnstable and was trucked to Clear Lake Duck Farm. A miniature railroad distributed the food to the sheds. Initially, a bread machine mixed water into a mash of bran and flour with a dollop of cod-liver oil. After World War II, pellets combined all these nutrients.

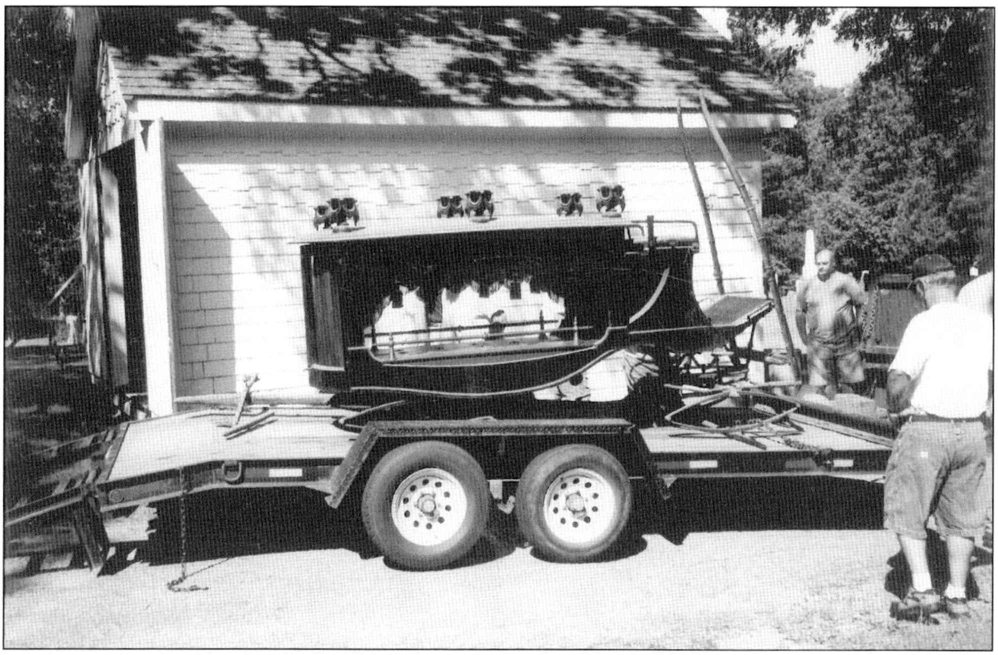

Marstons Mills Burial Ground dates back before the American Revolution, to 1774. Here are buried the early leaders of Cotuit and the famous Marstons Mills judges. There are stones for Revolutionary War veterans, captains of ships, farmers, and their wives and infant children. The 1885 hearse and hearse house are the last in the town of Barnstable, and perhaps Cape Cod.

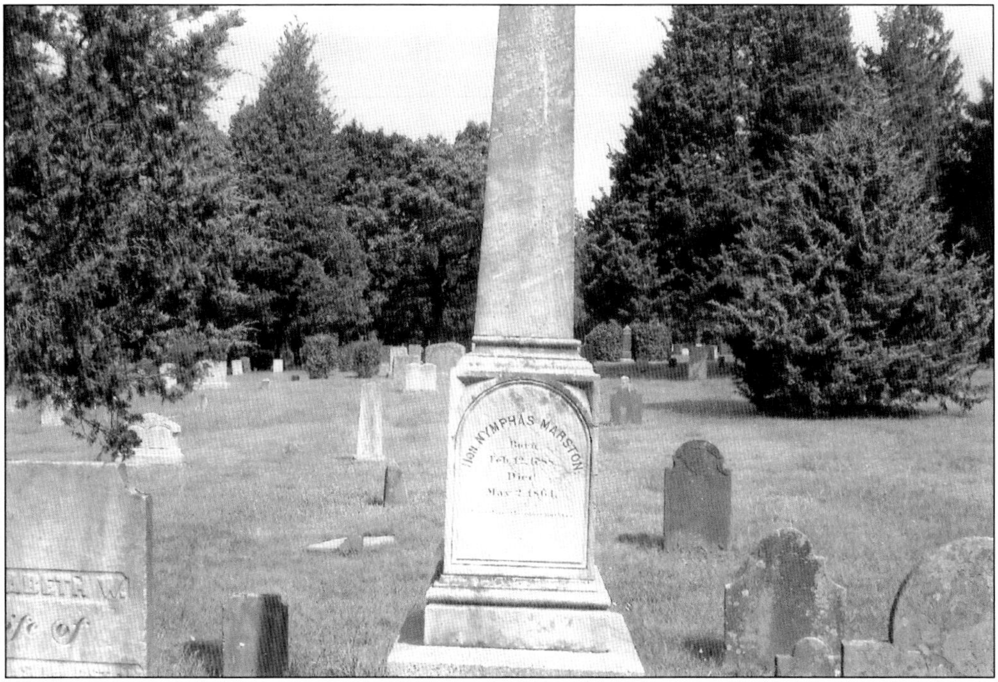

The noble obelisk honors Judge Nymphas Marston (1778–1864), a distinguished lawyer who became state senator and judge of probate from 1828 to 1854. The table gravestone nearby has lost its inscription honoring his famous uncle and namesake Nymphas Marston (1728–1788), who was a town moderator during the American Revolution, serving on the town's Committee of Correspondence. (Courtesy of Arthur Thifault.)

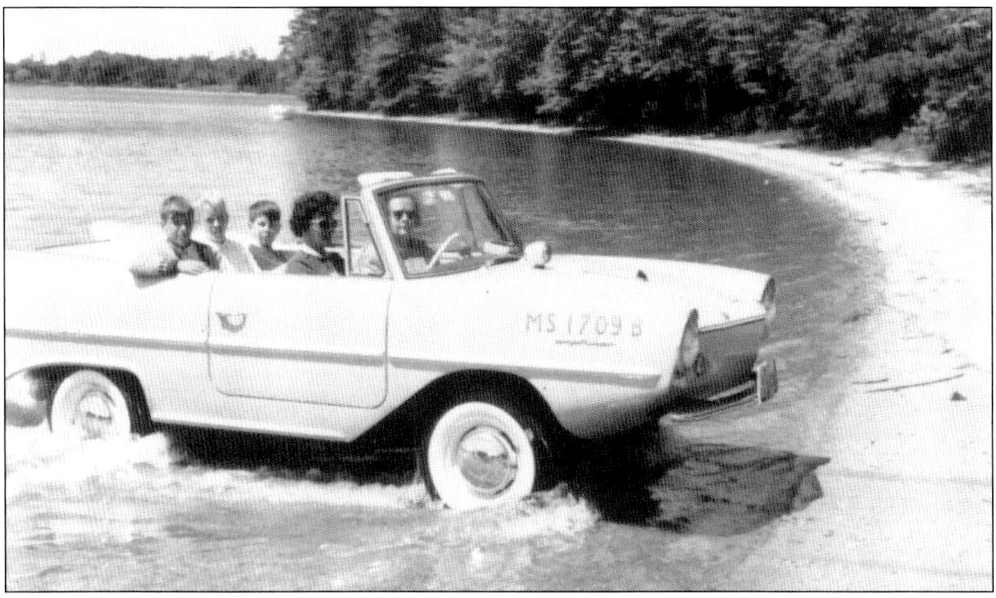

Next to the burial ground is the Town Beach, once the playground of Pekin ducks. In 1965, Ruth Rusher, a lifesaving heroine and tour guide, drove her amphibious Amphicar for a spin on Hamblin's Pond as a treat for new graduates of Marstons Mills elementary school. Made in Germany for the American market, the car could do 7 knots in the water and 70 miles per hour on land.

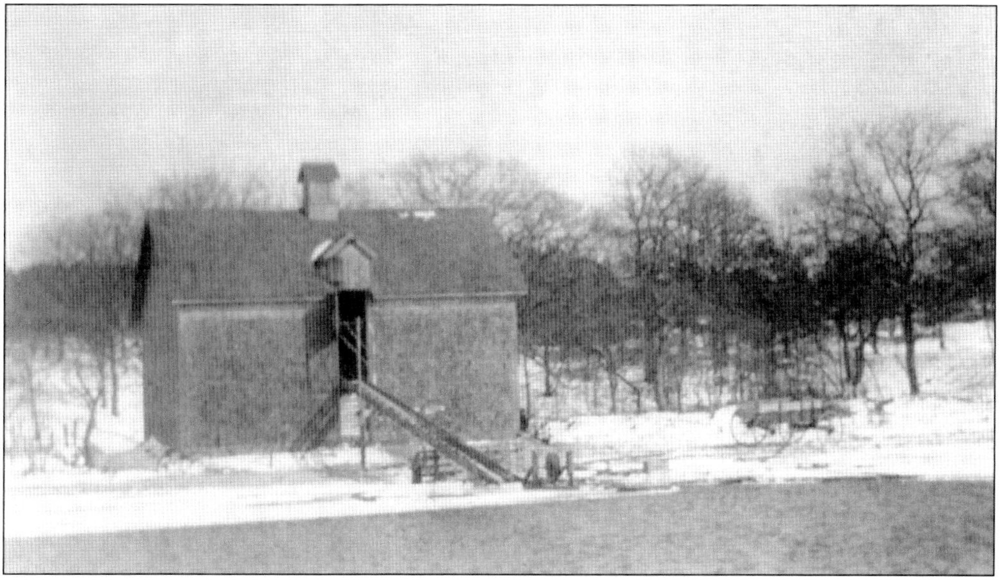

The icehouse on Hamblin's Pond in the 1890s was below today's Burgess House. Ice was cut into large blocks and dragged by horse and then up the ramp by wheel and tackle to be stored in the icehouse, whose double walls were insulated by seaweed or sawdust. The village held Fourth of July picnics here.

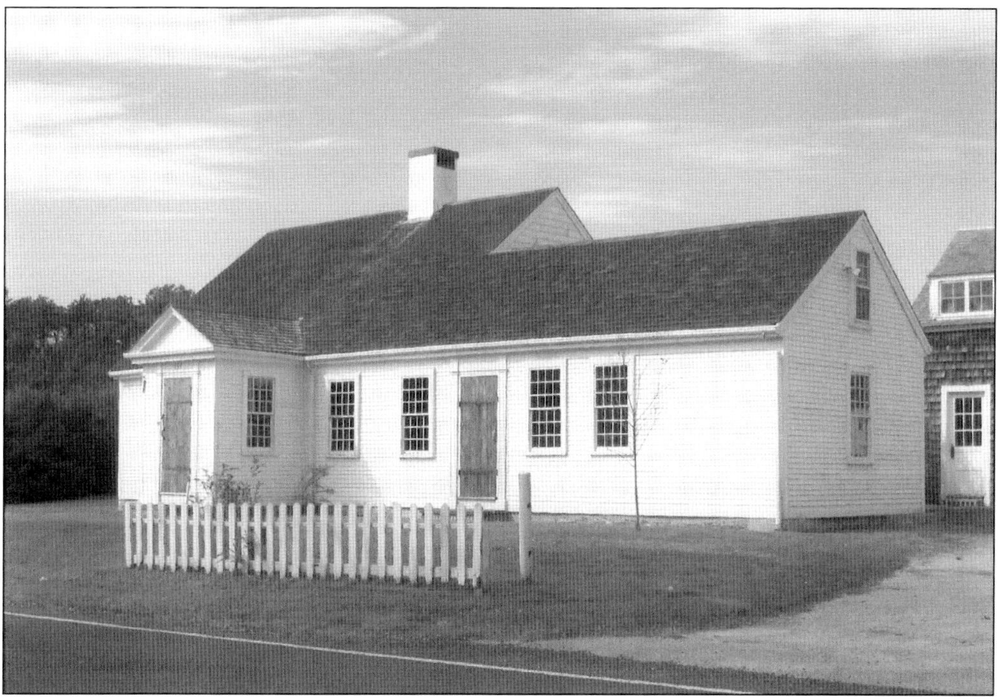

The Burgess house was built in 1823 as the home and office of two village doctors. In 1938, it became the garden showcase of Dr. Rachel Burgess. The January 1948 *House & Garden* magazine called it "the Prettiest House on Cape Cod," featuring hundreds of flowerbeds, a croquet court, a bowling green, a "Welsh Clock" blooming 12 months of the year, and a view of Hamblin's Pond across a field of red wheat.

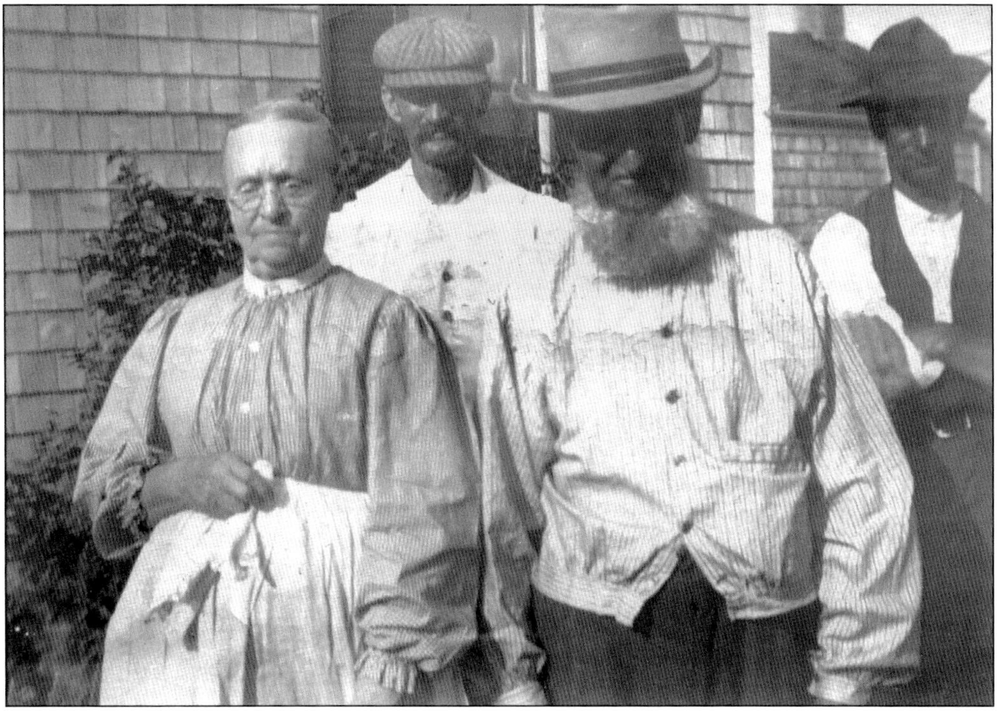

Bennett Wing Cammett (1835–1915) was named for the Quaker doctor who probably delivered him. Dr. Bennett Wing lived in the Burgess house, where he died of smallpox, which he caught from a brother he was caring for. Cammett was a dairy farmer who grew strawberries and cleared woodland. He and his wife, Elizabeth (Hamblin), were active leaders in the Methodist church.

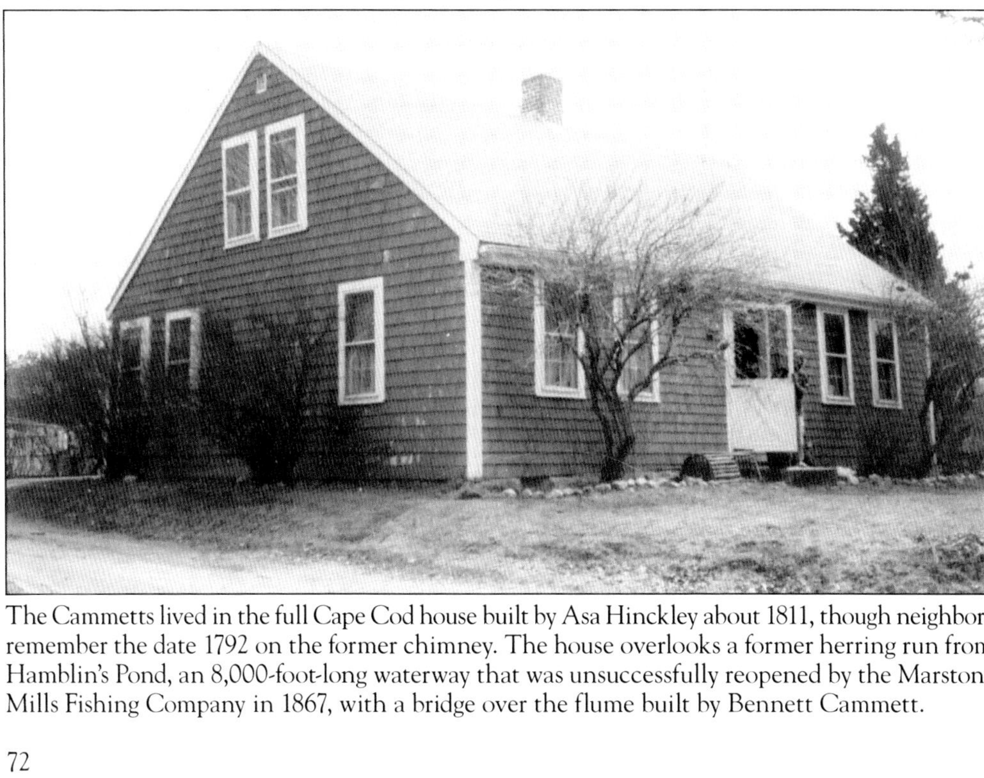

The Cammetts lived in the full Cape Cod house built by Asa Hinckley about 1811, though neighbors remember the date 1792 on the former chimney. The house overlooks a former herring run from Hamblin's Pond, an 8,000-foot-long waterway that was unsuccessfully reopened by the Marstons Mills Fishing Company in 1867, with a bridge over the flume built by Bennett Cammett.

Old Bill Signet (1846–1936) came from St. Helena on a whaling ship. He lived with the Cammetts doing stable work and odd jobs. After their deaths, he washed dishes in Osterville, walking two and a half miles and refusing offers of a ride. Ted Pierce remembered him as bowlegged, with eyes that snapped when someone teased him about baiting a whale with minnows.

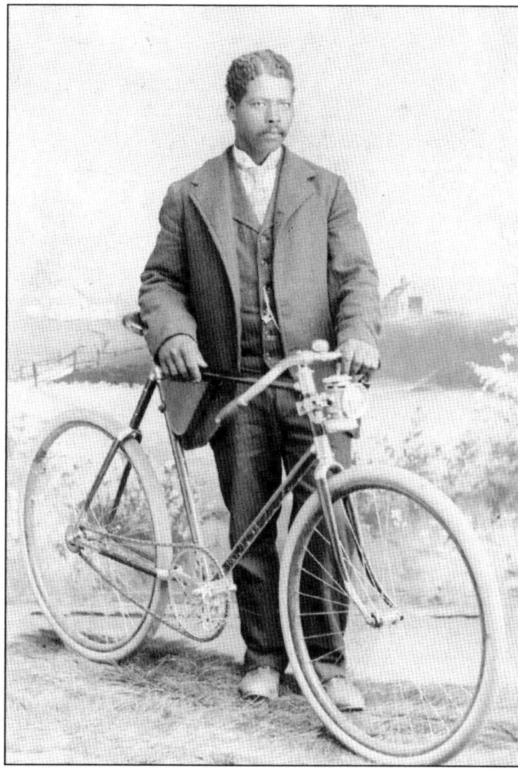

The Fuller farmhouse on the road to West Barnstable was built about 1800, rebuilt after a fire in 1887, when "Ma" Olive Hamblin Fuller (1844–1909) left clothes drying by the fire. The south wing was added in 1892, when this picture was taken, as a wing for the newlyweds Calvin Fuller (1869–1959) and his wife, Mary Hallett. This was one of the last working farms until the 1980s. (Courtesy of Harold Fuller.)

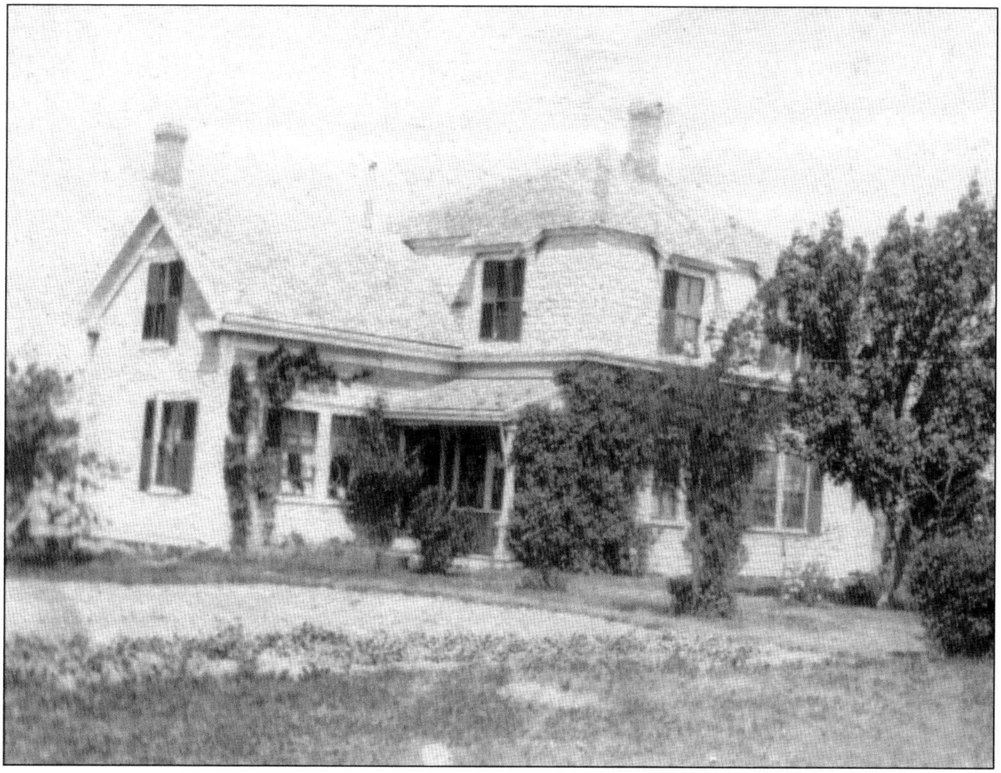

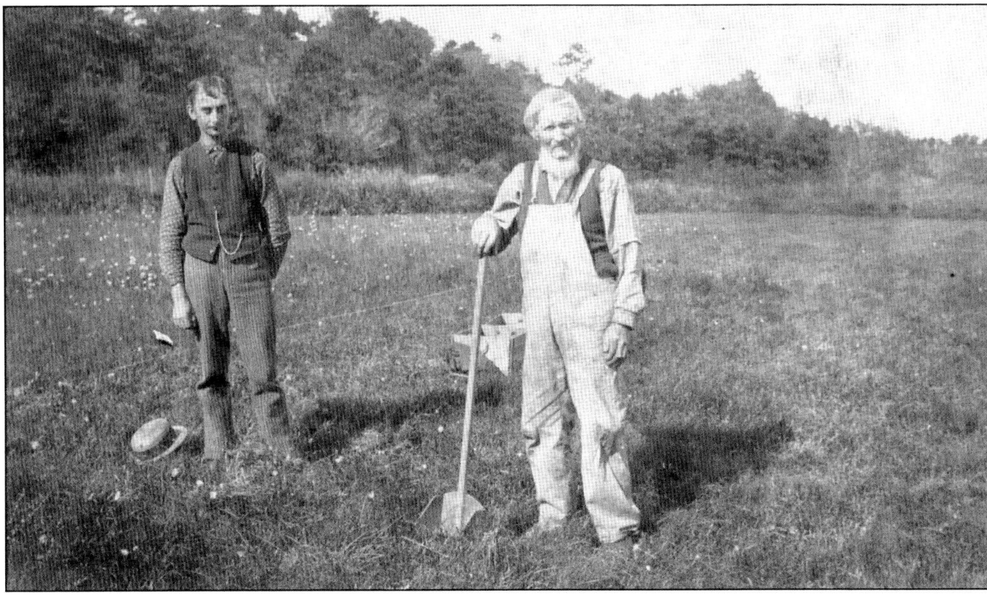

Ansel E. Fuller (1843–1924) is pictured working with his son Calvin in the Fuller cranberry bog south of the homestead along Cotuit Road. In 1903, the yield was 90 barrels. The Fullers were descendants of village founder Roger Goodspeed and Dr. Matthew Fuller, the hot-headed surgeon general of the Colonial troops in King Philip's War, whose parents came on the *Mayflower*. (Courtesy of Harold Fuller.)

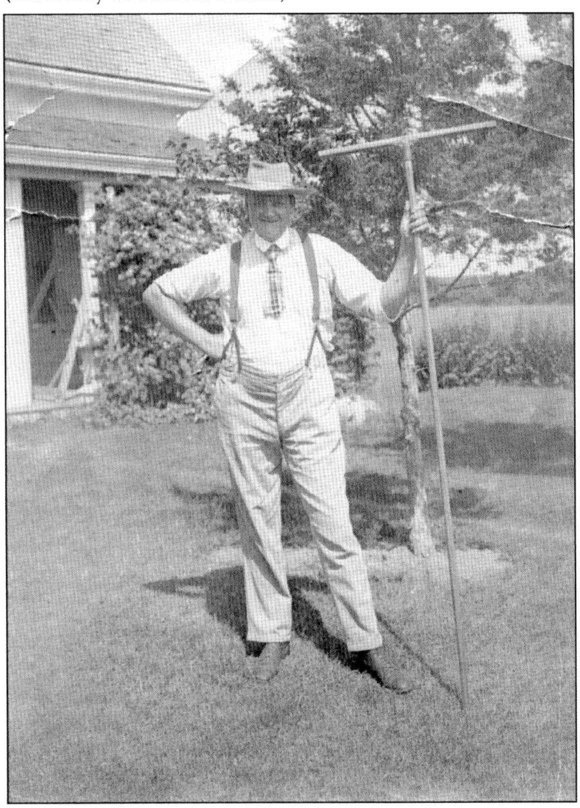

Ansel Austin Fuller (1874–1946), shown with a hay rake in 1915, was a working farmer, but he poses in Sunday gear of hat, tie, and dress shoes. In addition to the productive cranberry bog, the Fullers had a herd of cows whose milk was sent to the Mystic Lake Dairy. (Courtesy of Harold Fuller.)

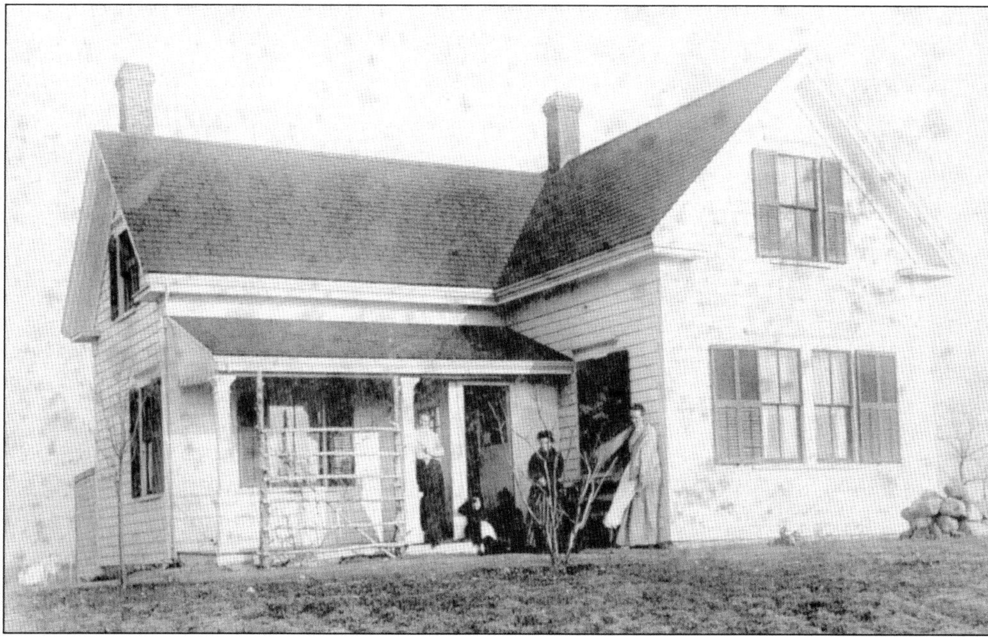

Across the road from the Fuller farm is the house built in 1889 by Wilton Bennett Cammett (1865–1923), son of Bennett Wing Cammett. In 1887, he had married Sarah A. Jones, 25 years his senior. When they got the job of running the Falmouth Almshouse in 1890, they sold their residence to their neighbor Calvin Fuller (1869–1959), who screened cranberries here and rented the house to William Thew, whose son later bought it.

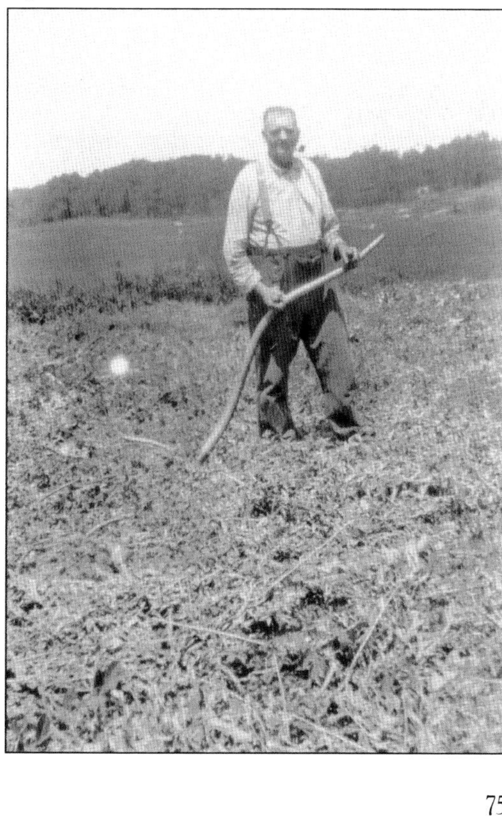

Ansel Austin Fuller is cutting hay with scythe, about 1915. In 1898, when he was 24, he married Rose Cartier (1874–1954) of Boston. They had four children—Elizabeth, who married Lorenzo Gifford Jr., and three boys, Carroll, Orrin and Alfred. Alfred (1918–2000), the youngest, kept the farm going until the end of the century. He and his wife, Barbara, were active members of the Santuit Grange. (Courtesy of Harold Fuller.)

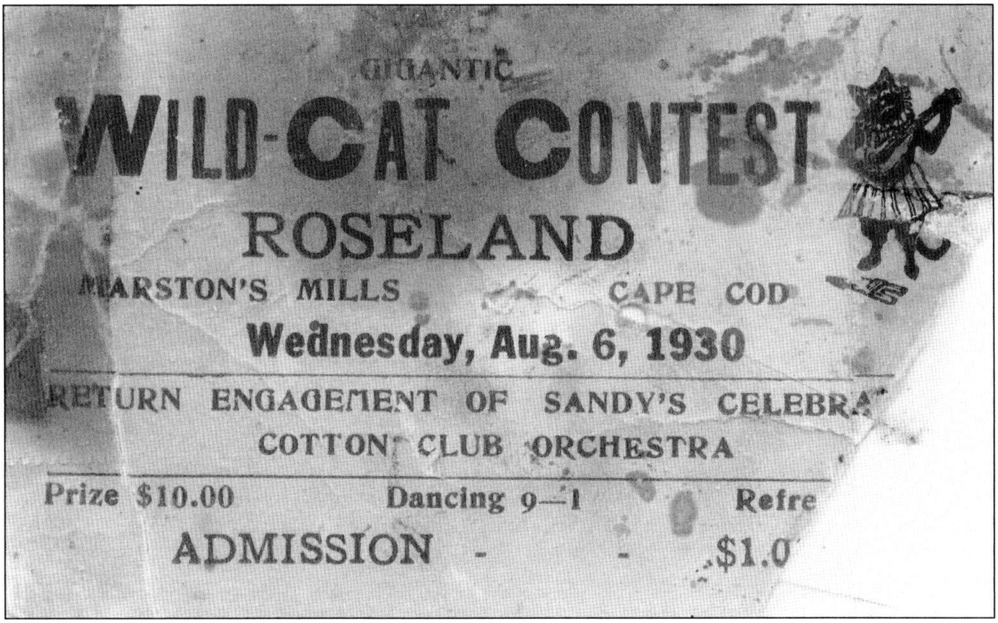

East of the Fuller farm was Roseland Ballroom, where Count Basie played and Ella Fitzgerald sang. The big, barnlike structure was built in the mid-1920s, during Prohibition, by "Ma" Elnora Rose (1908–1963), a descendant of South Carolina slaves. Cape Verdeans and others came from afar, bringing their own liquor to dance to the "mixed-up" bands, made up of banjo, guitar, violin, and drums.

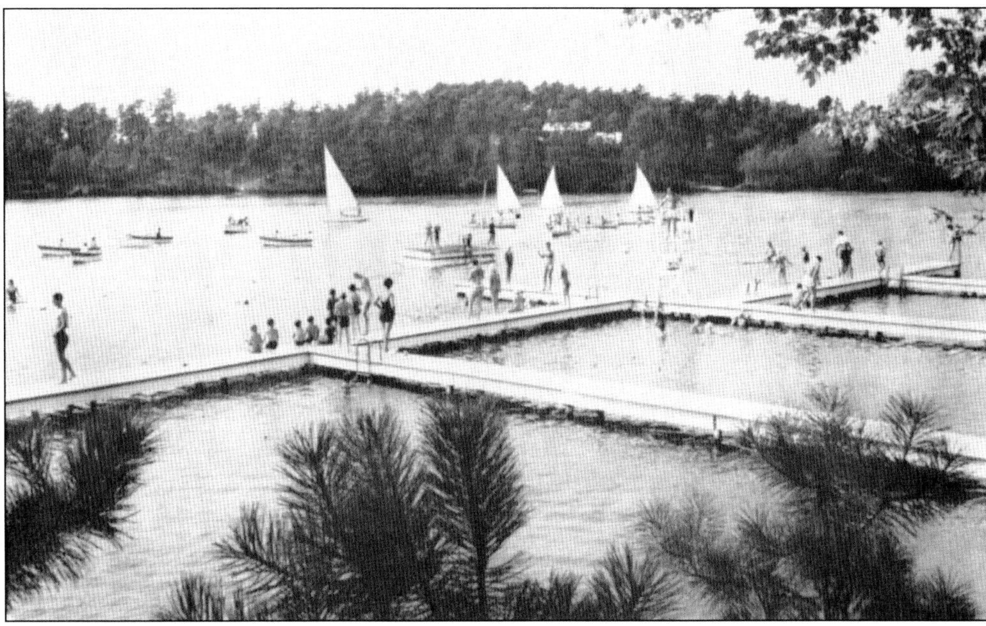

The first summer camp was started in 1934 by June Whittemore at the waterfront of what is now the Burgess house. The children enjoyed greatly swimming in Hamblin's Pond with the ducks that had escaped from the Clear Lake Duck Farm. The second camp was Camp Alpine, on the waterfront of the Fuller farm. The musicians Lillian and Mark Budd opened the camp for Jewish children in 1939; it was one of the first coed camps in New England. (Courtesy of Budd family.)

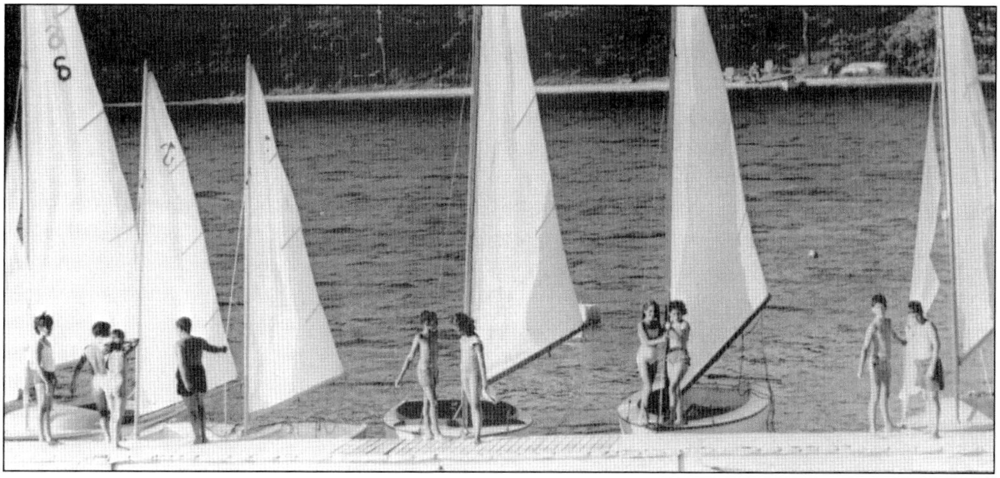

Gasoline rationing during World War II made Camp Alpine hard to maintain, but the camp flourished in the postwar years until 1975. Field trips were made to the Blue Hill for mountain climbing and to Bass River for canoeing, but the main outdoor activities were swimming and sailing. (Courtesy of Budd family.)

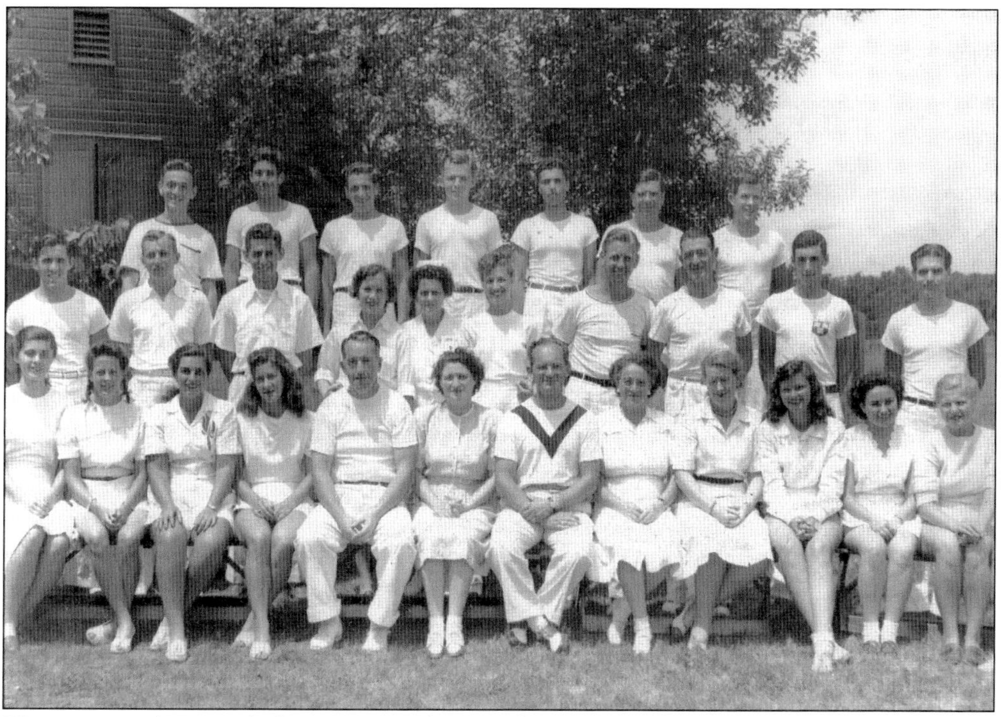

This postwar photograph shows Camp Alpine staff with director Mark Budd in the "V" shirt, his wife, Lillian, to his right, and head counselor Thomas O'Donnell on her right. Musical performances of shows such as *Oklahoma!* and *Oliver!* were produced by talented drama counselors, and the children were accompanied by Lillian Budd, a former concert pianist and teacher. (Courtesy of O'Donnell family.)

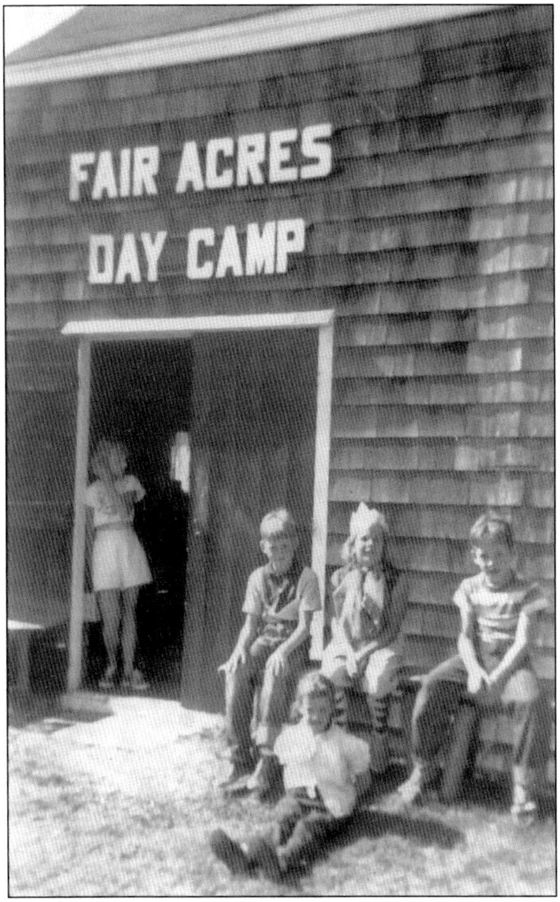

Nearby was Camp Fair Acres, on the west shore of Shubael Pond. Begun in 1950 by Cornelius and Arlene Fair in the old Morse dairy barn, to which they added surplus Army barracks, it was a weekday camp for the two summer months. The Larson family continued it from 1967 until 1987, when they began a year-round day school. (Courtesy Veronica Canning.)

Alfred Fuller came from his nearby farm to give the Fair Acres children a hayride. Another fun trip was made to the Oyster Harbors stables for horseback lessons by "Mister Bob." The camp week always ended with Friday treats of ice cream and bobbing for bottles in the pond. (Courtesy of Veronica Canning.)

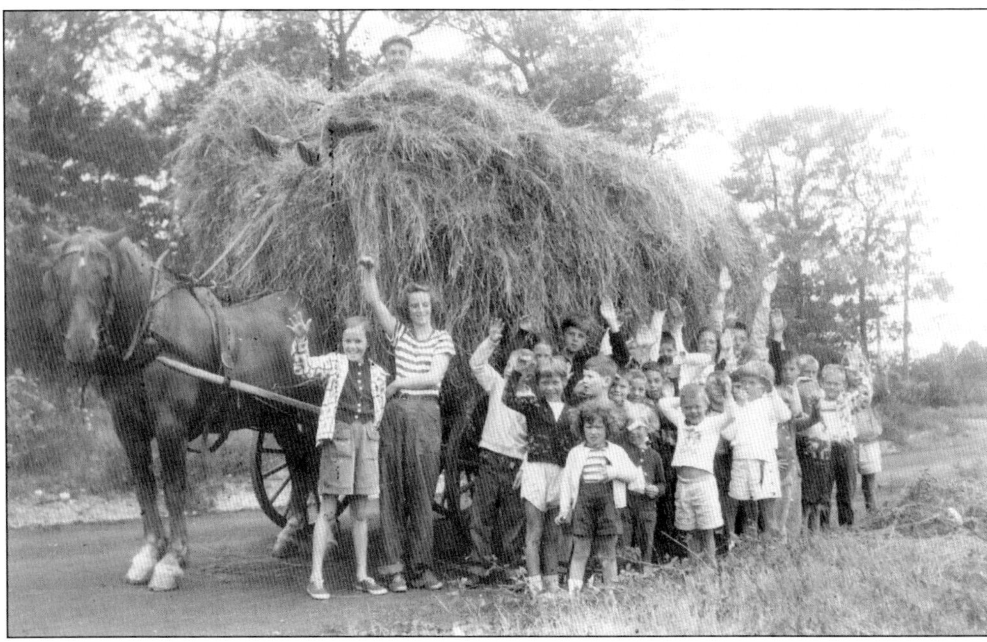

Seven

The Plains

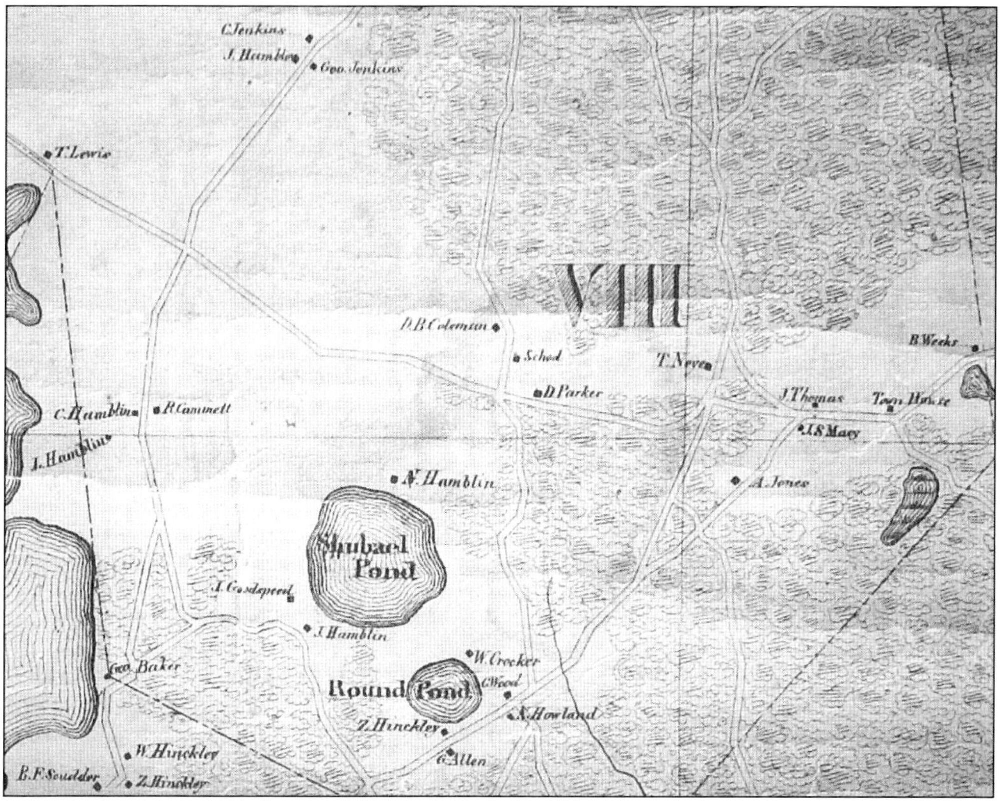

The Plains, or Hamblin's Plains, in 1856 lay at the foot of a glacial moraine and are a broad stretch of fertile soil that was tilled by Indians for corn and squash and taken over by Colonial settlers for farming. Well populated, it had its own schoolhouse at the junction of Race Lane and Osterville–West Barnstable Road (Roman VIII was the school district). Farmhouses faced southward onto the central cape highway, Race Lane. (Courtesy of Robert Frazee.)

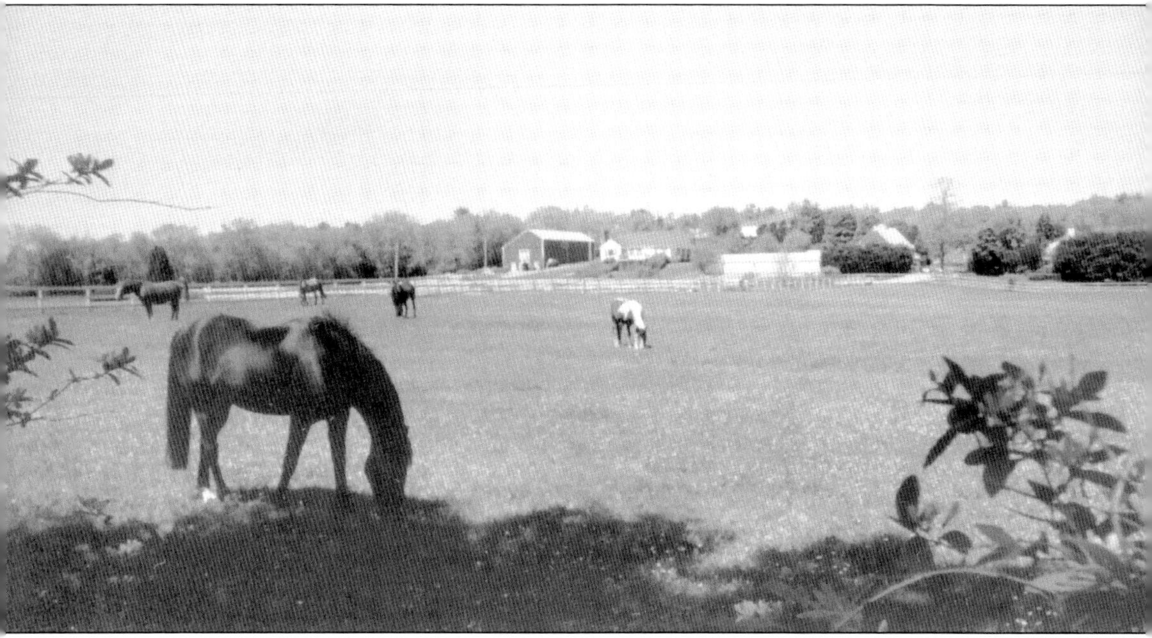

The northwest corner of Race Lane and Osterville–West Barnstable Road still retains the rural character of the past. In the 19th century, it was the Benjamin and Isaac Crocker farm, later David Coleman's, and after 1938 the pioneer veterinarian Dr. Daniel Leach's. The Barnstable County Sheriff's Youth Ranch is located here today. (Courtesy of Susan Leach.)

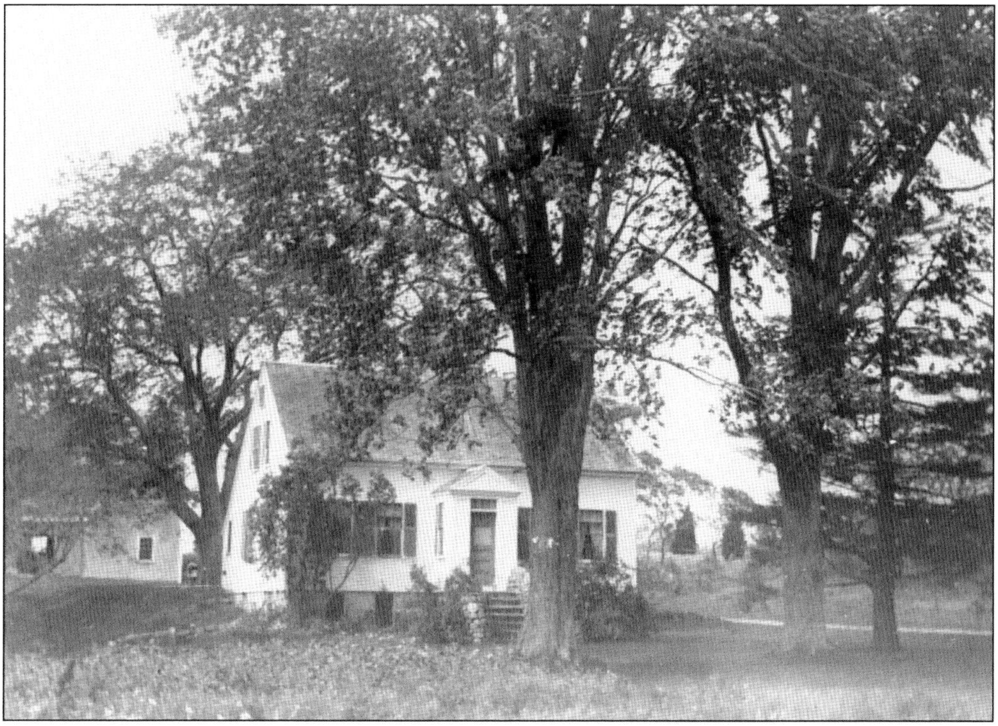

The Benjamin and Isaac Crocker farmhouse was built about 1808 as a full Cape Cod cottage. Later, it was the farm of Civil War veteran David Coleman, who married the Crocker heiress. This view, taken before World War II, shows the big elm trees and the barn, which Dr. Leach used for his veterinary practice. (Courtesy of Susan Leach.)

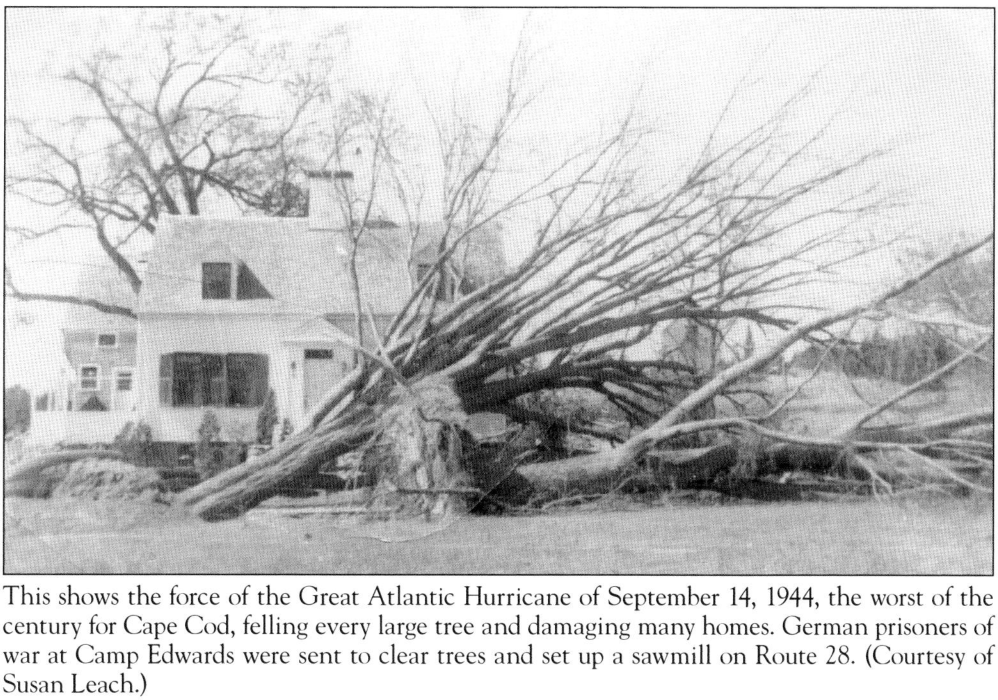

This shows the force of the Great Atlantic Hurricane of September 14, 1944, the worst of the century for Cape Cod, felling every large tree and damaging many homes. German prisoners of war at Camp Edwards were sent to clear trees and set up a sawmill on Route 28. (Courtesy of Susan Leach.)

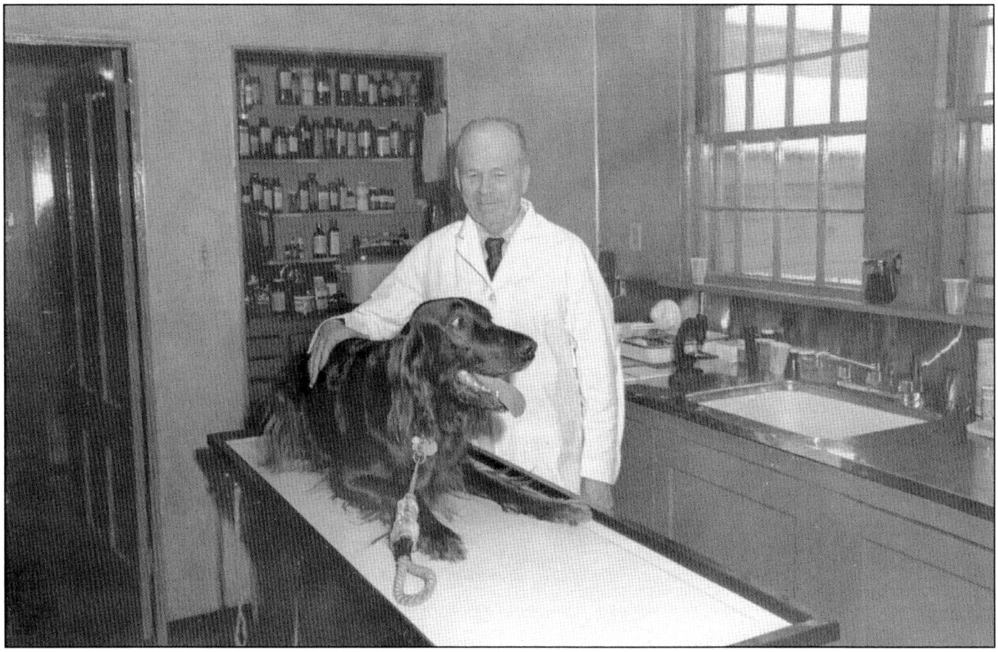

Dr. Daniel Leach (1903–1986) was the first veterinarian on Cape Cod. With a degree from the University of Pennsylvania School of Veterinary Medicine in 1933, he bought the 20-acre Crocker farm in 1938. He started his animal practice in the basement of the old house and later moved to the remodeled barn behind the house. (Courtesy of Susan Leach.)

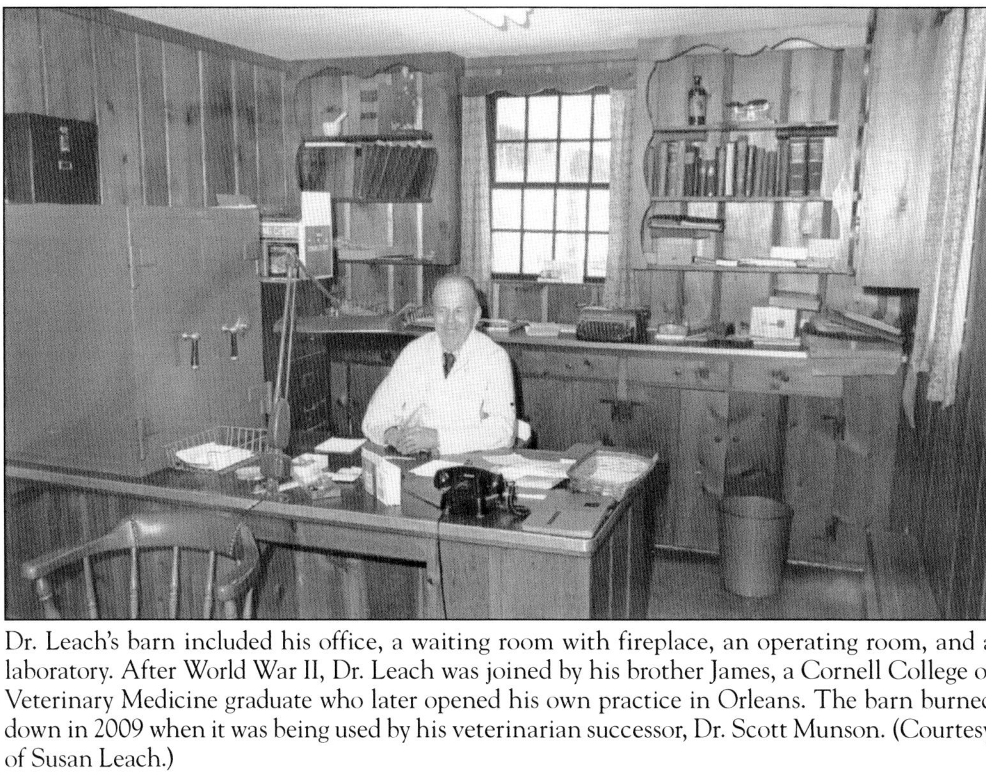

Dr. Leach's barn included his office, a waiting room with fireplace, an operating room, and a laboratory. After World War II, Dr. Leach was joined by his brother James, a Cornell College of Veterinary Medicine graduate who later opened his own practice in Orleans. The barn burned down in 2009 when it was being used by his veterinarian successor, Dr. Scott Munson. (Courtesy of Susan Leach.)

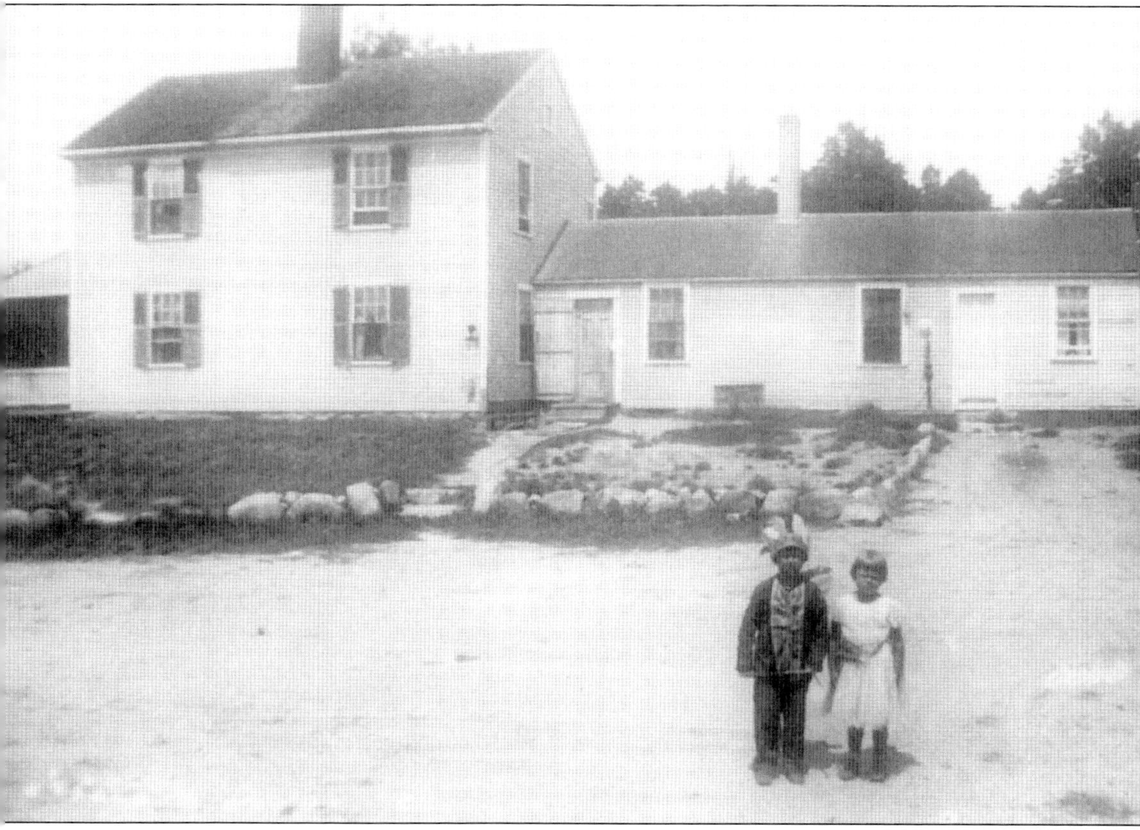

The James Jenkins house on the West Barnstable Road (Route 149) was the home of Elizabeth "Buff" Crocker Jenkins (1874–1956), known as "The Woman Who Saved a Meetinghouse" (the Rooster Church, a mile away). In 1922, the homestead on 25 acres was sold to the immigrant Finnish farmer Nestor Aalto (1869–1928), who raised 10 children there. Pictured in Indian garb is Edward Aalto with his sister Helen. (Courtesy of John Aalto.)

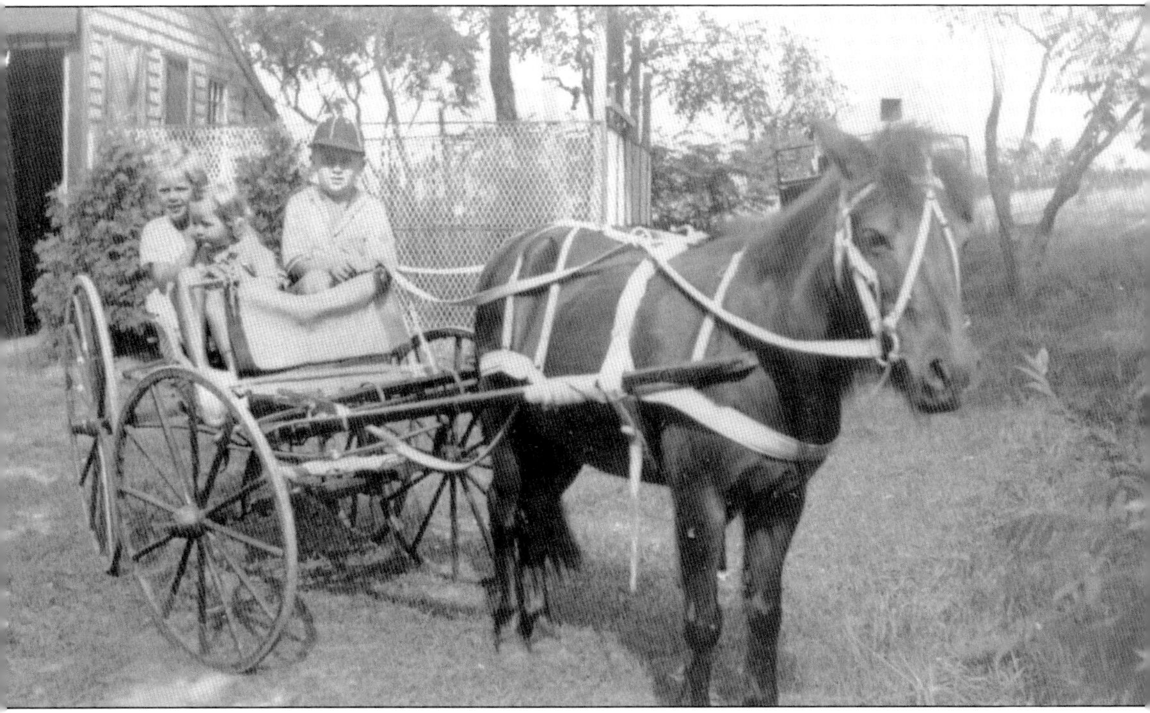

Nestor and Marion Aalto's 10 children grew up milking cows and tending the sheds. They learned to ride when they were young. Here, in 1932, six-year-old son Edward, the eldest child, takes his two little sisters, Helen and Betty, out for a ride. (Courtesy of Susan Leach.)

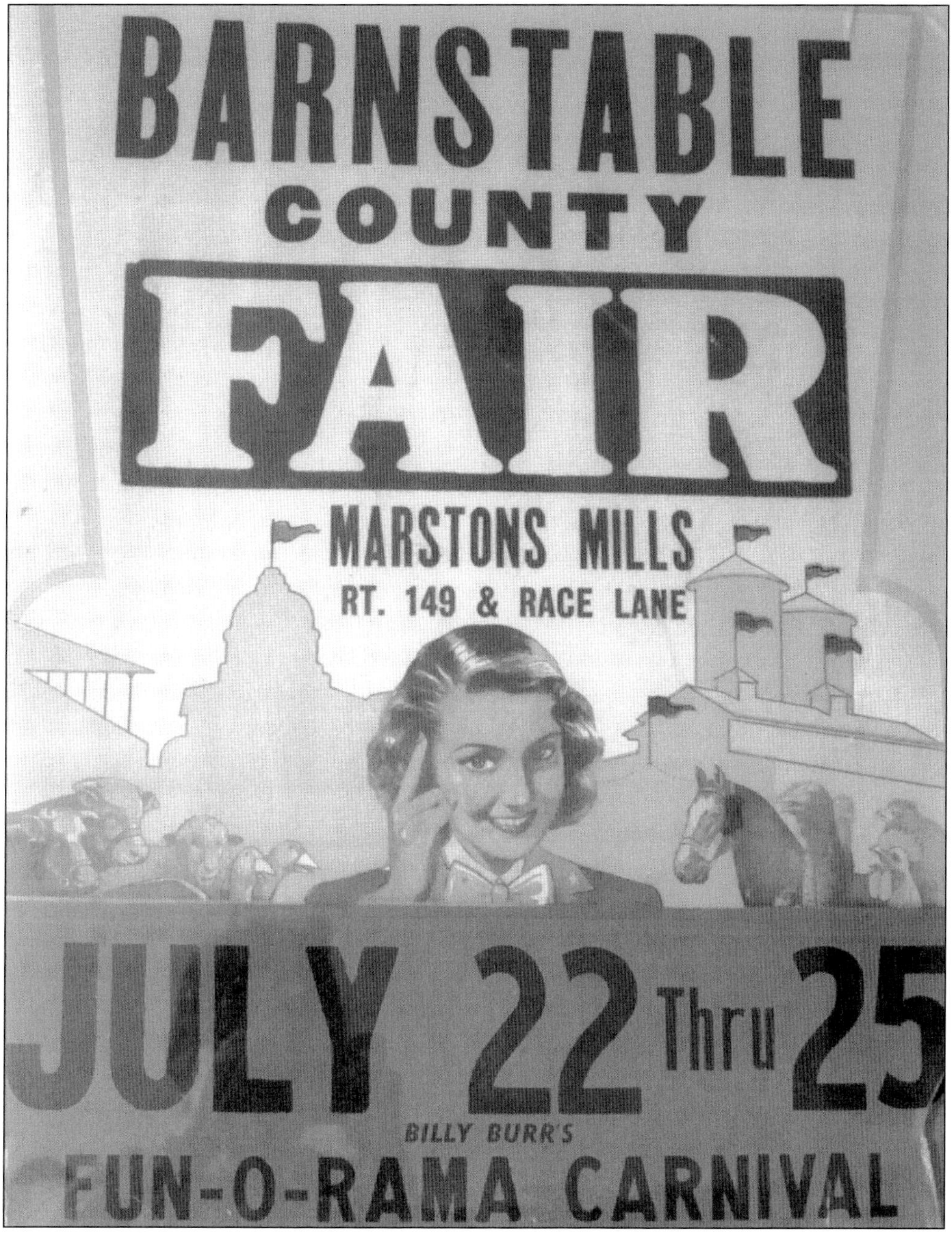

This poster advertises the first Barnstable County Fair in 25 years. It was revived on the south part of the Aalto farm in 1954. Charles D. Meyer (1911–2001), an advance agent for circuses, had summered on Cape Cod and raised funds from neighbors Dr. Daniel Leach, Hilding Hord, and others to revive the fair, which had been dormant since 1931. (Courtesy of John D. Meyer.)

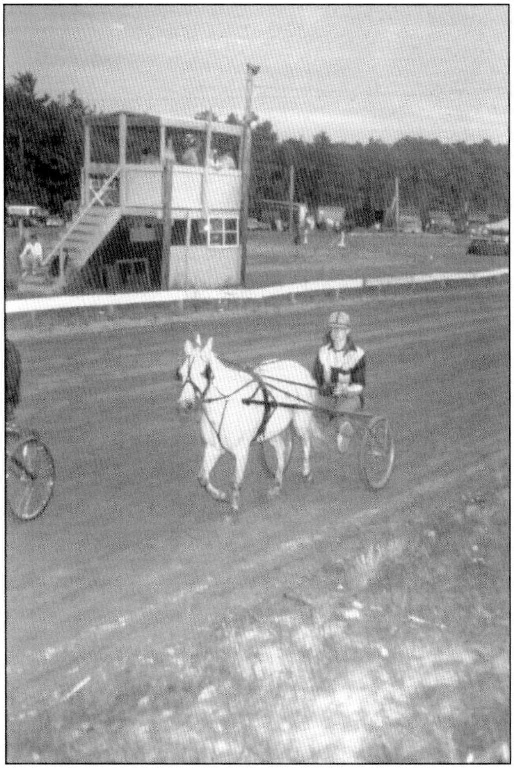

Nestor Aalto built a sulky track for the fairgrounds. His children offered pony rides, horse rides in the corral and on the trails, and a ride on a donkey, which had a blinder on one eye so he would not get dizzy going in a circle. The favorite animal was the intelligent mule Bugsy, who would sit down in front of the grandstand and not move until given a Pepsi. (Courtesy of Diane Aalto Long.)

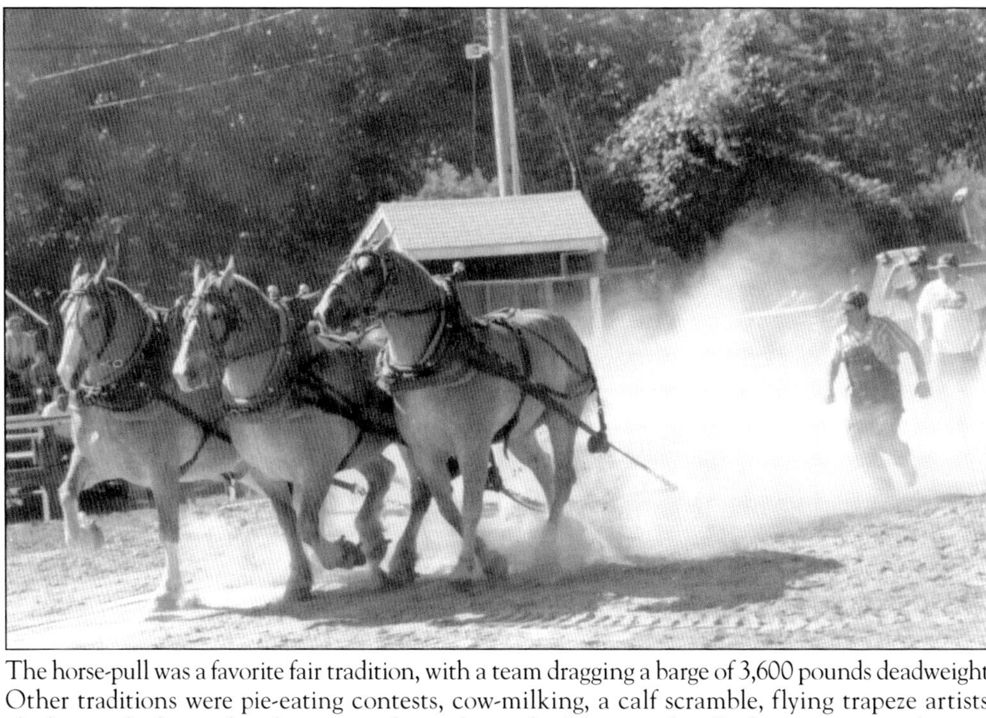

The horse-pull was a favorite fair tradition, with a team dragging a barge of 3,600 pounds deadweight. Other traditions were pie-eating contests, cow-milking, a calf scramble, flying trapeze artists, elephants, skydiving, band concerts, fireworks, and a "clean midway" of merry-go-round, circus rides, and games of skill. (Courtesy of John Aalto.)

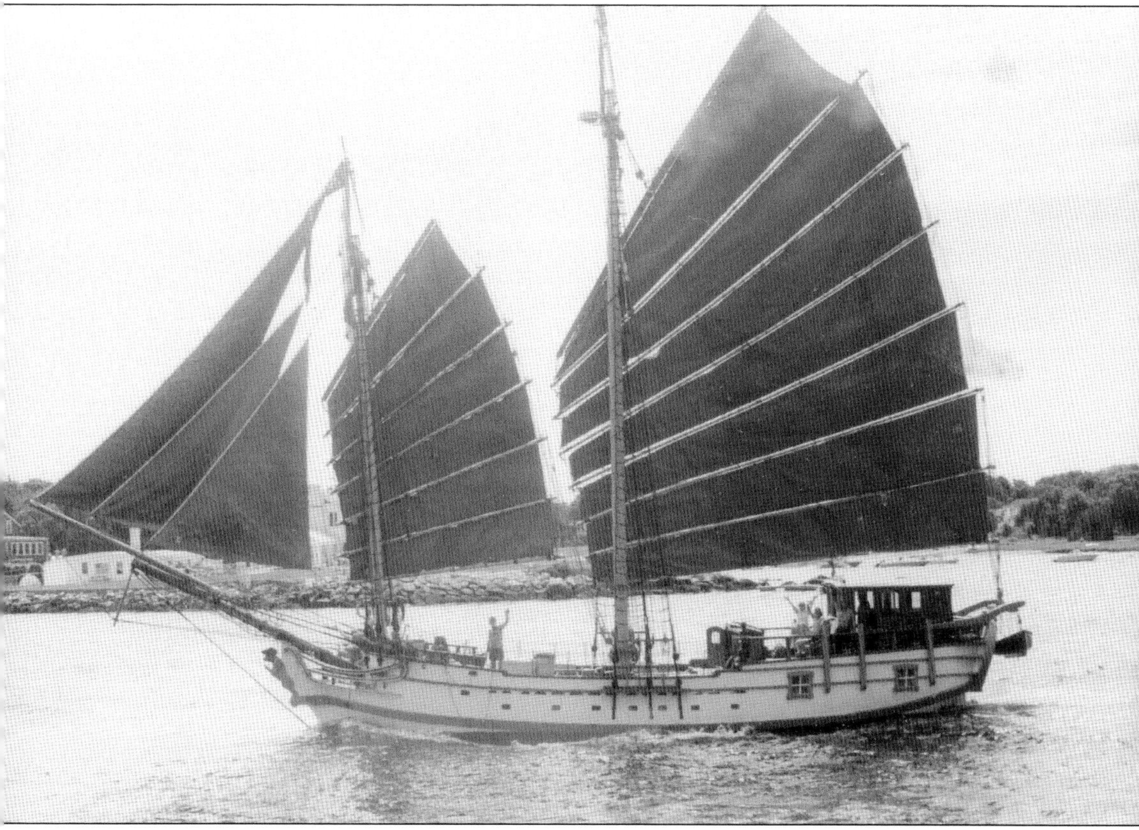

Across Race Lane from the fairgrounds was the shipyard of Larry Mahan (1942–2005), where, starting in 1968, he spent 25 years building the 62-ton ferro-cement-hulled *Larinda*, based on a 1767 packet boat. Launched in Falmouth in 1996, she sailed to the Marstons Mills River, to salute with her 300-pound brass cannon. The *Larinda* sank in 2003 in Halifax, Nova Scotia, during Hurricane Juan, but the wreck was sold and raised. (Courtesy of Marlene Mahan.)

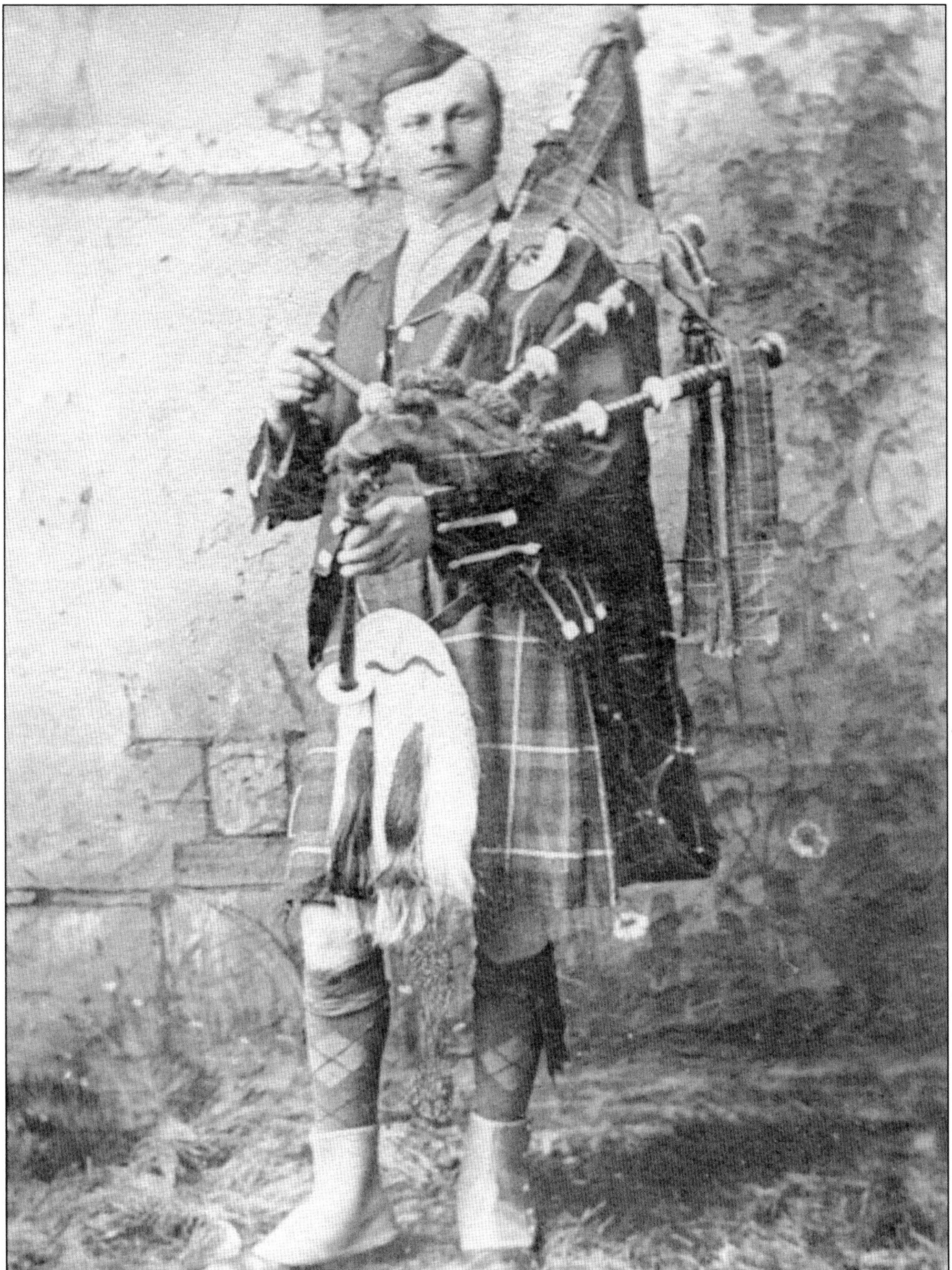

Nurseryman Charles Hay Reid (1872–1948) was born on the east coast of Scotland and learned gardening at Slains Castle, which is said to have inspired Bram Stoker's *Dracula*. At 18, he joined the famed Queen's Own Cameron Highlanders, and he later established his own nursery business. Reid brought his family to the United States before World War I and to Marstons Mills after the war. (Courtesy of Betsy McIntyre.)

Charles Hay Reid planted gorgeous rhododendrons and azaleas when he was foreman of the Farquahar Nursery here from 1919 to 1926, and later as head of his own nursery on Osterville–West Barnstable Road. A collaborator with the famous grower Charles Dexter of Heritage Plantation, Reid created his own varieties, including Reid's Red, a low-growing rosy-colored azalea. (Courtesy of Gerda Reid.)

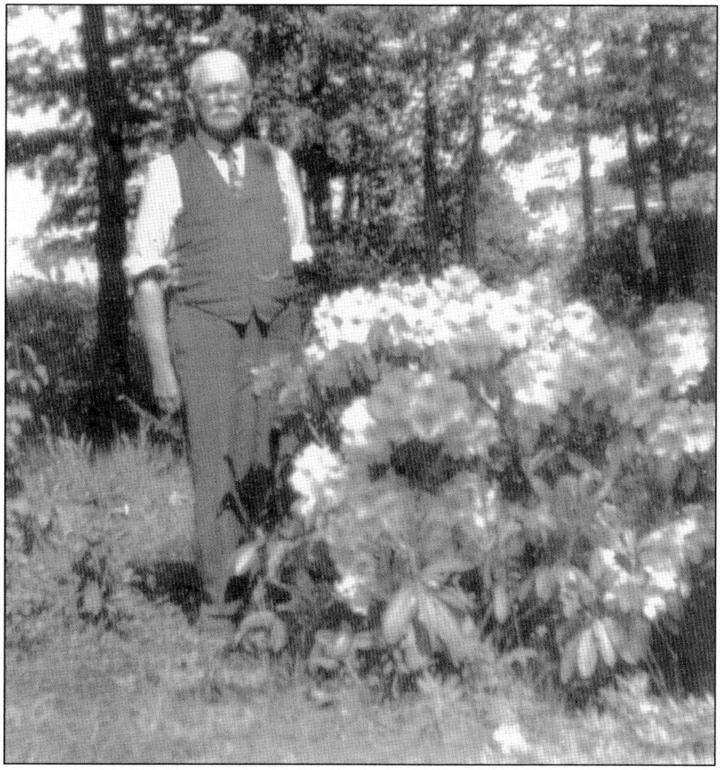

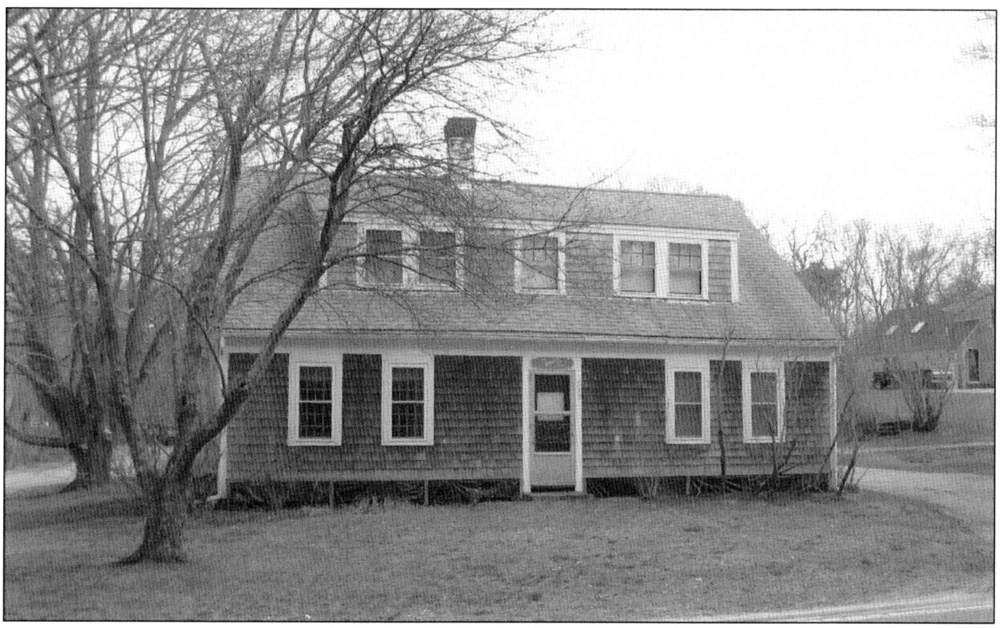

This full Cape Cod house was built about 1830 on Old Falmouth Road by Capt. George Allyn (1804–1892) and his wife, Asenath Hinckley, whose family were housewrights. Their son C. Howard Allyn (1848–1932) was born here and later became mate of the clipper *Glory of the Seas* and master of the clipper *Expounder* for a decade. He was the last clipper captain in the town. (Courtesy of Holly Hobart.)

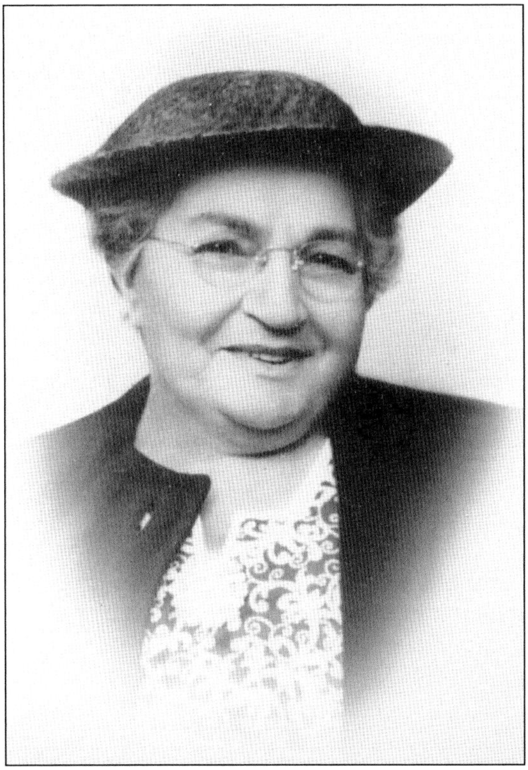

Annie Pearlstein (1872–1961) and her husband, Max, bought the Capt. George Allyn house and moved here in 1901, when they were welcomed as the first Jewish residents, immigrants from persecution in Russian-occupied Poland. Max was a teamster who hauled heavy loads such as a Crosby boat overland to Boston. (Courtesy of Cindy Van Wagenen.)

Max Pearlstein was killed in 1904 when a piece of heavy machinery he had brought from Osterville to load onto a freight car slipped and crushed him, leaving a widow and four little daughters. Annie supported her family by selling women's clothing and opened a successful store on the northwest corner of Main Street and Barnstable Road in Hyannis. (Courtesy of Cindy Van Wagenen.)

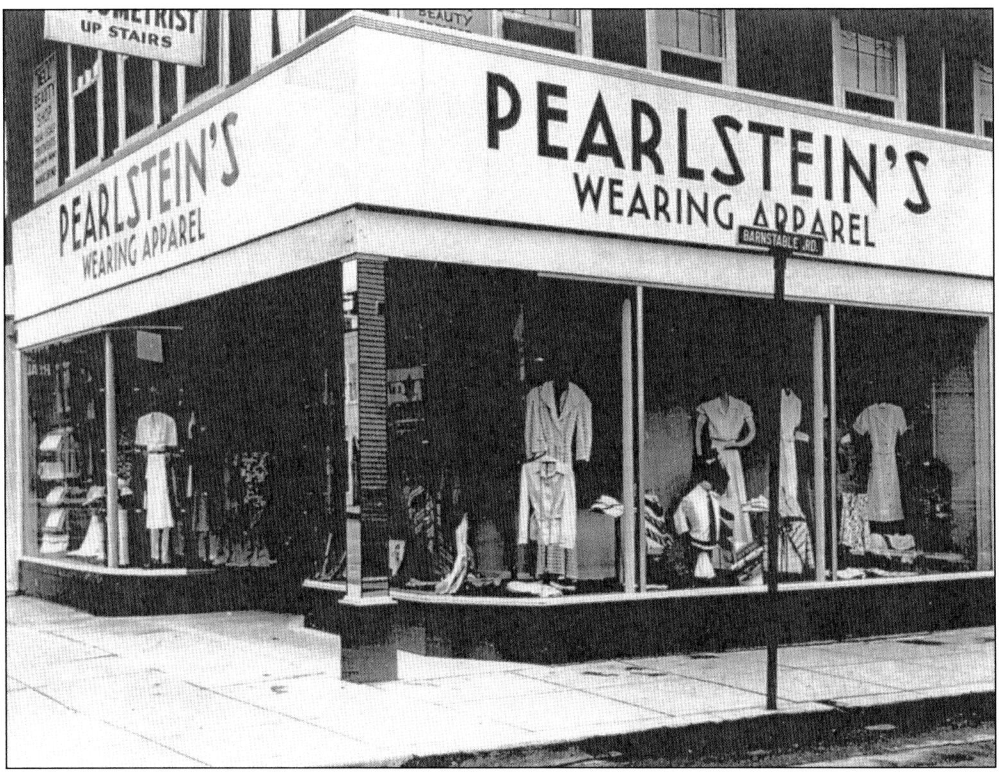

An aerial view of Round Pond shows Shubael Pond at the left, with Camp Fair Acres below on Edgewood Road (renamed Flint Street), the Pearlstein/Allyn house to the right on Old Falmouth Road, the Crocker farm on the top of Round Pond, and the Howland homestead on the intersection of Falmouth and West Barnstable Roads at top right. (Courtesy of Anne Thomas.)

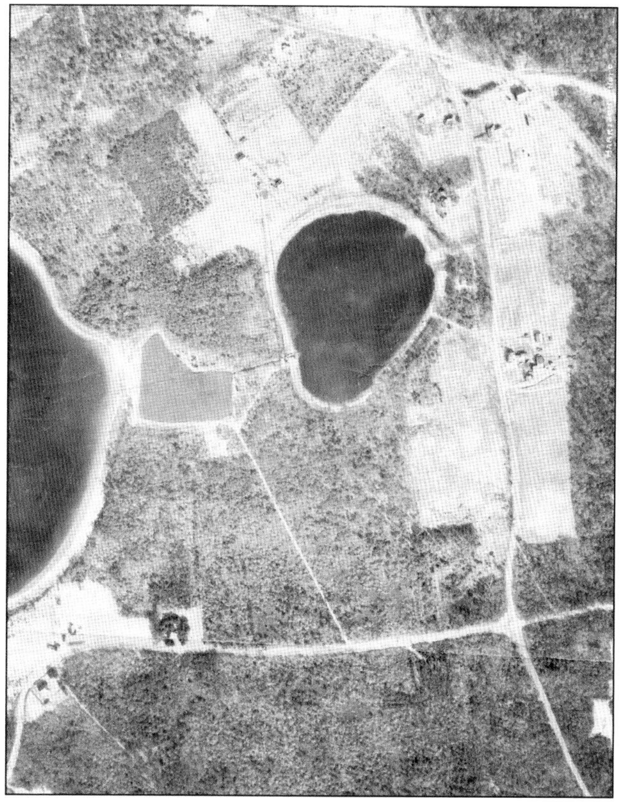

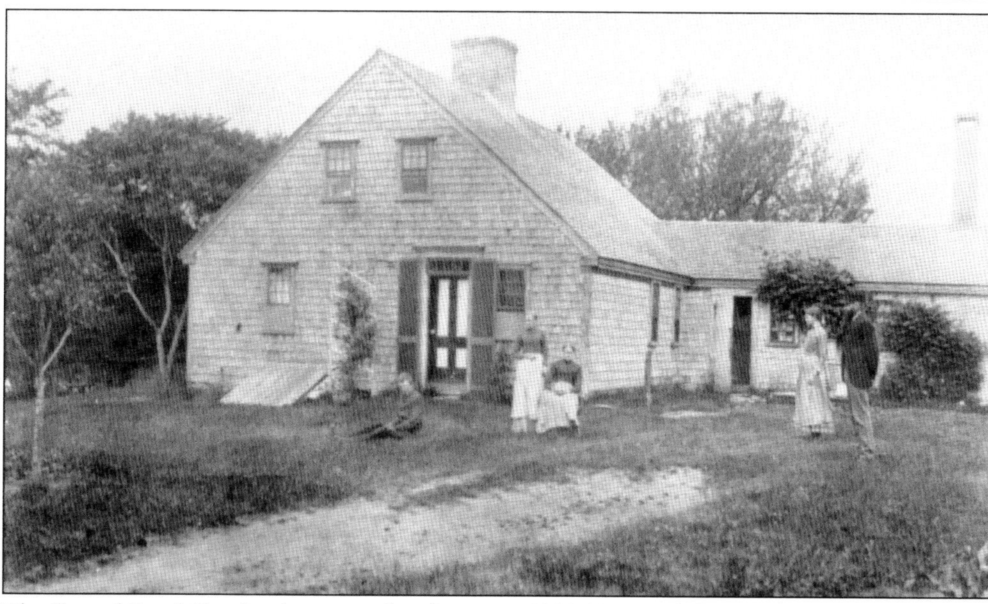

The Round Pond Crocker homestead is shown in 1888. Pictured, from right to left, are Nelson Crocker (1846–1914); his daughter Cora (born 1872); Nelson's mother, Betsey Wright Crocker (1811–1895); his wife, Lydia "Nettie" Phelps Crocker (1848–1905); and son Allen "Allie" (born 1874). Betsey was the sister of William Wright, the whaler who survived the sinking of the *Essex* by a whale. (Courtesy of Anne Thomas.)

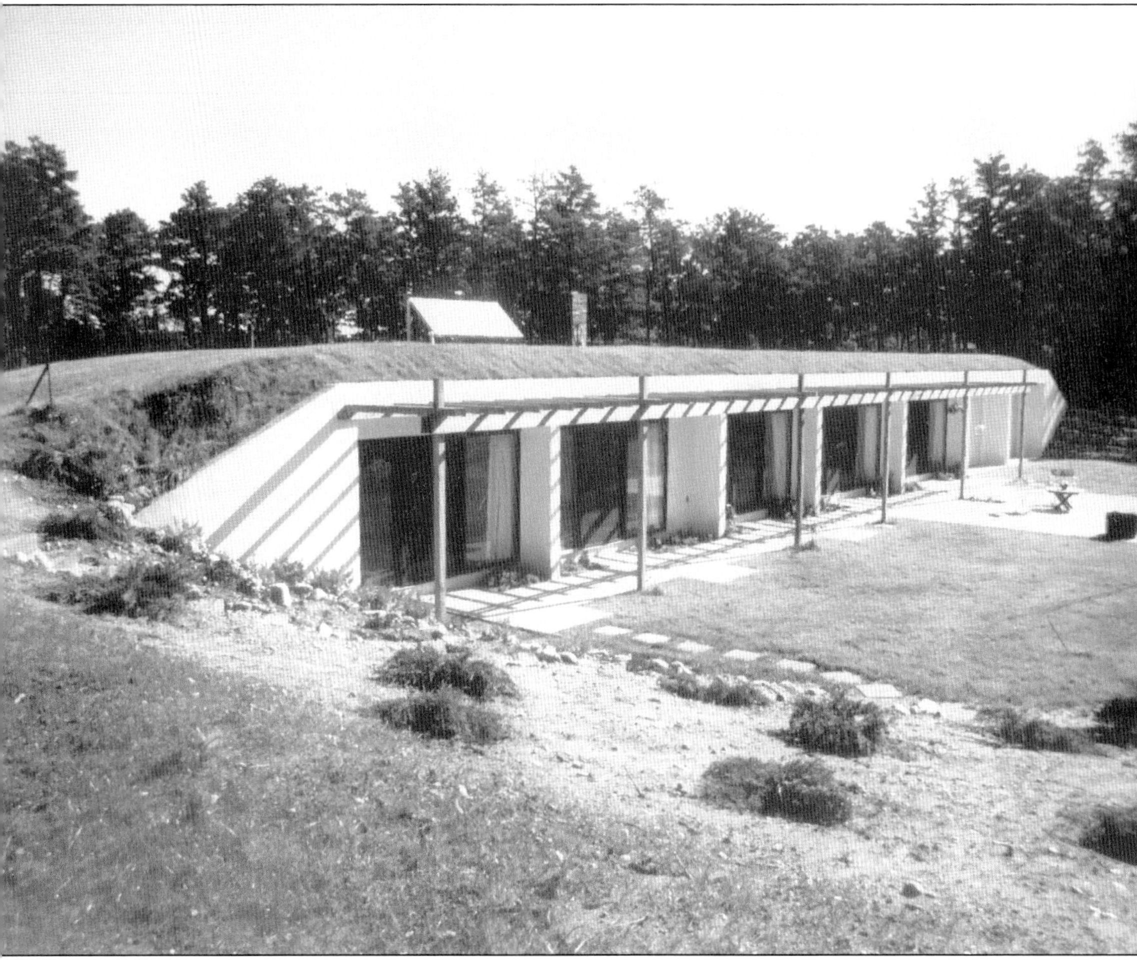

The Ecology II House designed by John Barnard Jr. (1918–1999) was a pioneer model of energy efficiency, inspired by the oil crisis, under construction in 1973. It faced south like the Colonial Cape Cod cottages to maximize solar exposure, with the rear a foot underground. It was built south of Race Lane on Wheeler Road for $20,000, about 60 percent of the cost of a comparable frame house. (Courtesy of Alex Bally.)

Eight

The Ponds and Airfield

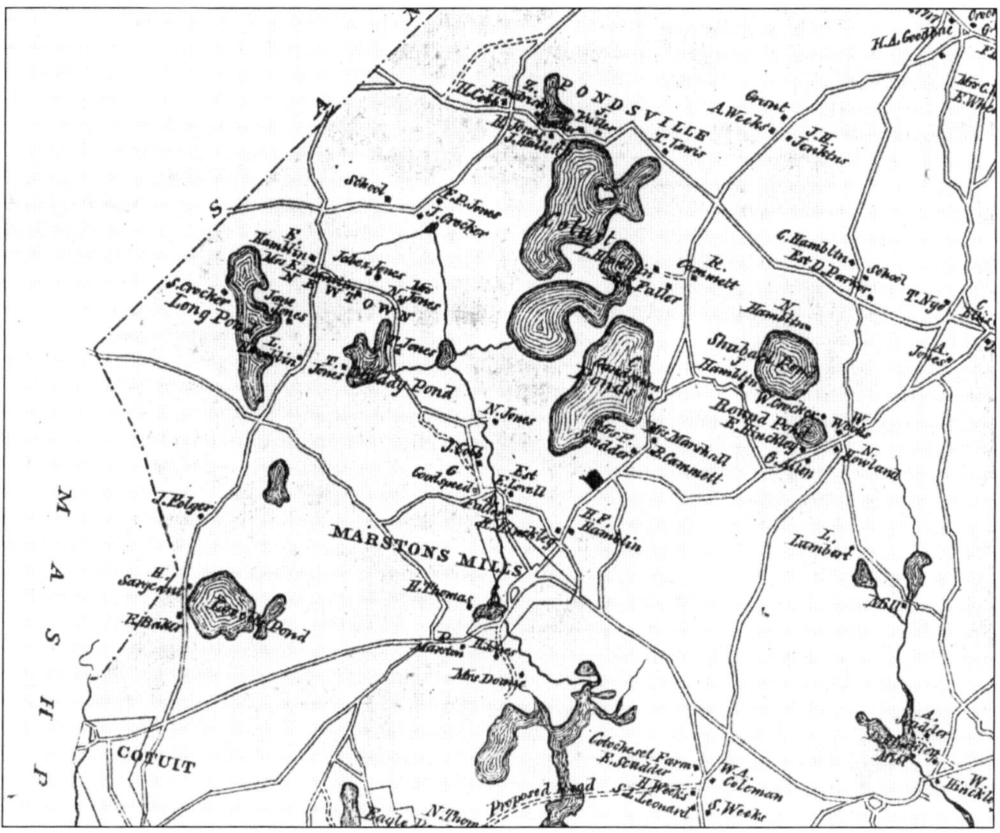

The Ponds area is paired with The Plains, but it formed its own farming village called Pondsville between the head of Mystic Lake and Little Pond. At this west end, Race Lane no longer ran on a straight line as it did farther east, but zigzagged along fence lines between farms. Rural roads like Crooked Cartway and Crocker Road ran north to West Barnstable over the woodlots on the glacial moraine.

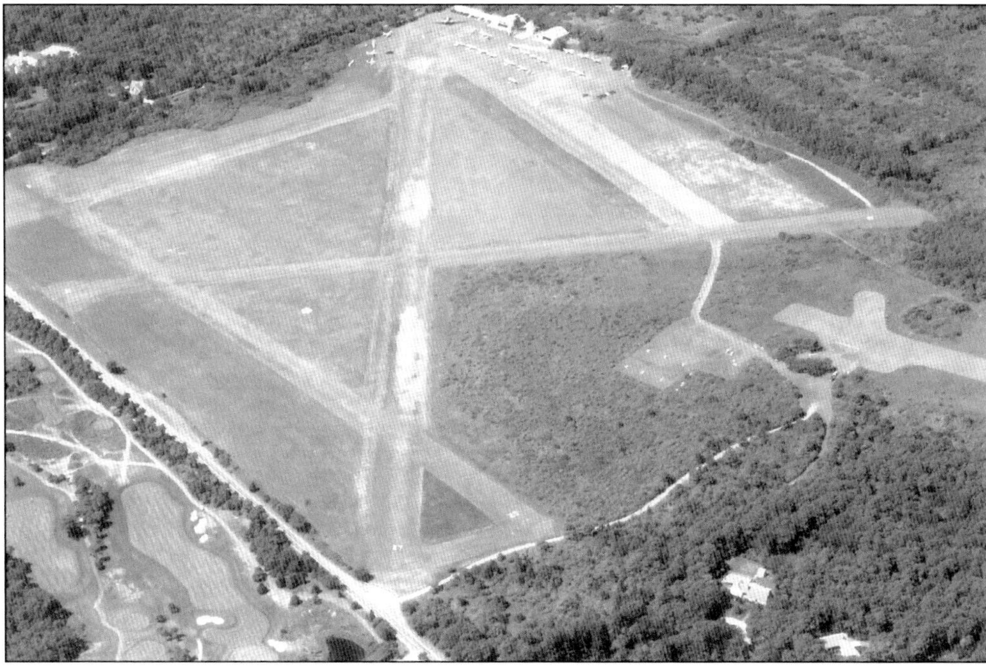

The first airfield on Cape Cod opened here on an old potato field on July 4, 1929, with an air show by World War I pilot Zenas Crocker, stunt flyer Crocker Snow, formation flights of National Guard planes, seaplane landings on Mystic Lake (top left), and parachute drops. Crocker added a racecourse for cars and motorcycles and a polo field. (Courtesy of Chris Siderwitz.)

Daredevil flyer Crocker Snow (1906–2000) was a pioneer in New England aviation who started the first commercial air service at Boston's Logan Airport in 1928. Snow later became the first head of aeronautics for the state and established a ferry route across the North Atlantic before World War II. (Courtesy of Crocker Snow Jr.)

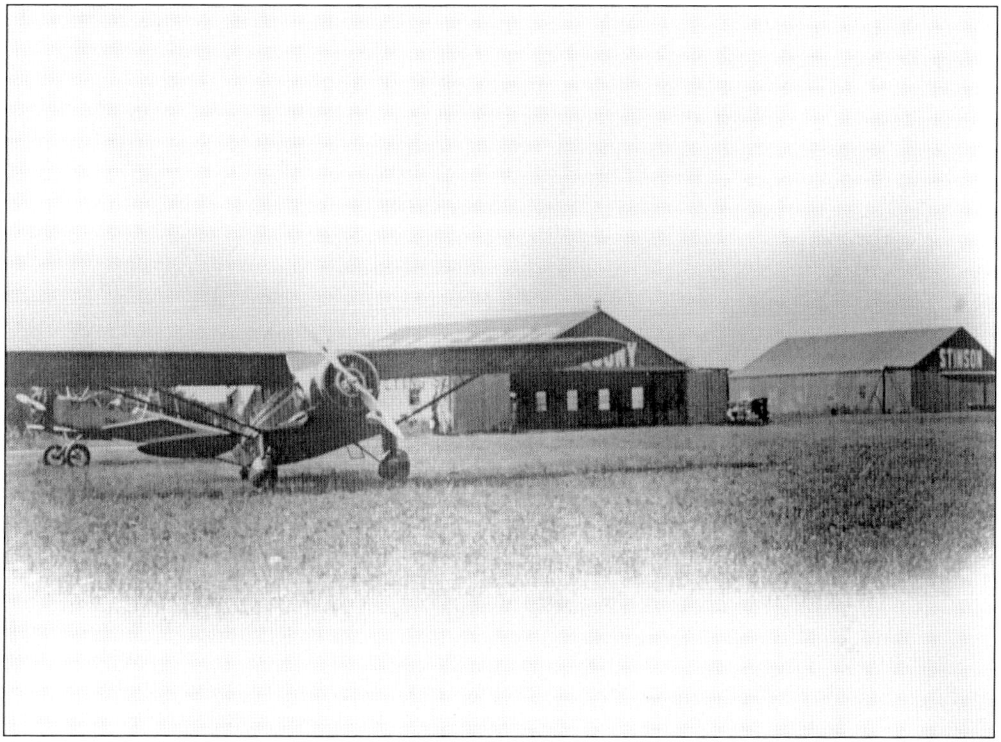

A Stinson airplane rests in front of the two hangars built by Zenas Crocker on the west side of Cape Cod Airport about 1930 for Skyways Summer Flying School run by Crocker Snow. The Stinson was a popular plane of the interwar era, built by the stunt flier Eddie Stinson. Between the hangars, Zenas Crocker built an office, which was a replica of the gatehouse windmill at Oyster Harbors, where he lived. (Courtesy of Chris Siderwitz.)

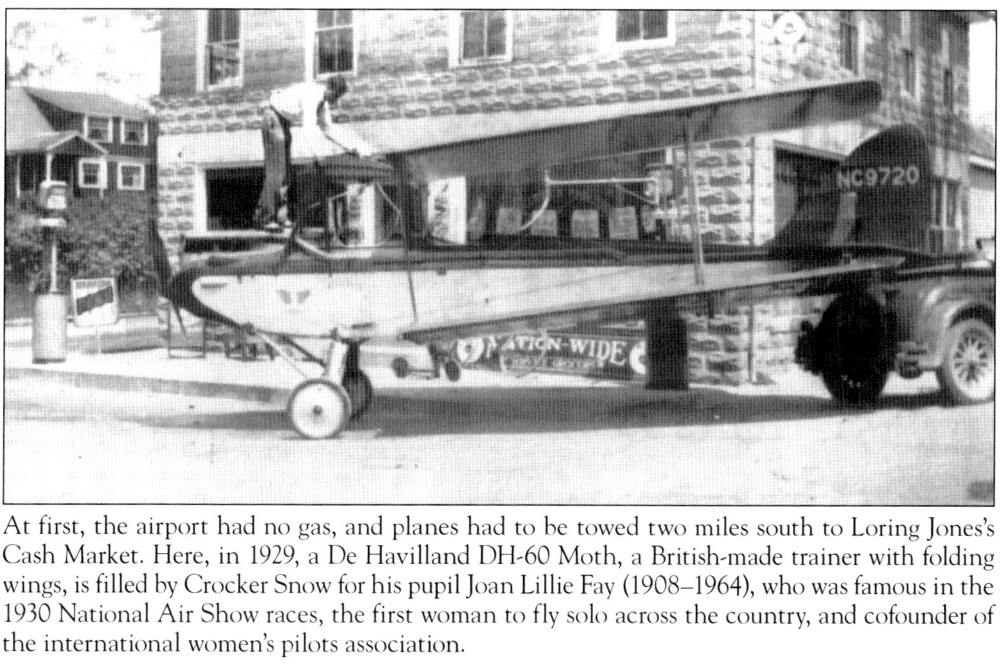

At first, the airport had no gas, and planes had to be towed two miles south to Loring Jones's Cash Market. Here, in 1929, a De Havilland DH-60 Moth, a British-made trainer with folding wings, is filled by Crocker Snow for his pupil Joan Lillie Fay (1908–1964), who was famous in the 1930 National Air Show races, the first woman to fly solo across the country, and cofounder of the international women's pilots association.

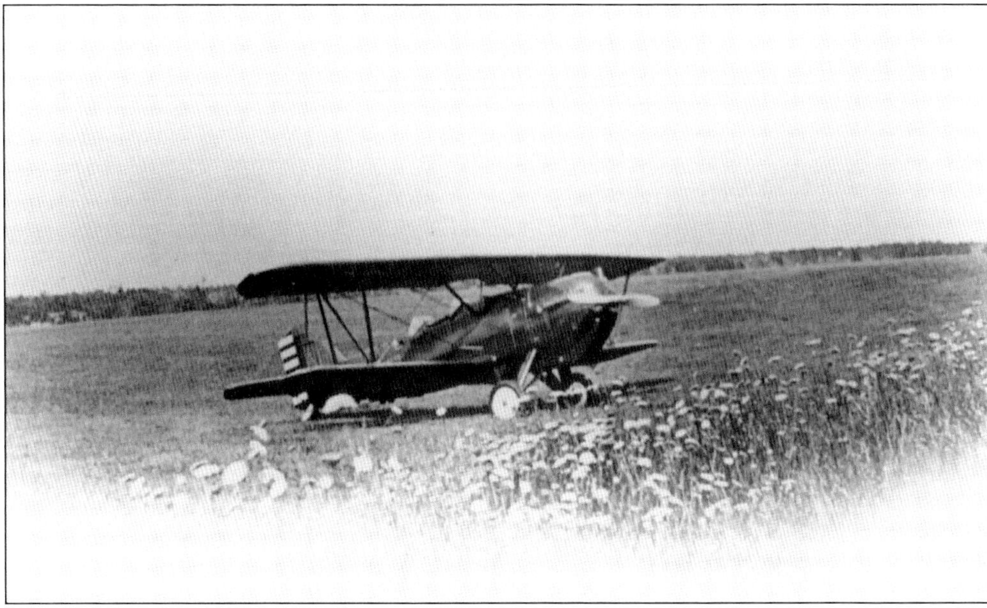

The Curtiss Falcon was built as a military plane for bombing and observation, finding service in South American wars in Brazil, Paraguay, and Colombia. Here, it was used for training civilian pilots and for air shows such as this one in 1934. These air shows were popular summer events, bringing crowds of cars lined up on Race Lane and West Barnstable Road. (Courtesy of Chris Siderwitz.)

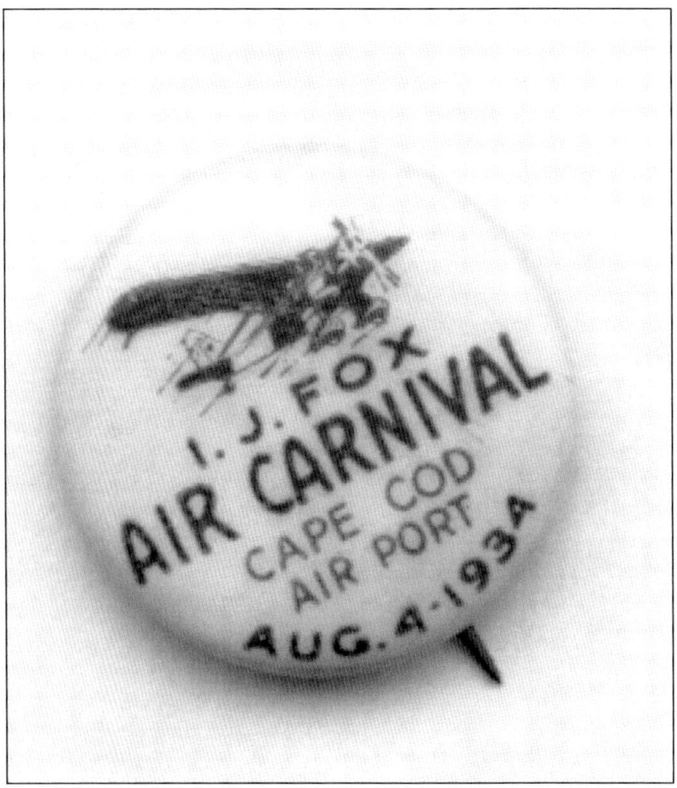

The sponsor of the 1934 air show was one of the nation's largest furriers, I.J. Fox of Huntington Avenue in Boston. An aggressive advertiser, Fox is cited as the having put on the first ad on television in 1930, although it did not comply with current regulations. At this event, a silver bombing trophy was awarded and souvenir buttons given to spectators.

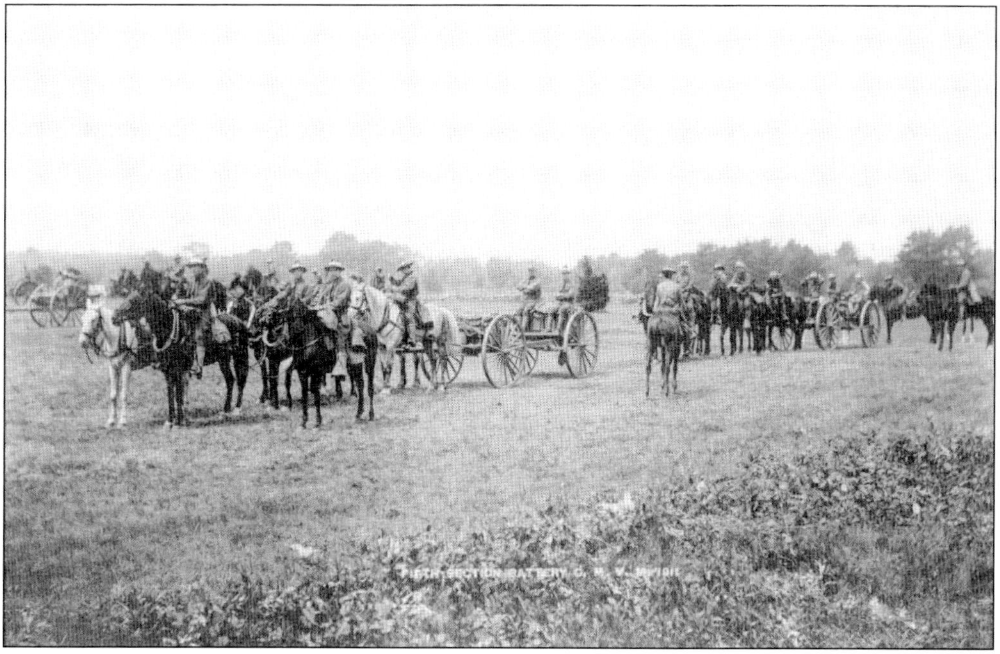

War games in The Plains came in July 1908, when artillery of the state National Guard "attacked" Pondsville from Sandwich and ended firing its guns into the Great Marshes. A full encampment was established in the summer of 1910, with Battery C shown here in 1911. Local farmers later complained that the soldiers had wrecked their peach orchards.

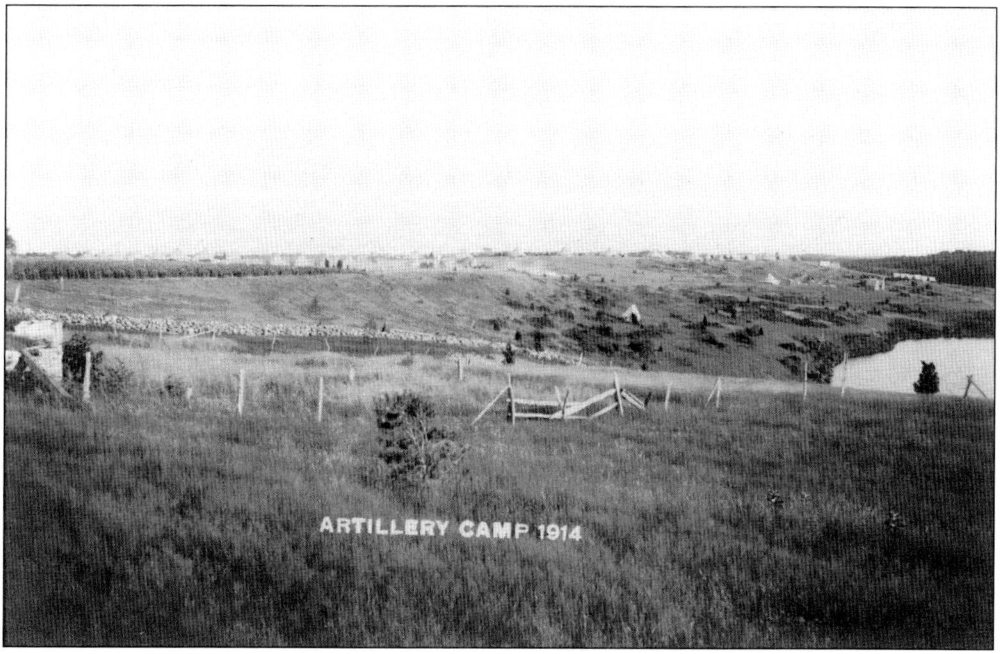

On July 20, 1914, the 1st Battalion of the Massachusetts National Guard arrived by train from Boston, Lawrence, and Worcester for the annual Field Day under Maj. John H. Sherborne. The location is Pickerel Cove, at the top of Mystic Lake. Zenas Crocker V later opened a popular tavern nearby that his brother Sheriff Lauchlan Crocker had to close for violation of Prohibition.

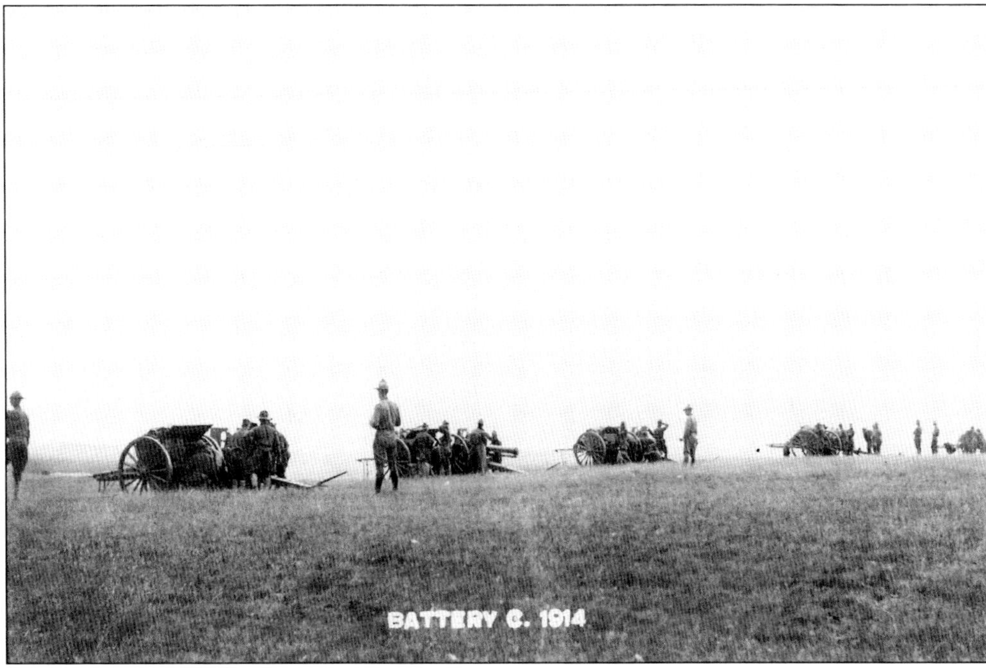

Battery C of the National Guard was equipped with the M1902 three-inch gun, whose 2,500 pounds was towed by horses. Some Massachusetts units took part in the Mexican Expedition in 1916. During World War I, this American gun was replaced by the French 75. A relic M1902 can be seen in Danvers cemetery.

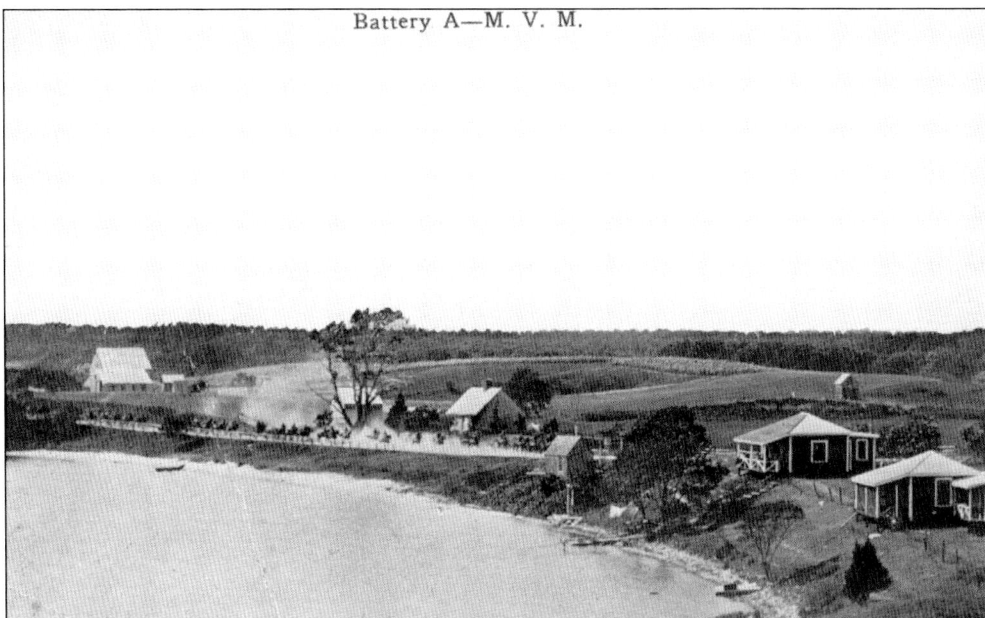

Infantry and cavalry units joined the artillery for the big Barnstable war maneuvers in 1913, attended by Gov. Eugene Foss. Here, a cavalry unit gallops through Pondsville village, along the shore of Mystic Lake, and past the Thomas Lewis homestead that became the Mystic Lake Dairy Farm.

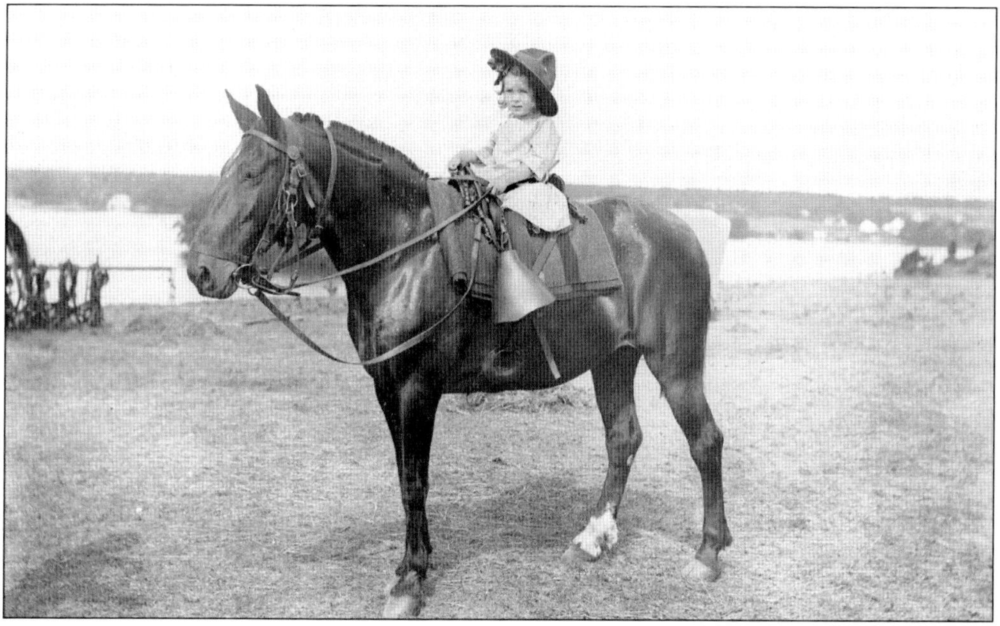

If the governor could watch the games, so did everyone in Marstons Mills—at a safe distance. In an off-duty moment, a guardsman let Marion Lovell put on his campaign hat and mount his horse. Marion, born in 1909, was the daughter of Winfred Lovell and Minnie Mecarta Lovell and granddaughter of the postmistress. Mystic Lake is in the background, with Pondsville to the right.

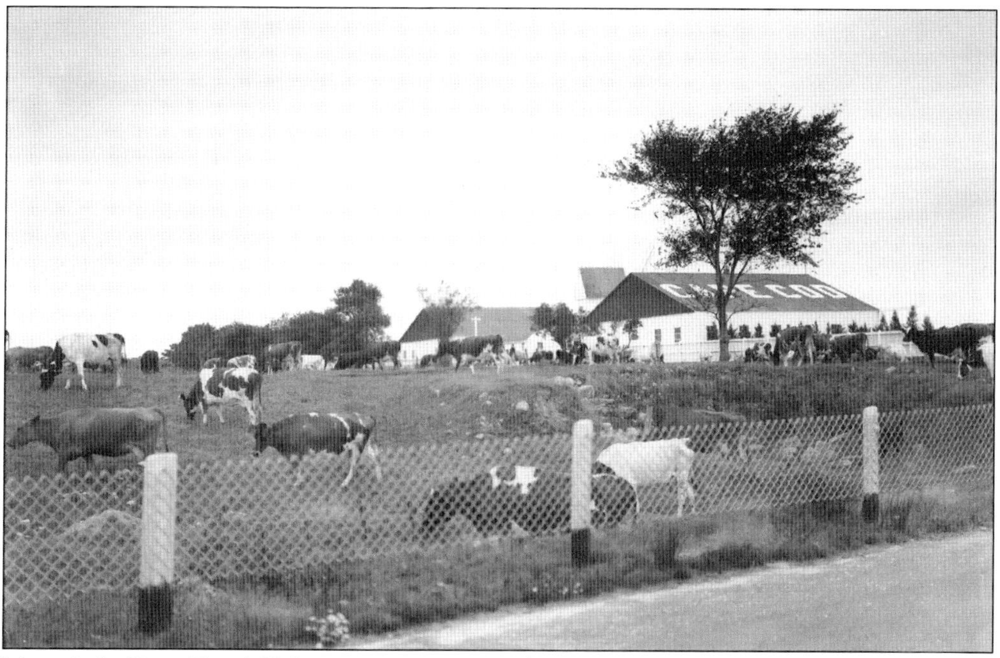

Mystic Lake Dairy Farm's Holstein cows are pastured next to the hangars of the Cape Cod Airport, with the peak of the windmill seen between hangars. The black-and-white Holstein breed was the favorite for its high milk production. Veterinary care came from Dr. Daniel Leach, only half a mile away. The farm operated from 1922 to 1962 and grew to 92 acres.

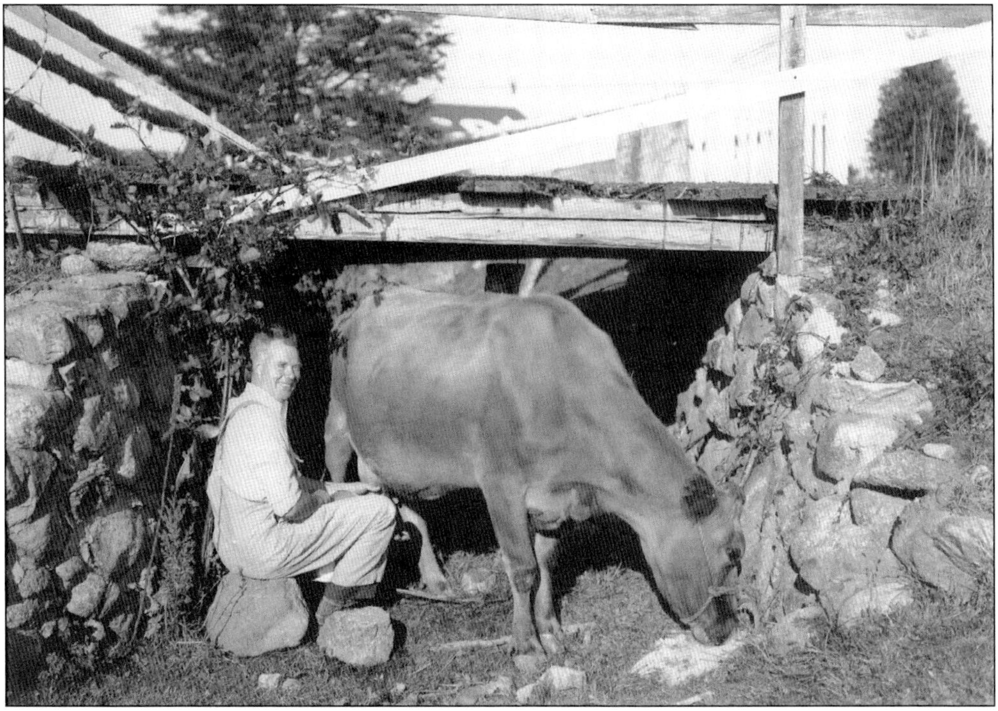

Hilding Hord (1885–1964) milks a Jersey cow like his first one, which he stabled under the so-called Lawrence Bridge, an ancient cow passage under Race Lane. Lawrence Bridge dates back to at least 1818, when it formed a landmark separating the school districts of Newtown, The Plains, and Marstons Mills. Born in Sweden, Hord came to the United States in 1909 and got jobs as lumberman, stonecutter, and valet.

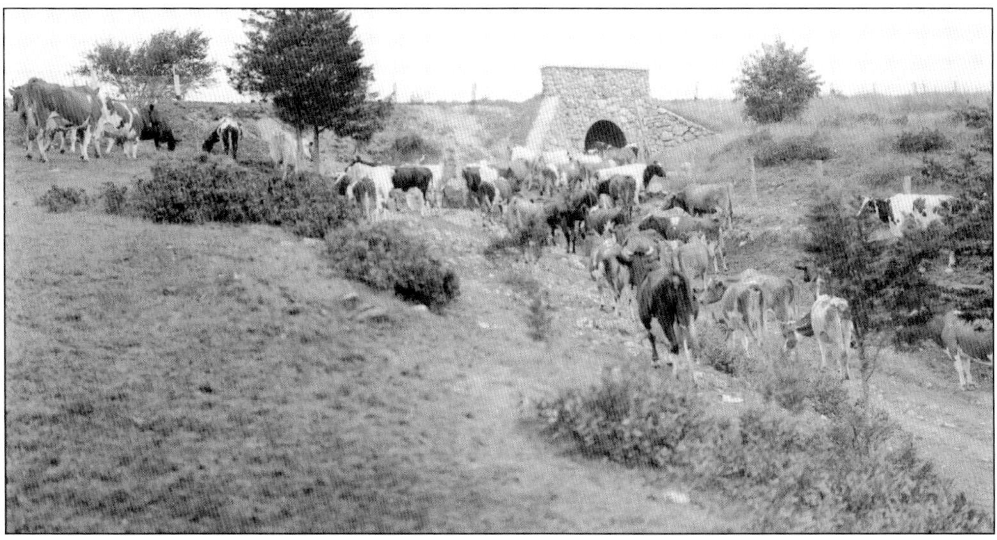

Lawrence Bridge is shown as it was rebuilt over Race Lane, with Hord's Jersey cows heading home from the shore. Hord married a Swedish farm girl, Helga Dahlberg (1899–1924), who got him to buy the 75-acre Lewis farm in 1919 and showed him how to milk that first cow. Helga died of tuberculosis at age 24, leaving him with a two-year old boy who was raised by his second wife, Hanna Bergstrom Hord.

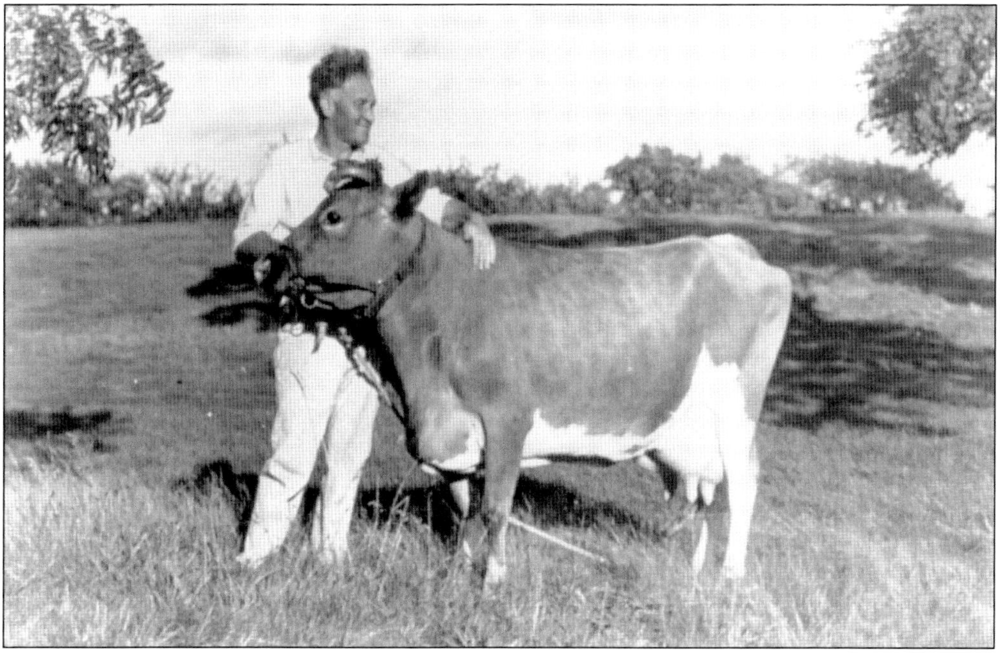

Ernest Cameron worked at Hord's Mystic Lakes Dairy. At its peak, it had 150 milk cows and dozens of calves. It received milk from neighbors Nestor Aalto, Dr. Daniel Leach, and Alfred Fuller. Six milk trucks delivered 1,500 quarts of pasteurized milk from Eastham to Woods Hole and supplied schools with 5,000 half-pints.

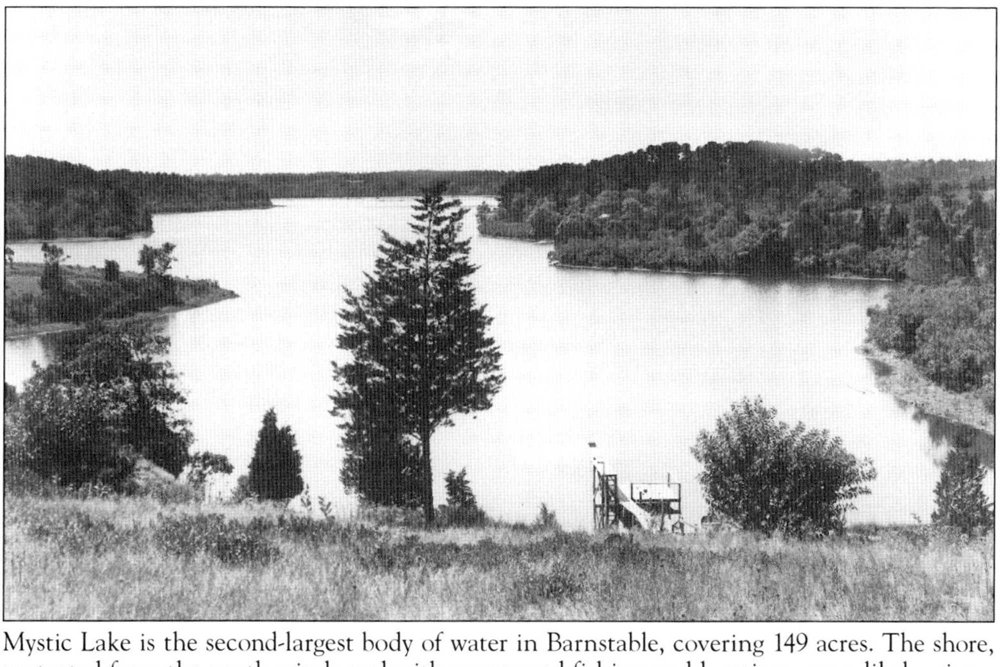

Mystic Lake is the second-largest body of water in Barnstable, covering 149 acres. The shore, protected from the north winds and with year-round fishing and hunting, was a likely winter refuge for Indians. Ram Island, at the left, was uninhabited but later had a summer cottage. Like the river and lakes of the same name in Boston, the name may derive from the Wampanoag word *mass*, meaning "large waters."

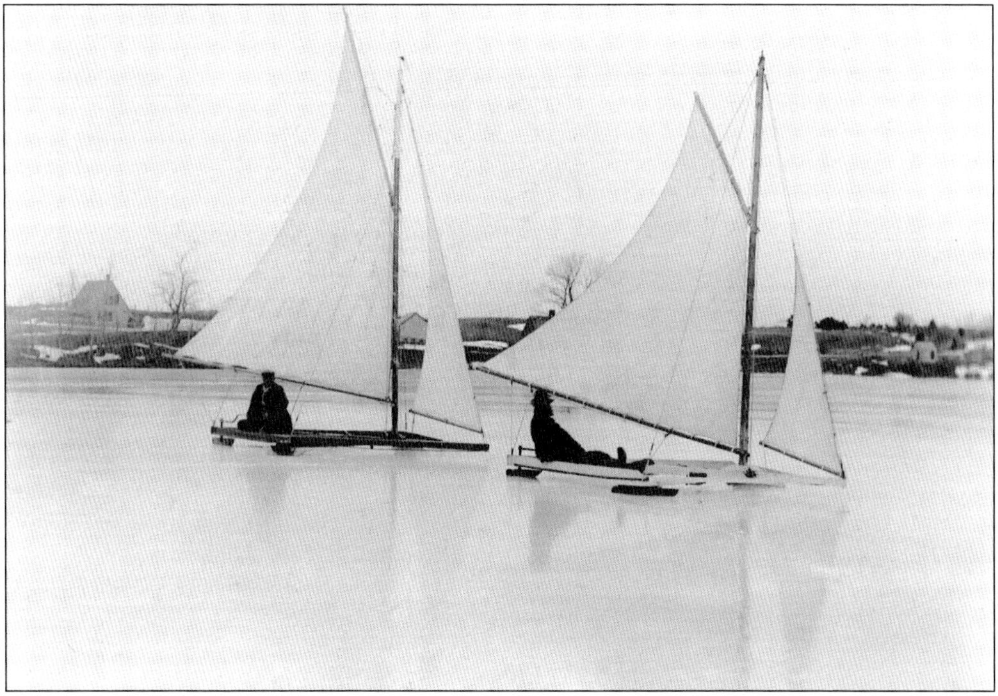

Winter on the Mystic Lakes brought fun on the ice: skating, iceboat races, and fishing. Homemade iceboats were usually built in one's own yard, taking an old boat and rigging it with a sail. Ice fishing was done by sawing a hole in the ice, which could be as much as 15 inches thick, and mighty nice perch and pickerel often came out of that hole.

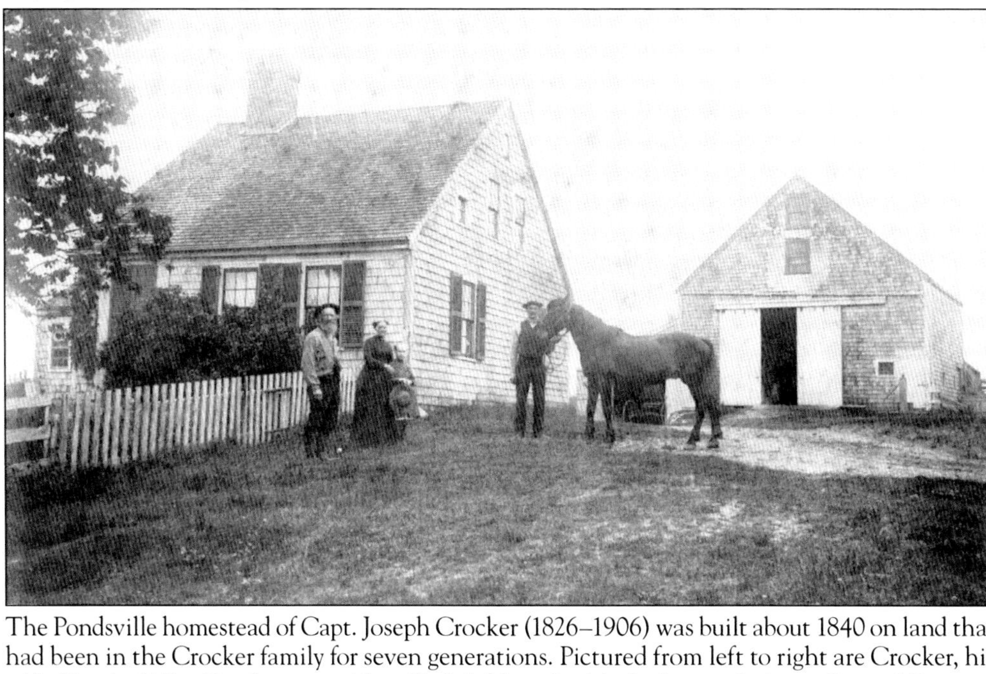

The Pondsville homestead of Capt. Joseph Crocker (1826–1906) was built about 1840 on land that had been in the Crocker family for seven generations. Pictured from left to right are Crocker, his wife, Harriet Stiles Crocker, an unidentified child, and, with the horse, their son Samuel Fremont Crocker (1865–1931), who inherited the place.

Samuel Fremont Crocker, usually called Fremont, was named for John C. Fremont, the western explorer and first Republican Party presidential candidate. Although Crocker's ancestry was almost entirely English, there were many Scottish immigrants like the Reids, Camerons, and Bremners, who celebrated St. Andrews Day. Fremont, who never married, inherited the family farm on Race Lane. He was active in the Grange movement.

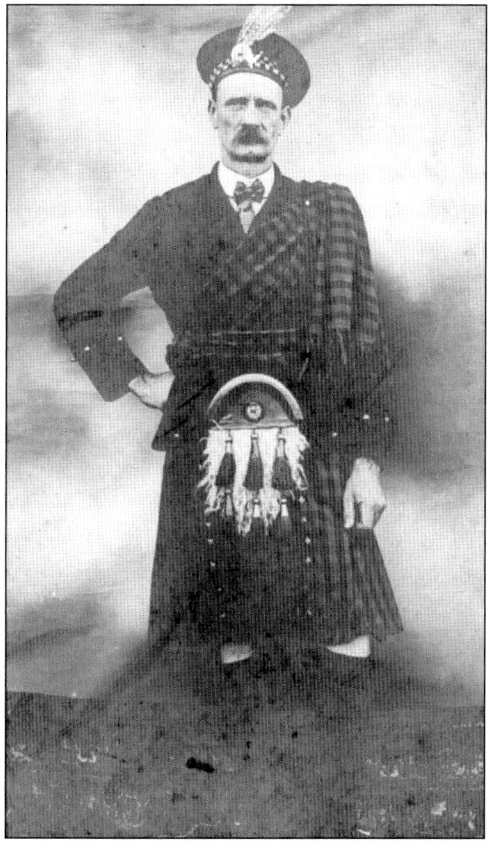

Fremont Crocker created this unusual map of Cape Cod from fragments of Sandwich glass, showing each of the 15 towns in a different color. He was a successful farmer who installed a pump to lift water from Mystic Lake to his cranberry bog and sawmill. It also watered a variety of crops, including apples, turnips, corn, kidney beans, and mangel beets; and watered his cows and pigs.

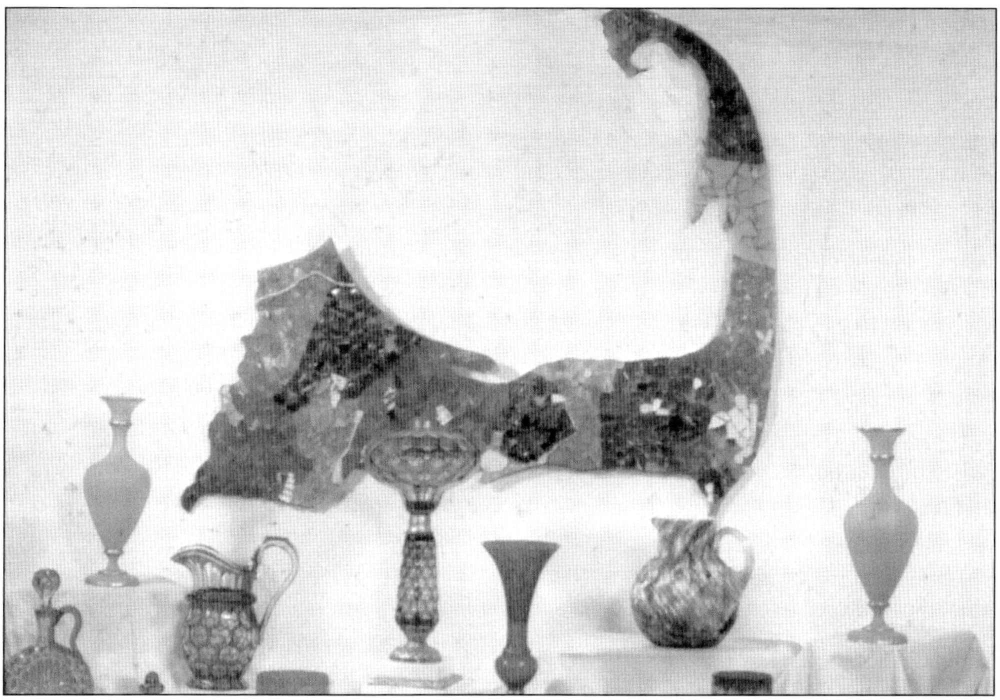

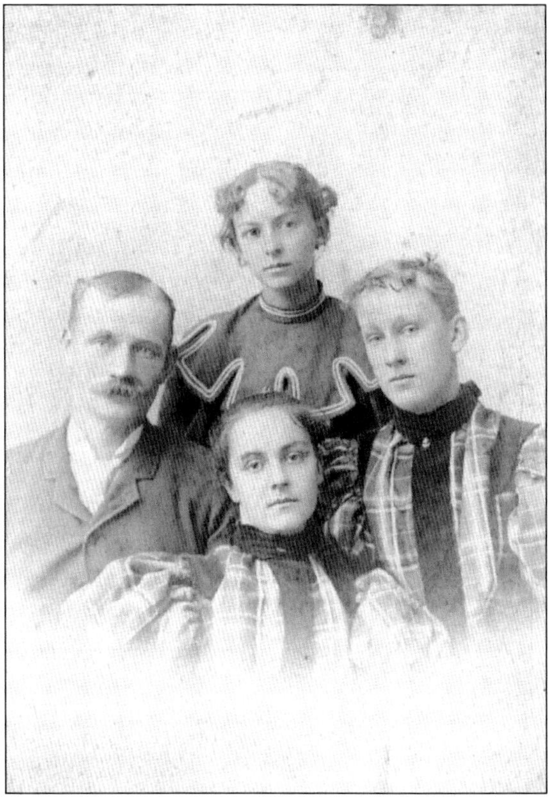

Fremont Crocker is pictured with his two nieces, Estelle Mecarta (above) and Minnie Emily Mecarta (below), and their maiden aunt, Fremont's sister Josephine Maine Crocker (1879–1967). "Aunt Josie" was the last Crocker to live on this farm, which the family had first tilled in the 17th century.

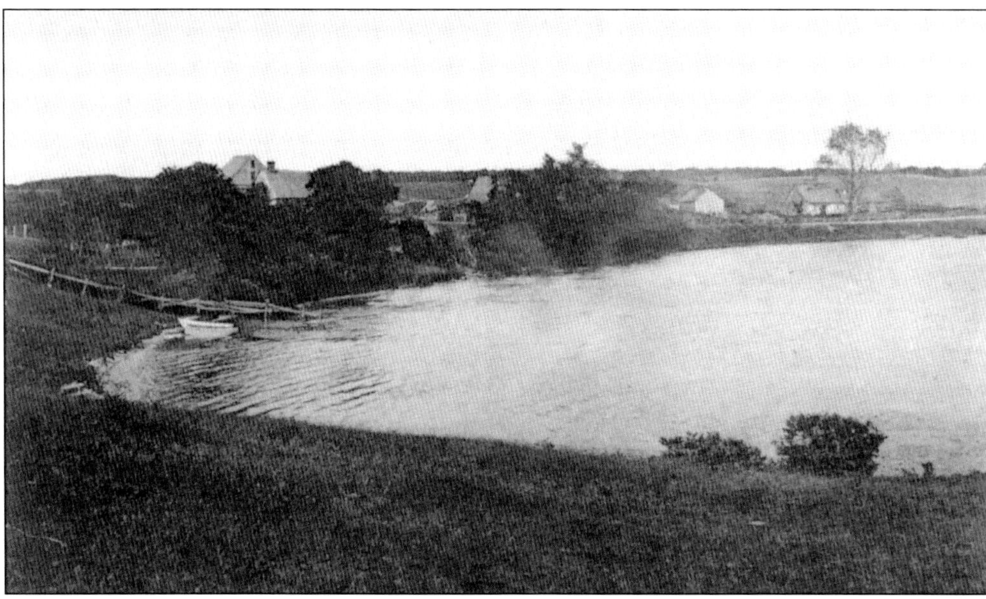

Pondsville village about 1905 had houses of Cobb, Kendrick, Hallett, Jones, Wright, Crocker, and Fuller families. The soil is a fertile loam without stones, said to be the best east of the Connecticut Valley. Probably cultivated by Indians, this was part of a 100-acre farm that Deacon William Crocker endowed in 1692. The ponds were used by Colonial farmers to wash their sheep and water their crops of flax.

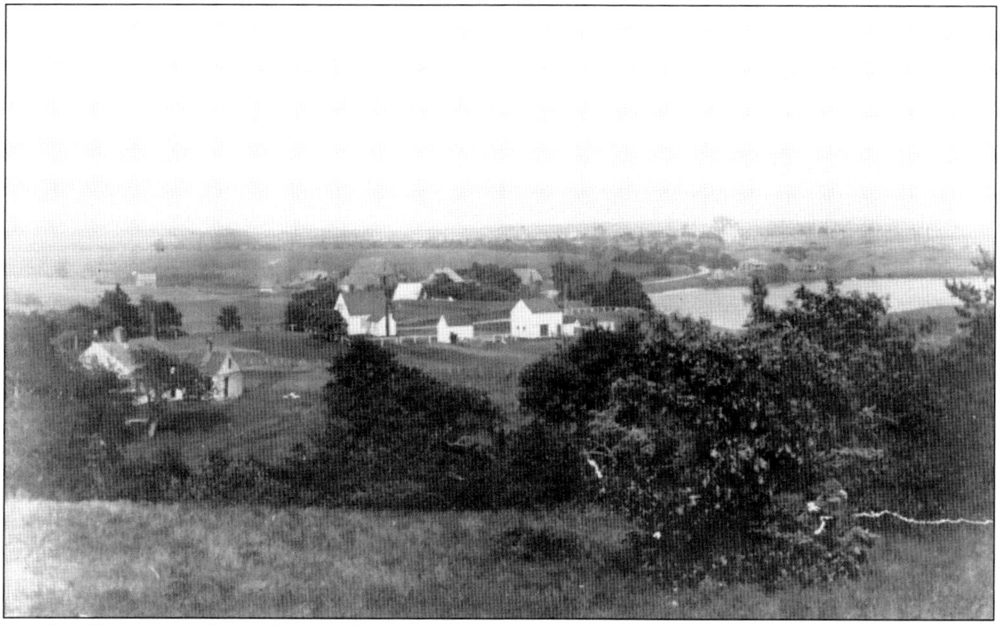

Pondsville is seen from the southwest about 1905, with Mystic Lake on the right with The Plains stretching to the horizon. On the left is the Wing house that claims to be the oldest in the area, dating to 1750. Later, it became the home of retired captain Zemira Kendrick. The next house is the 1780 Capt. William Wright house, which may have been the original Crocker homestead. To the far right is the Capt. Joseph Crocker house.

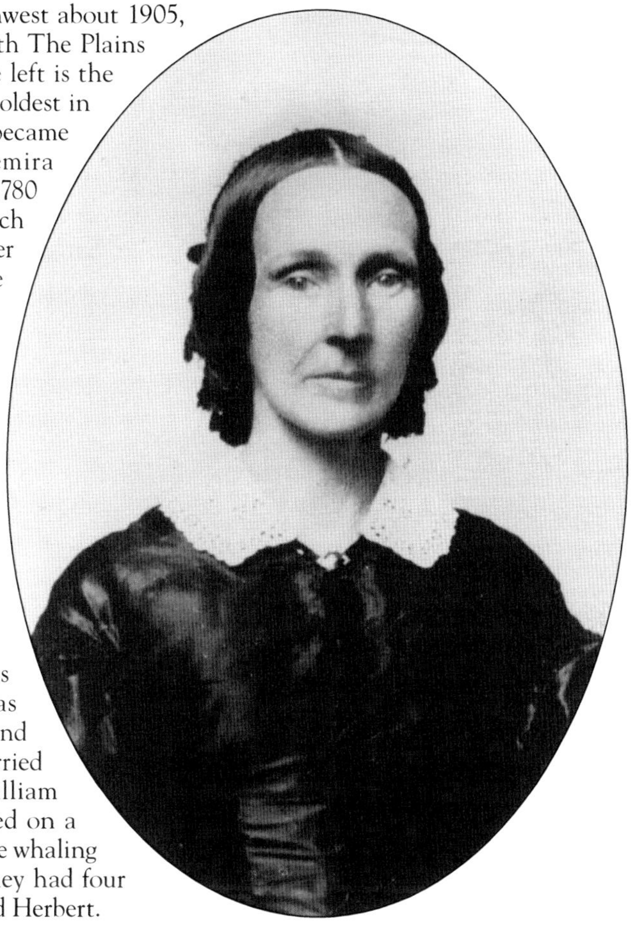

Pondsville resident Hodiah Jenkins Crocker Wright (1815–1908) was the daughter of Samuel Crocker and Thankful Percival. In 1837, she married Capt. Asa Wright, brother of William Wright, who in 1820 had survived on a Pacific island after the sinking of the whaling ship *Essex* by an angry whale. They had four sons—Nelson, Asa, Chessman, and Herbert.

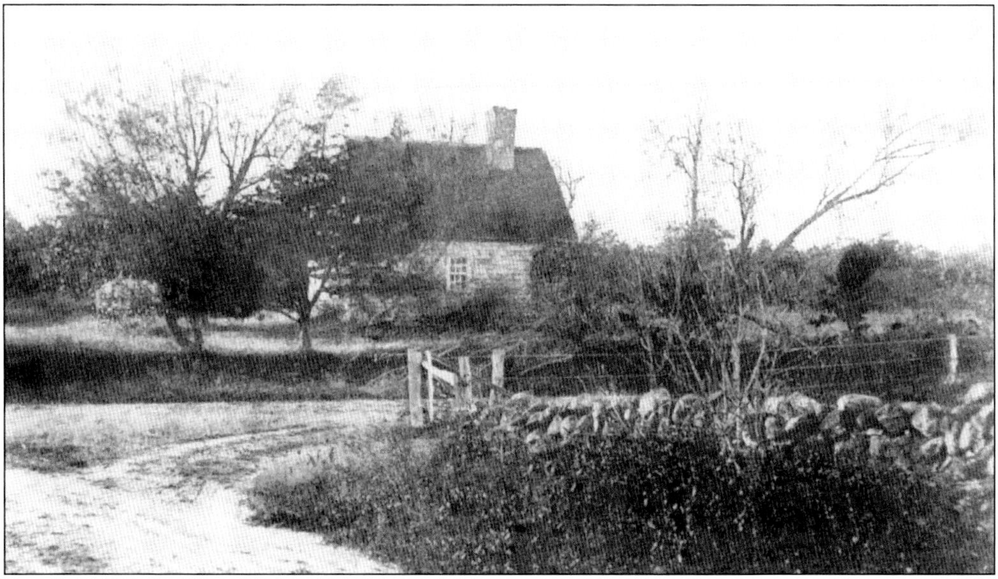

Cobb's Corner is at the junction of Crooked Cartway with Race Lane. Henry Cobb (1797–1892) and his wife, Patience, ran a grocery store for Pondsville residents, who included well-to-do sea captains, prosperous farmers, and South Sandwich families a short distance across the town line.

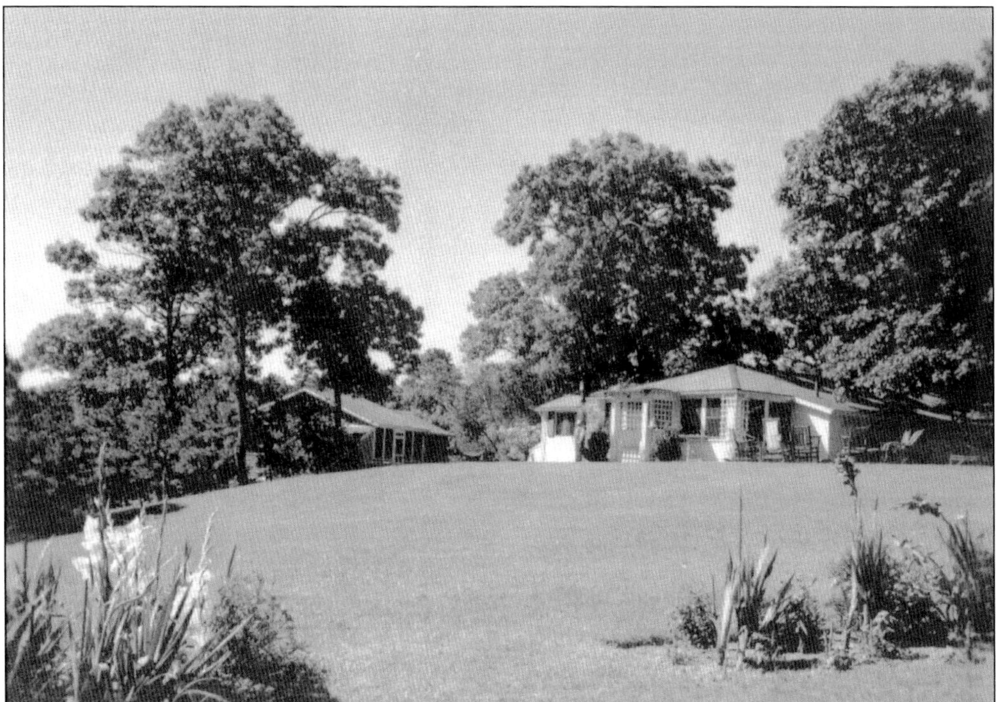

After World War I, Maurice Klouse of Brookline and his wife, Adelaide, bought 70 acres on Mystic Lake and built this summer home called Camp Adelaide. After their deaths, it was sold in 1937 to Abraham Lincoln Filene (1865–1957), who owned the leading Boston department store. He renamed it Lynxholm, an obvious pun on his name. Filene died here in the summer of 1957.

Nine

Cranberries in Newtown

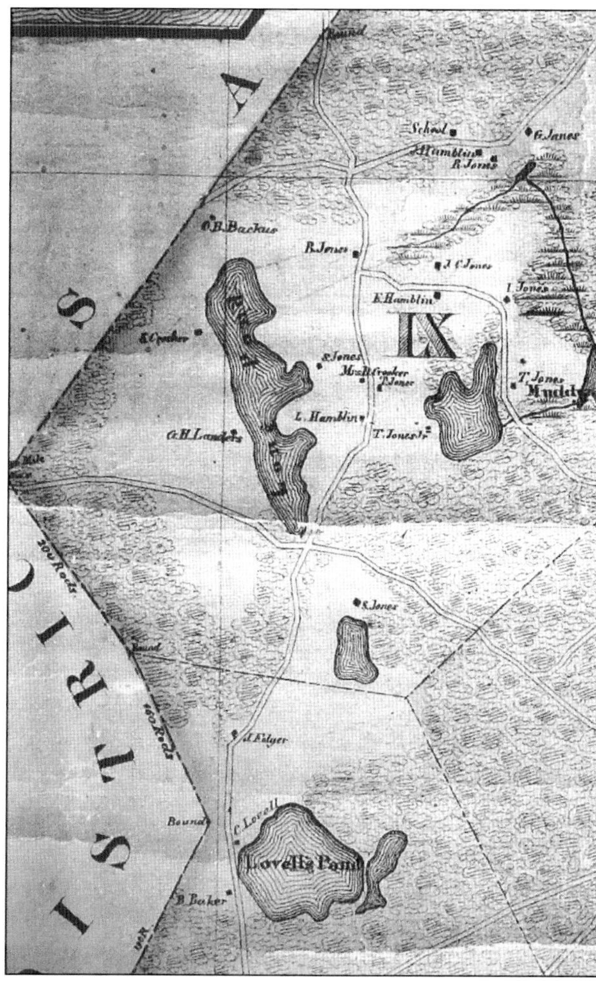

The western part of Marstons Mills bordering on Mashpee and South Sandwich had been called Newtown since at least 1800. Although there were scattered farms, large parts were heavily wooded or swampy meadowland where the Marstons Mills River rises. The wetlands were converted to cranberry farming in the second half of the 19th century, largely through the efforts of A.D. Makepeace. (Courtesy of Robert Frazee.)

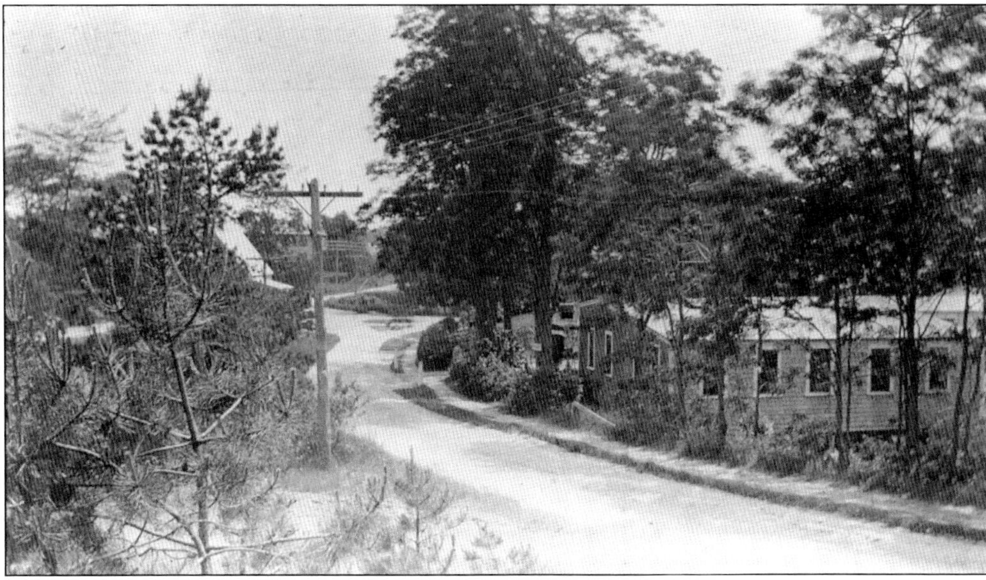

The road to Newtown, now called River Road, left the village center at Hamblin's grocery (at the left) and Isaac Greene's paint shop (on the right). Greene (1849–1918), a mariner and farmer in his early years, became a painter of signs and carriages. For funerals, he drove the hearse. He built this shop in 1891 and shared the front part with G. Webster Hallett's tin shop, where his son George Greene later opened a bicycle shop.

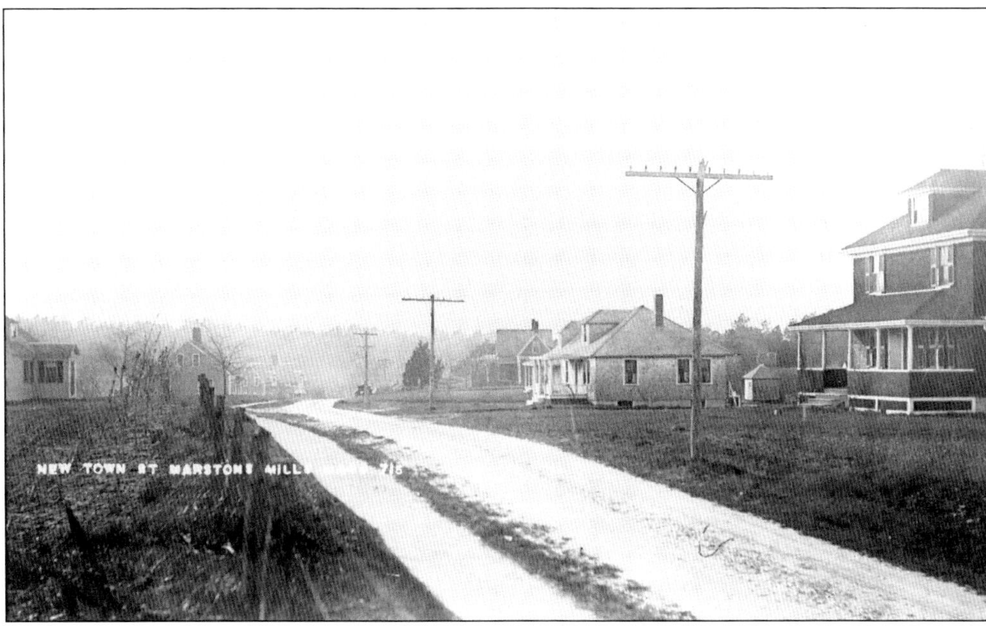

This is the unpaved road to Newtown, now called River Road, about 1911. The American Foursquare house on the right was built in 1910 by William T. Makepeace, himself a cranberry grower and the brother of the so-called Cranberry King, Abel Makepeace. In the middle is the Craftsman-style bungalow constructed the same year by the builder Leonard Hamblin, last owner of the gristmill.

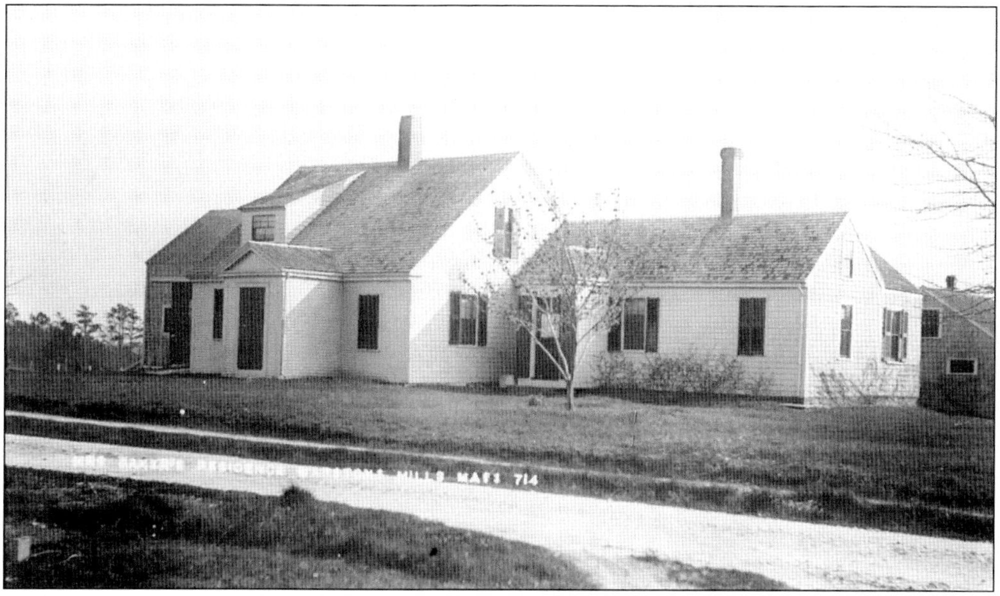

Arthur B. Marston (1797–1888) built this Cape Cod cottage in 1819 on the hilltop above the fulling mill he ran with clothier Robert Francis. There was a store on the land in 1840. Later, for 17 years, it was the office and home of the local physician Dr. Henry E. McCollum (1800–1867), a graduate of Bowdoin Medical School.

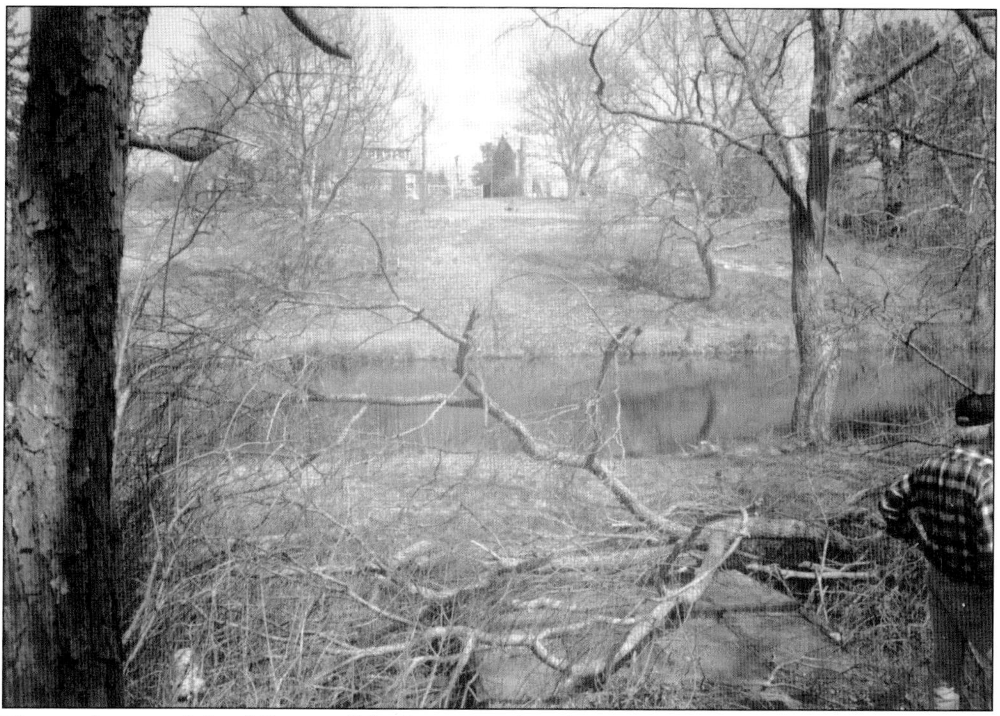

This is the site of the fulling mill built in 1689 by Thomas Macy to process the raw wool by pounding it with huge wooden hammers in water with detergent fulling earth. It was improved by Benjamin Marston, and activity expanded to include carding and weaving. Floods washed all remains away by late 19th century.

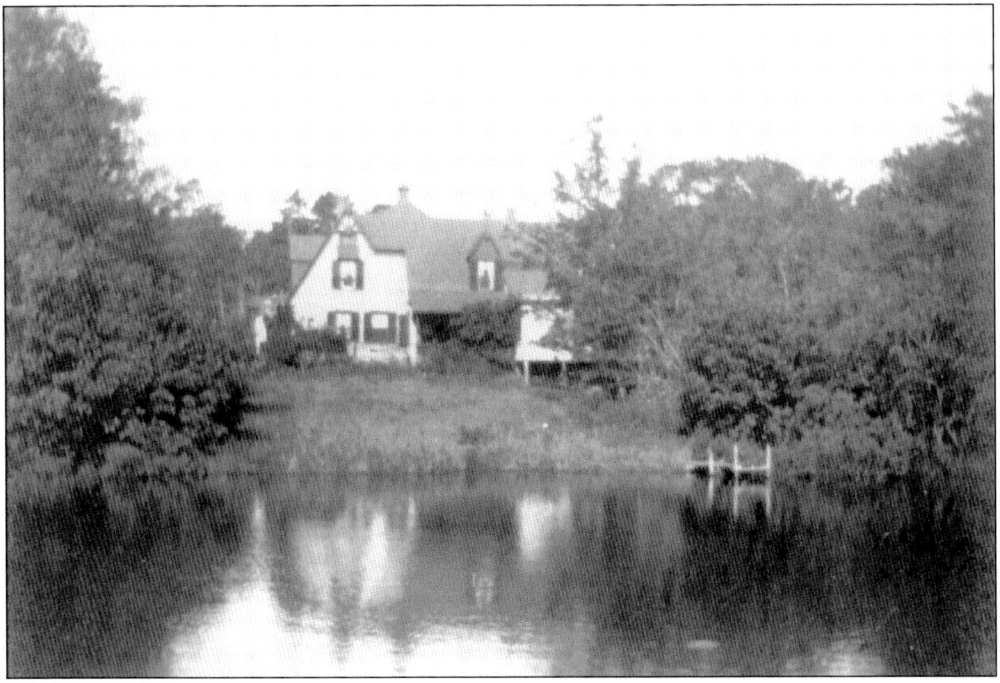

Willow Dell, the first summer home, was built in 1866 by prominent Boston lawyer Henry A. Scudder (1819–1892) on his wife's Goodspeed family land. Access to the west bank of the river was created by a bridge over the abandoned fulling mill dam and flume. Scudder became judge of the highest state court in 1869.

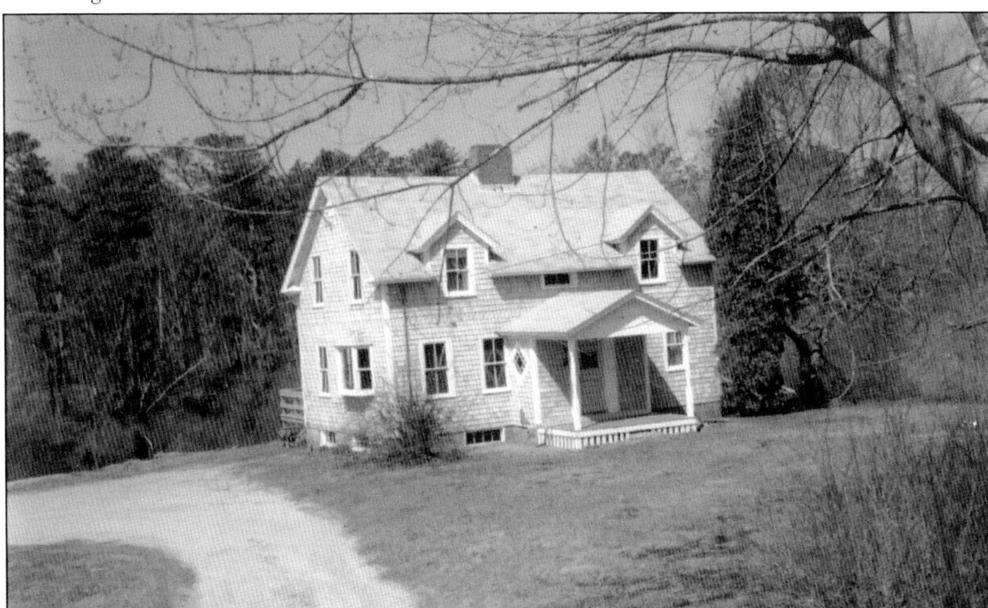

The riverside home of farmer Ansel B. Fuller (1808–1892) was built before 1856. When Andrew Jackson Bodge (1834–1912) sold the Gifford farm in 1898, he and his wife, Caroline "Carrie" Pearson Bodge, retired to this place. Carrie was a popular Sunday school and temperance leader. After World War I, it was the home of Loring Jones Sr., owner of the general store and auto agency.

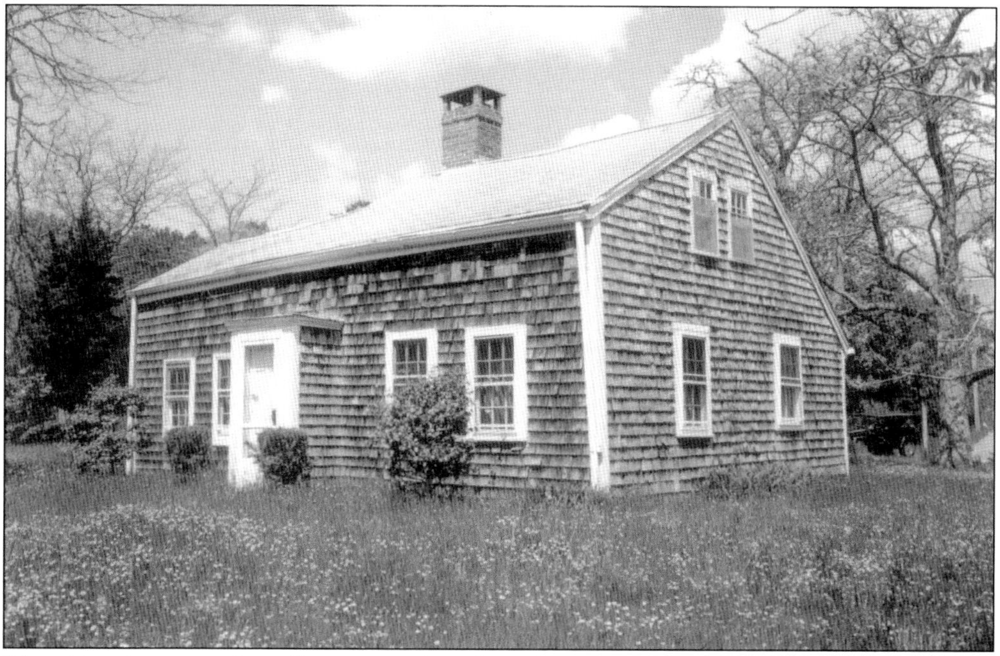

The oldest house in the village, once thought to have been the first house of pioneer Roger Goodspeed, was proven to have been built before 1708 by Roger's youngest son Ebenezer Goodspeed Sr. Born in 1655, he lived to be 91 years old. Recently, it was the summer home of Joseph Muranyi, the jazz clarinetist who played with Louis Armstrong. (Courtesy of Robert Frazee.)

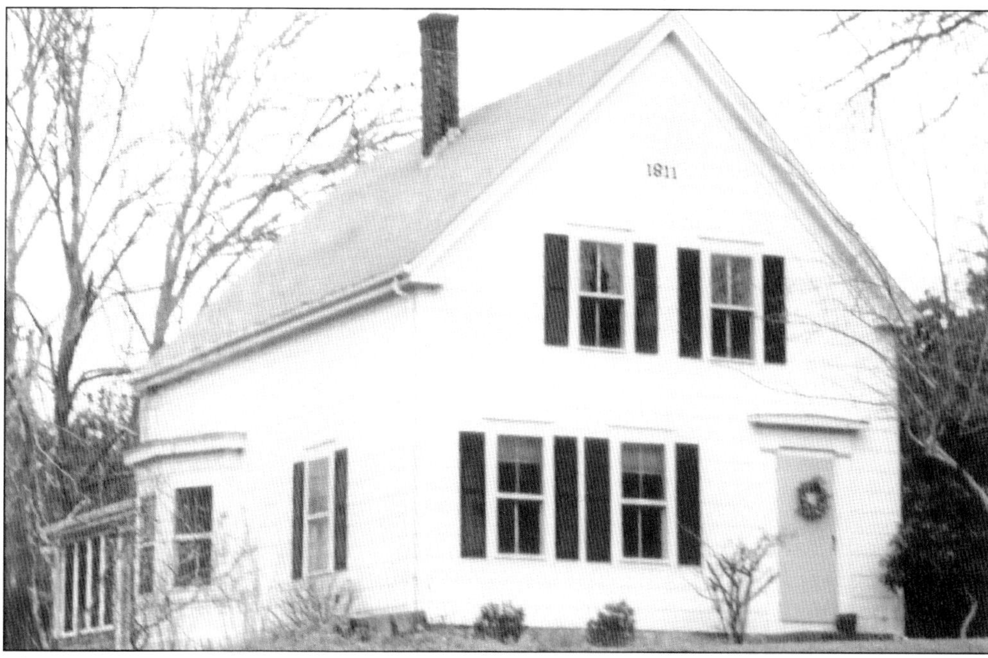

The core of the David Jones house on Rosa Lane may have been built in 1811 by Cornelius Jones. The house as seen today was built in Greek Revival style in 1861 by mariner David Jones, who farmed the fertile bottomland. In 1905, the house was bought by Jose de Gracie Rosa, an immigrant farmer from the Azores. (Courtesy of Arthur Thifault.)

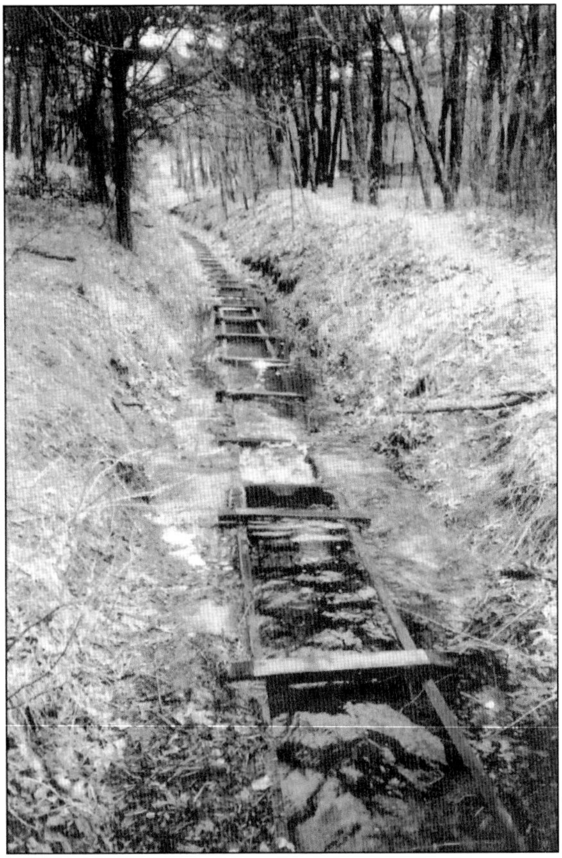

In 1875, Abel D. Makepeace drained Muddy Pond to create the biggest cranberry bog on Cape Cod, an obstacle to the herring run to Middle Pond. In 1880, the town cut a shortcut over the hill on David Jones's farm. In spite of periodic clearing, the number of herring continued to decline until the fishery was declared "worthless" in 1897. (Courtesy of Lindsey Counsell.)

Rebuilding the herring run was done after World War II by Taisto Ranta, who opened the lower run that had been blocked by the David Leland's hydroelectric plant. Another major clearing was done in 1978. In 1992, the Liberty Hall Men's Club rebuilt the 1,200-foot ladder, which climbed up to Middle Pond, once called Run Pond. (Courtesy of Lindsey Counsell.)

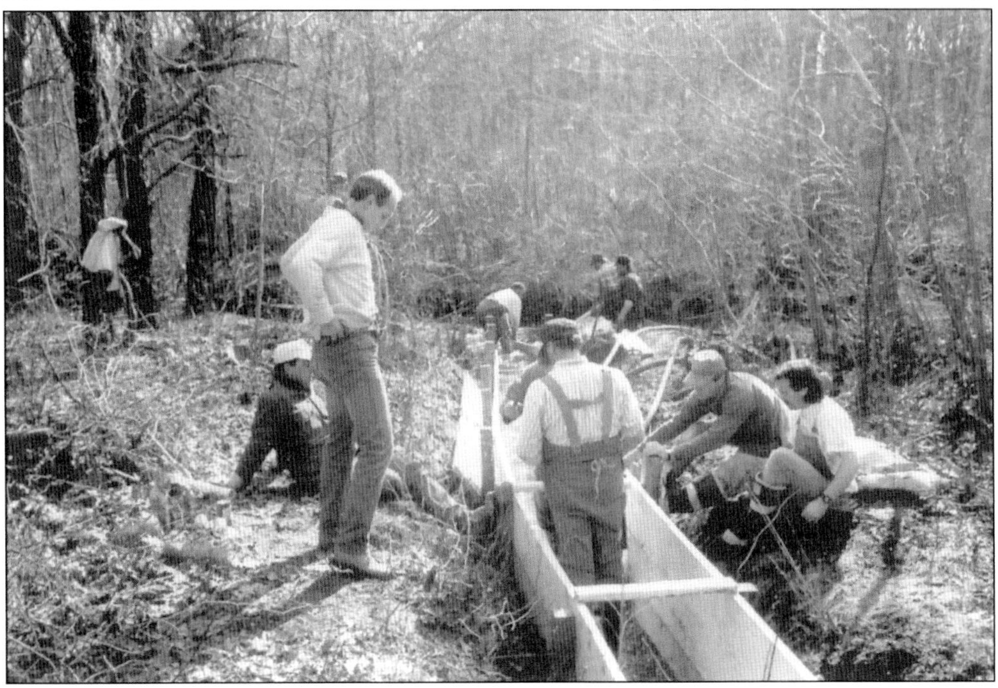

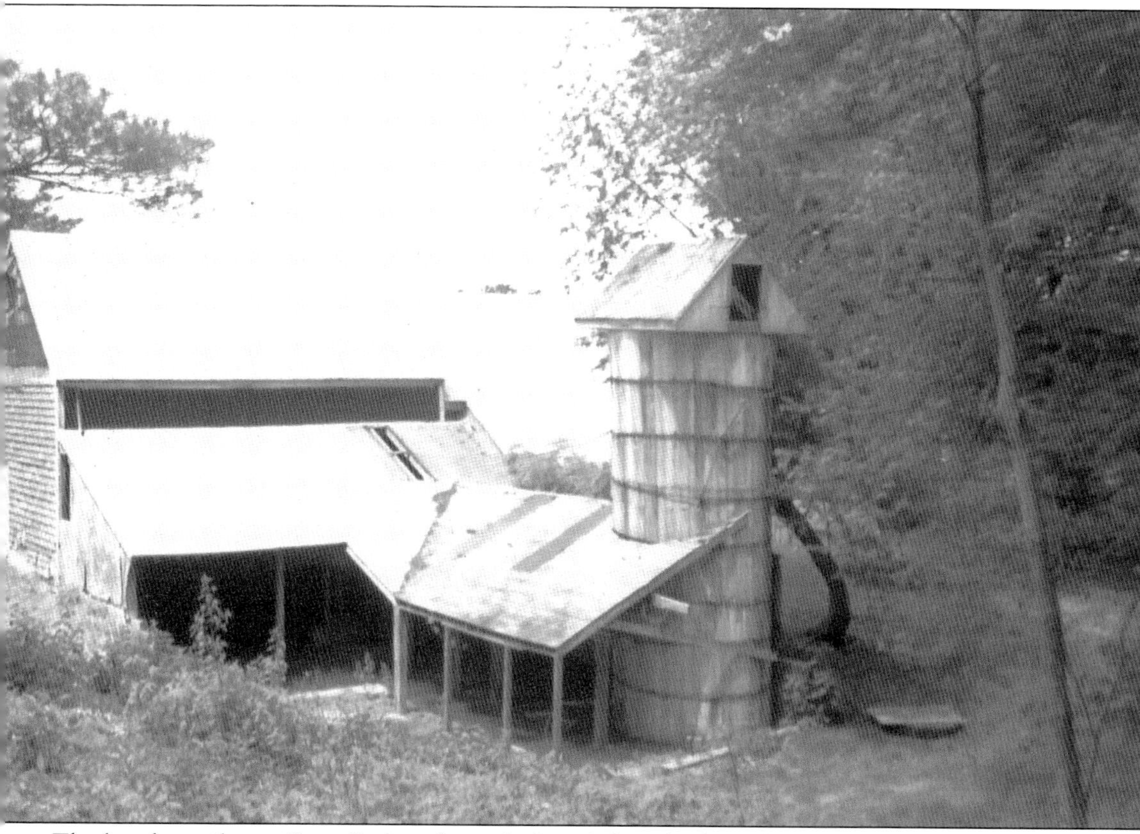

The last farm silo on Cape Cod, with its shed roof, dates back to the 19th century, when the farm was run by Bethuel Crocker. After longtime owner John Warner's death, the homestead, barn, and silo were preserved in 2008 by Cape Abilities, which uses the farm for the training of persons with disabilities. (Courtesy of Anne Thomas.)

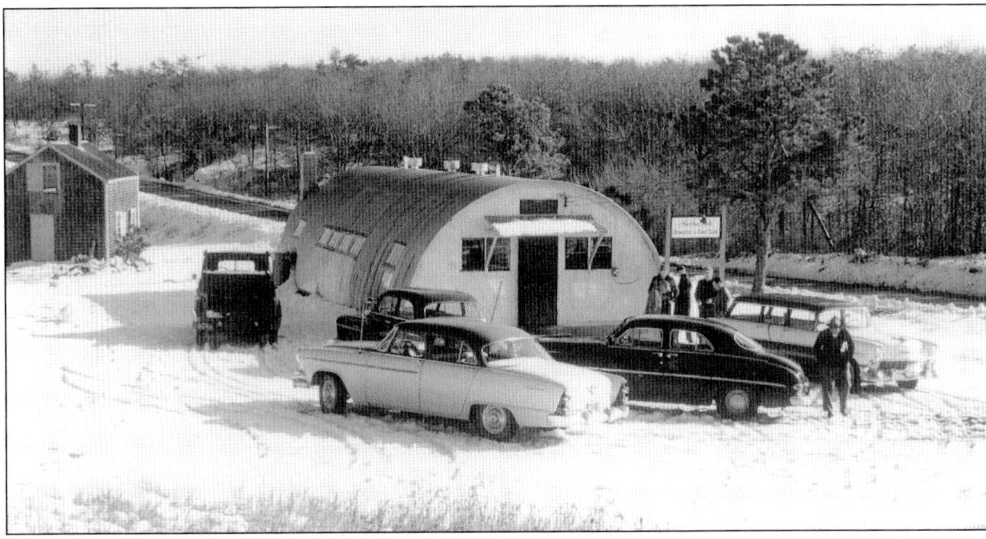

Nicknamed "The Snake Pit," a surplus Quonset hut was moved after World War II to Tom Jones Cove along River Road as a meeting place for the Marstons Mills Athletic and Civic Club. To the left is the wooden barracks Makepeace built before the war for cranberry workers, many from Cape Verde. The Quonset hut was sold when the Men's Club moved back to Liberty Hall in 1960. (Courtesy of Kay Dick.)

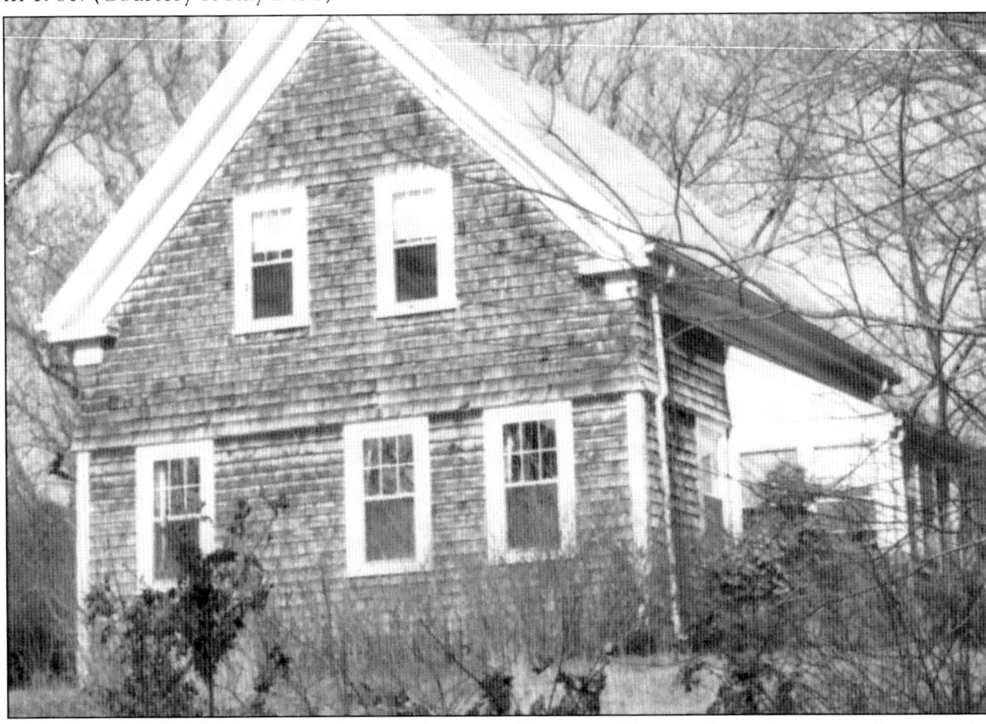

Surrounded by cranberry bogs, the Greek Revival Deacon Thomas Jones homestead was in the family for over a century and a half, housing six generations. It was built before 1857 by Jones (1823–1896), a yeoman farmer whose Quaker ancestor Ralph Jones first settled nearby in the 17th century. The deacon's grandson Ephraim was a pioneer cranberry grower in the bogs adjoining Muddy Pond.

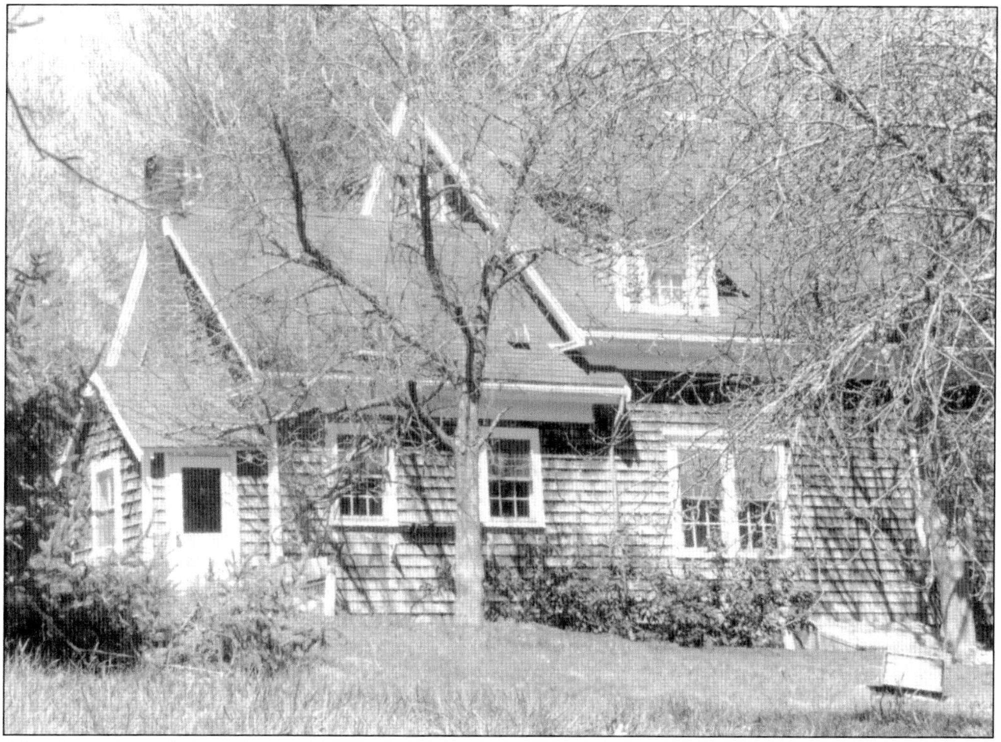

The Zenas Crocker IV house was built in 1880 by Stephen Crocker Hamblin (1851–1881) for Abel Makepeace. Chief engineer of Makepeace's bogs, Hamblin died at age 30 constructing the big Wankinko bog on the mainland. The house was later the home of Zenas Crocker IV (1864–1963), the town road-grader, who raised his sons Lauchlan, a future sheriff, and Zenas V, a future World War I pilot and founder of Cape Cod Airport, here.

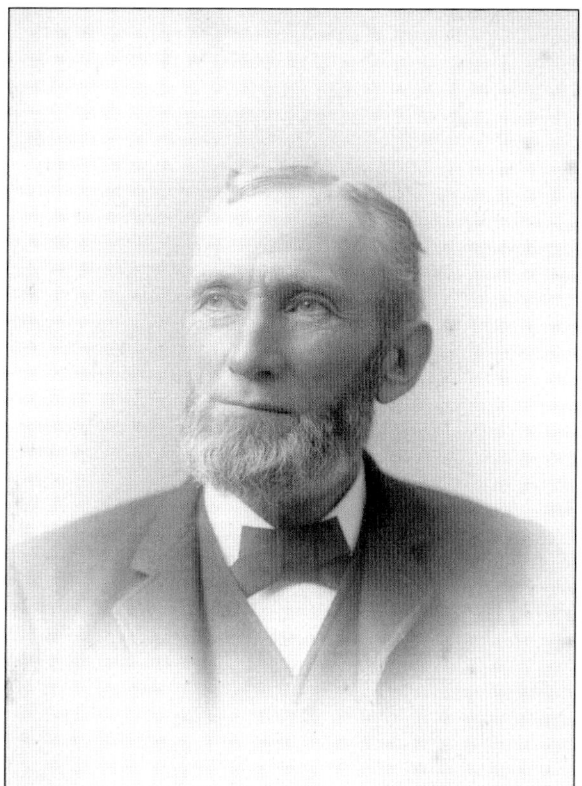

The Cranberry King, Abel D. Makepeace (1832–1916) and his wife, Josephine Crocker Makepeace, moved to Stephen Hamblin's house on River Road in 1880 before moving permanently to West Barnstable. The house looks out on the Baker Bog, named for Makepeace's financier, George T. Baker of Hyannis. It was one of the first large-scale cranberry bogs. (Courtesy of Betty Nilsson.)

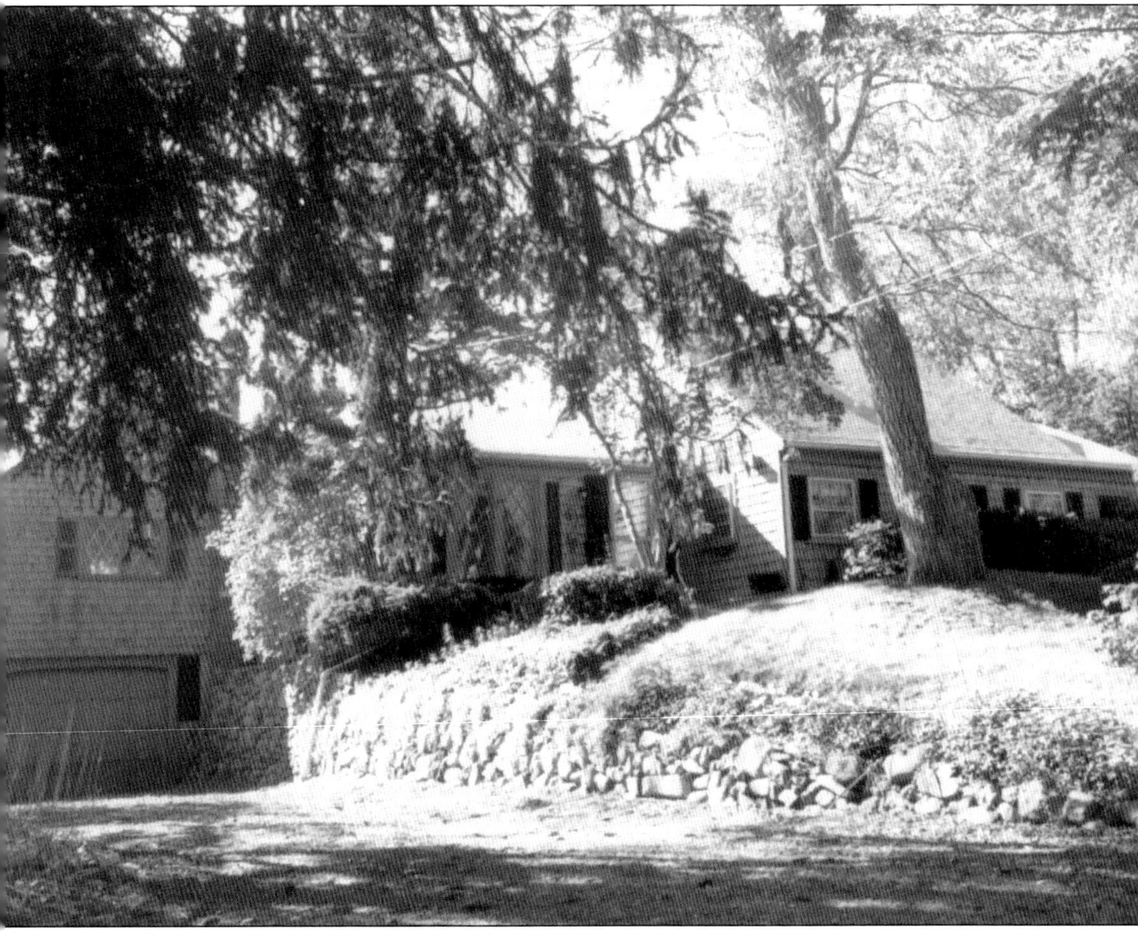

The three-quarter Cape Cod homestead of Ellis Hamblin (1806–1871) was built in 1838 on the west side of River Road. It was inherited by his son Henry, who was supervisor of works for A.D. Makepeace, who opened the Baker bog next to the house in 1877 and contracted with Hamblin to build the Wankinko bog in Wareham—one of his most successful and still producing.

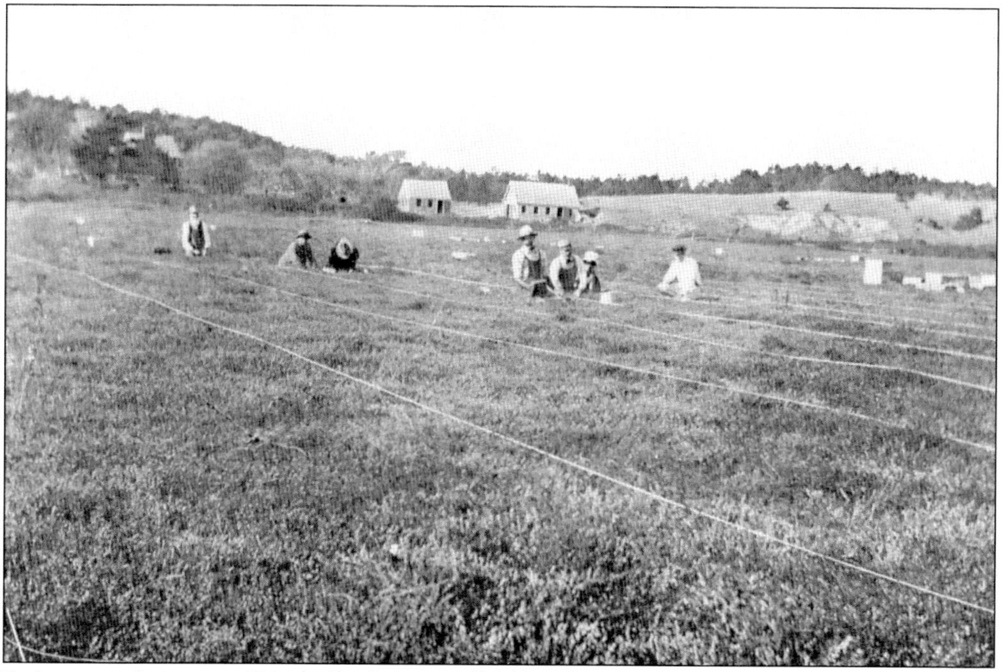

Picking cranberries on "Uncle Fred's Bog" off Old Mill Road was done by stretching strings to separate lanes for pickers with snap scoops (picker in center) to harvest the ripe berries. Pay was 2¢ or 3¢ per quart, so one could take home a couple of dollars after picking 100 quarts a day. Alonzo Hamblin held the record for 196 quarts one day in 1881. (Courtesy of Charles F. Crocker.)

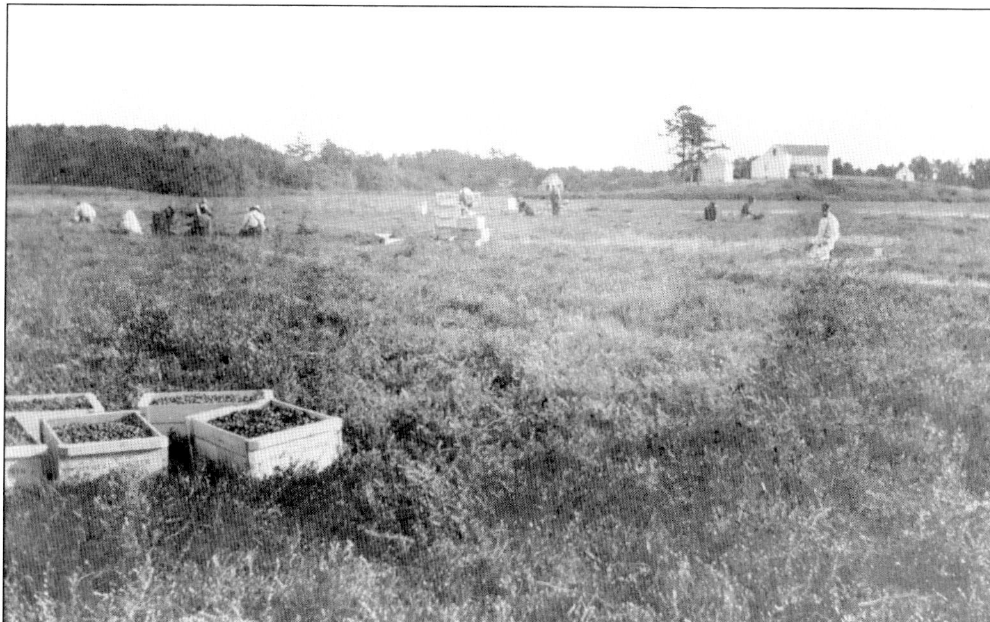

This image of Jedidiah Jones's Bog shows boxes of cranberries stacked at the side. The large barn in the background is the separator house; the others are bog houses. The sandy hill itself was mined for sand and gravel to build the Mid-Cape Highway. The Jones family had been in this area since 1643, as cattle farmers and Quakers. (Courtesy of Charles F. Crocker.)

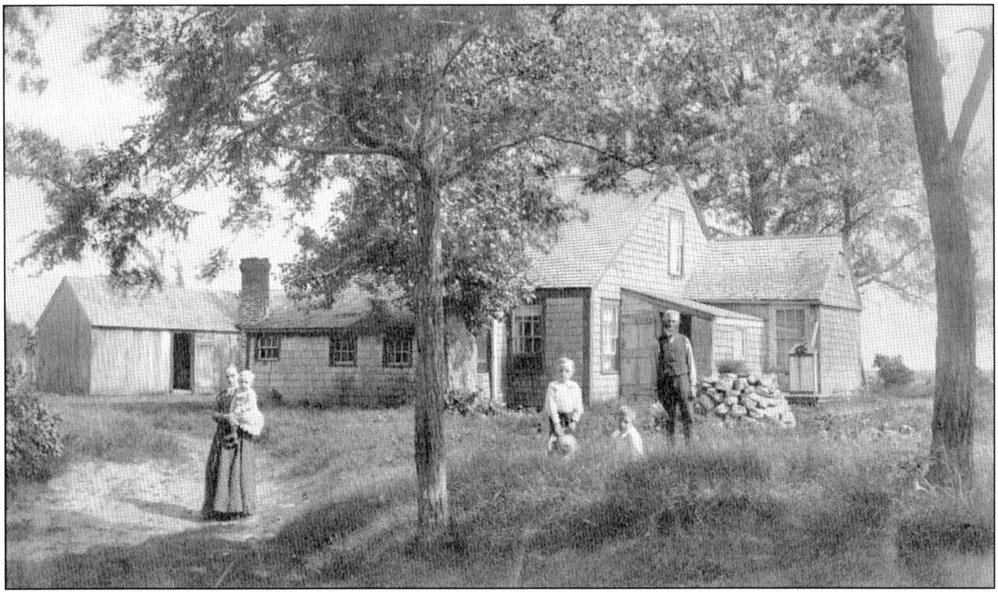

Jedidiah Jones's half Cape Cod house, built in 1814, is seen in 1890. From left to right are Cora Crocker (1858–1911), holding Mary Crocker (Sinnett) (1889–1939); son Chester (1881–1962), a longtime selectman; son Harvey (1884–1963); and James Harvey Crocker (1850–1928). (Courtesy of Charles F. Crocker.)

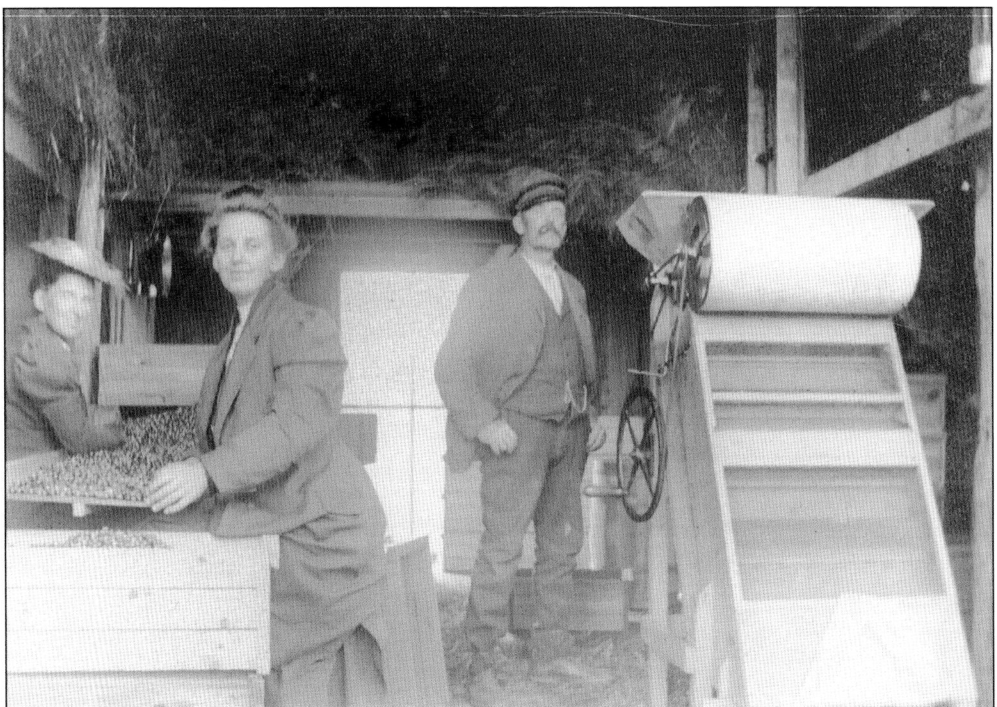

At the right is a screening machine, which separated spoiled berries from good ones by a bouncing process but still required skilled women to handpick the berries before they went into shipping boxes. Many local women earned a few extra dollars during cranberry-picking season.

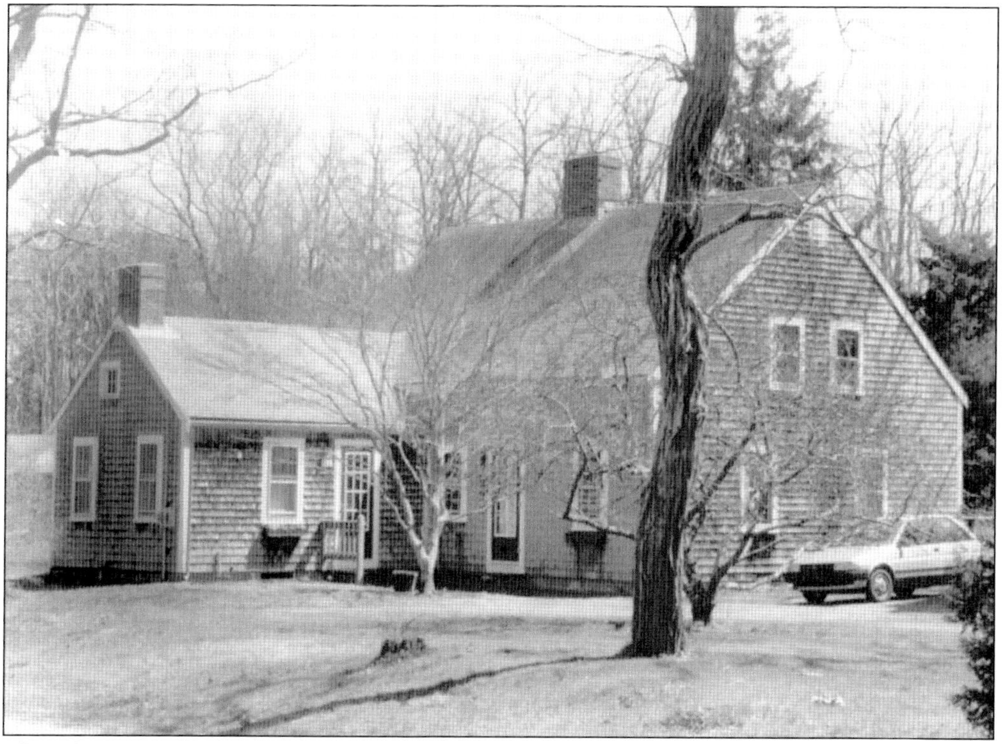

The John Hamblin house on School Street overlooks the Hamblin bogs. It was built about 1828 of parts that may date back to the 18th century by yeoman farmer Reuben Hamblin (1803–1860). The house and 500 acres was inherited by the cranberry farmer James "Uncle Jikker" Crocker (1850–1928), marked by his flowing white beard, who owned the Osterville ice cream store.

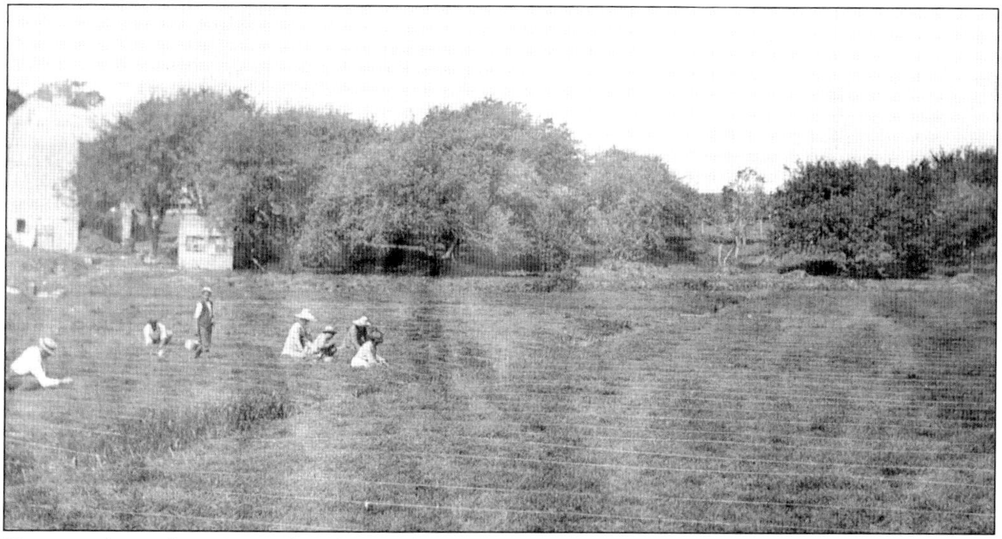

Here, in the early 1920s, a family is picking cranberries, probably on their own farm. From left to right are the father, boys with a pail, and two women in hats with younger children. Harvest usually falls in late September, so school closes, and teachers join their students in the bogs. Bigger bogs required itinerant labor, often from New Bedford or Fall River, and many men newly arrived from the Azores or Cape Verde Islands.

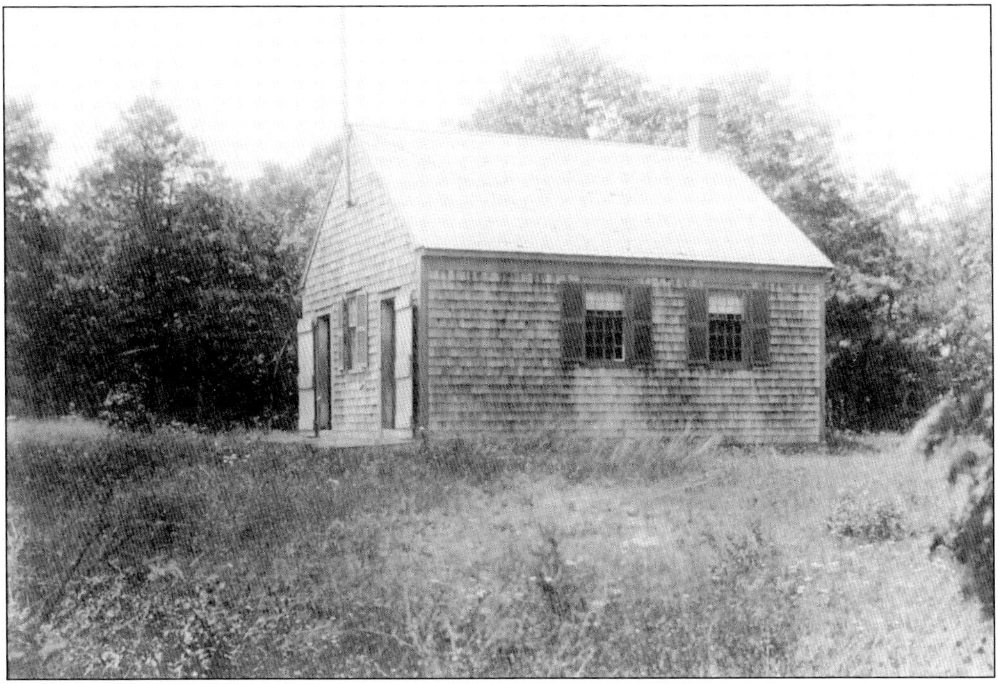

Newtown School was built in 1839 for $250 for District IX Pondsville and Newtown. Consolidation of schools closed it in 1901, coincidently with the death of its last teacher, 19-year-old Edward Bearse, who died of pneumonia after patiently waiting in wet ground to see the reaction of his girlfriend to his doorstep gift of mayflowers.

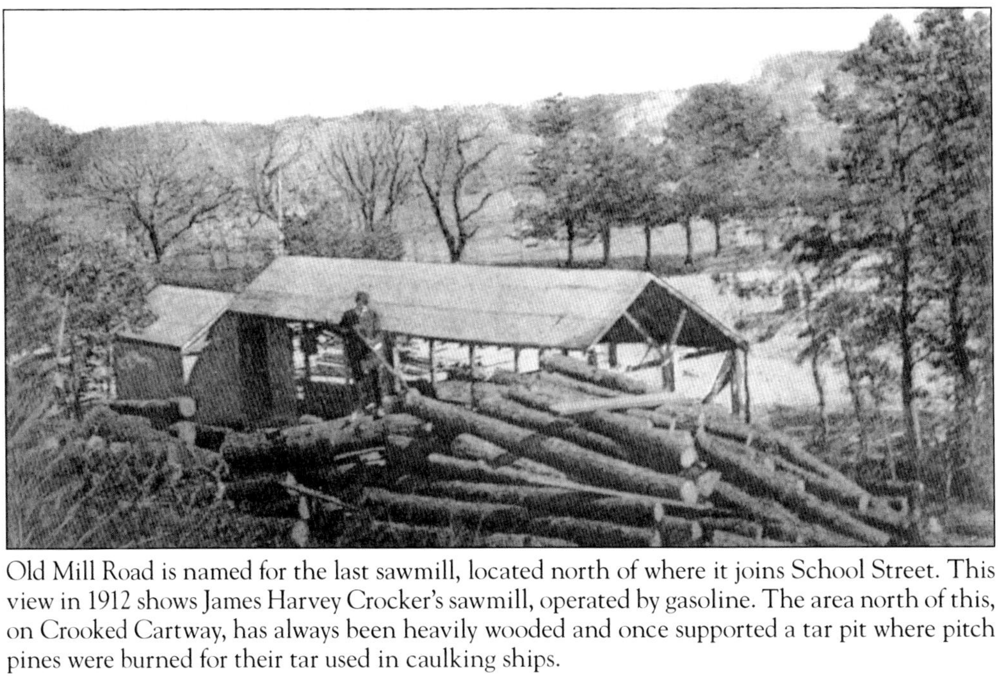

Old Mill Road is named for the last sawmill, located north of where it joins School Street. This view in 1912 shows James Harvey Crocker's sawmill, operated by gasoline. The area north of this, on Crooked Cartway, has always been heavily wooded and once supported a tar pit where pitch pines were burned for their tar used in caulking ships.

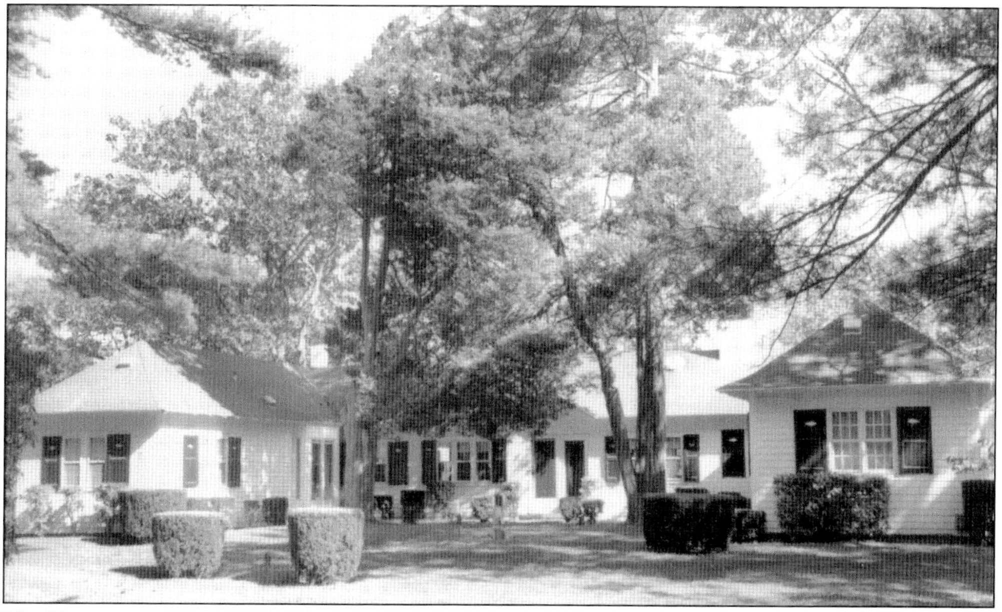

The Tanampo Club flourished here on Middle Pond between the wars, with Wampanoag gamekeeper Ferd Mills and cook Eben Quippish. The hunting club took its name from the Choctaw word for "gun and rifle," the name suggested by Mills's son-in-law, a Choctaw native, according to according to Chief Earl Mills of Mashpee. The club took over the summer home the Boston Conservatory's pianist Carlo Buonamici built in 1913. The Halperts converted it to a comfortable home.

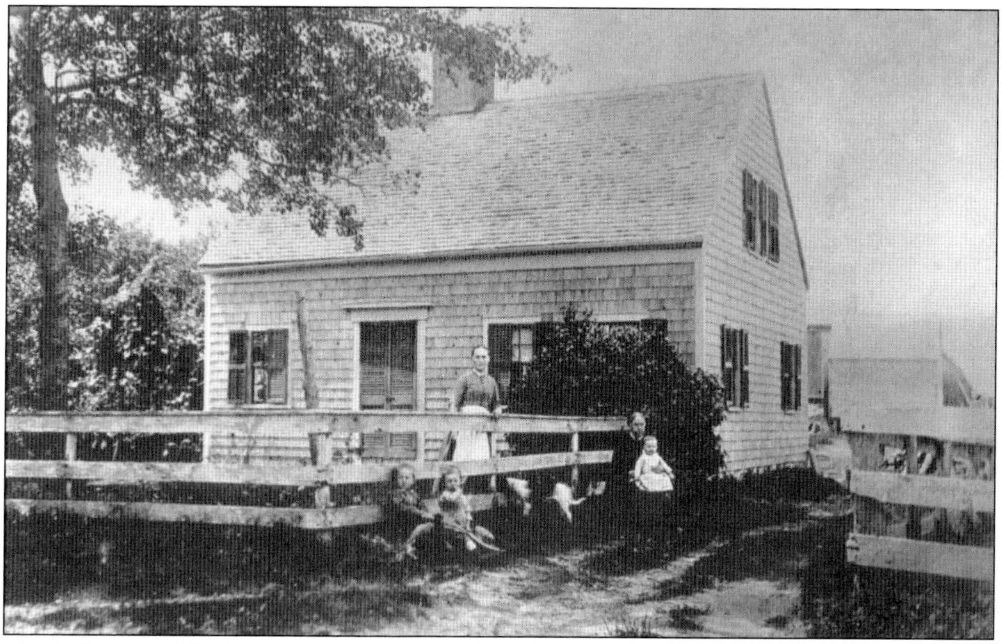

The Luther Hamblin house on Newtown Road is a three-quarter Cape Cod cottage built in 1836. In this picture taken about 1889, Luther's widow, Caroline (Crocker) Hamblin (1814–1895), stands above son Ezekiel's wife, Helen (Lewis), holding Charles Luther Hamblin (1889–1974, a future builder), with Stephen Francis (1884–1962, a future Harvard professor of botany) and Nellie (1886–1925). (Courtesy of Charles E. Hamblin.)

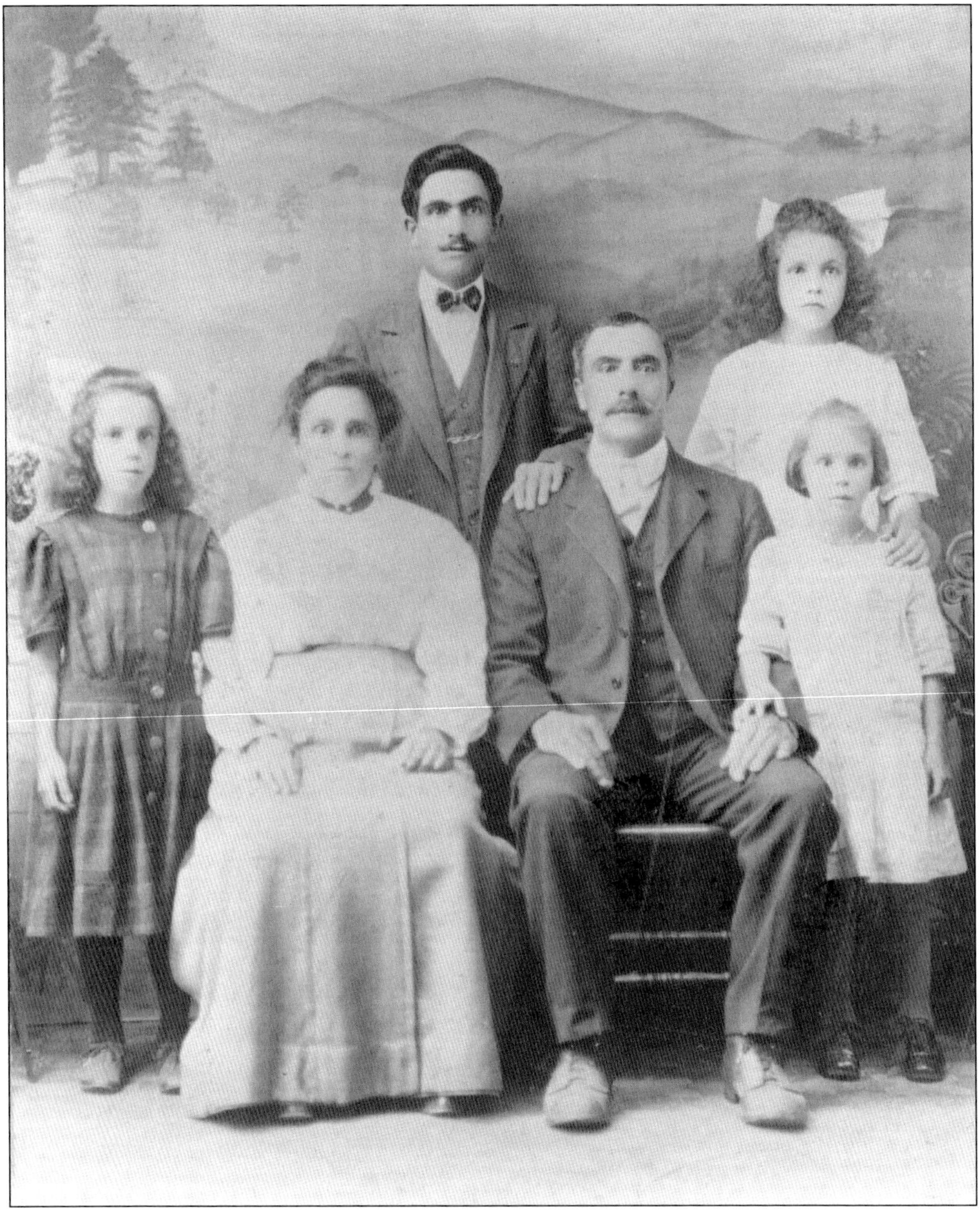

Wheelwright John Rogers (1858–1922) came from the Azores in 1903 with his schoolteacher wife, Harriet (1864–1926). They settled on the west side of Long Pond. Pictured in 1917 from left to right are Mary Angel, Harriet, Ernest, John, Mary Carm (who married Charles L. Hamblin), and Myra. The Rogers family contributed their woodworking skills to fine finish carpentry in boats and homes. (Courtesy of Charles E. Hamblin.)

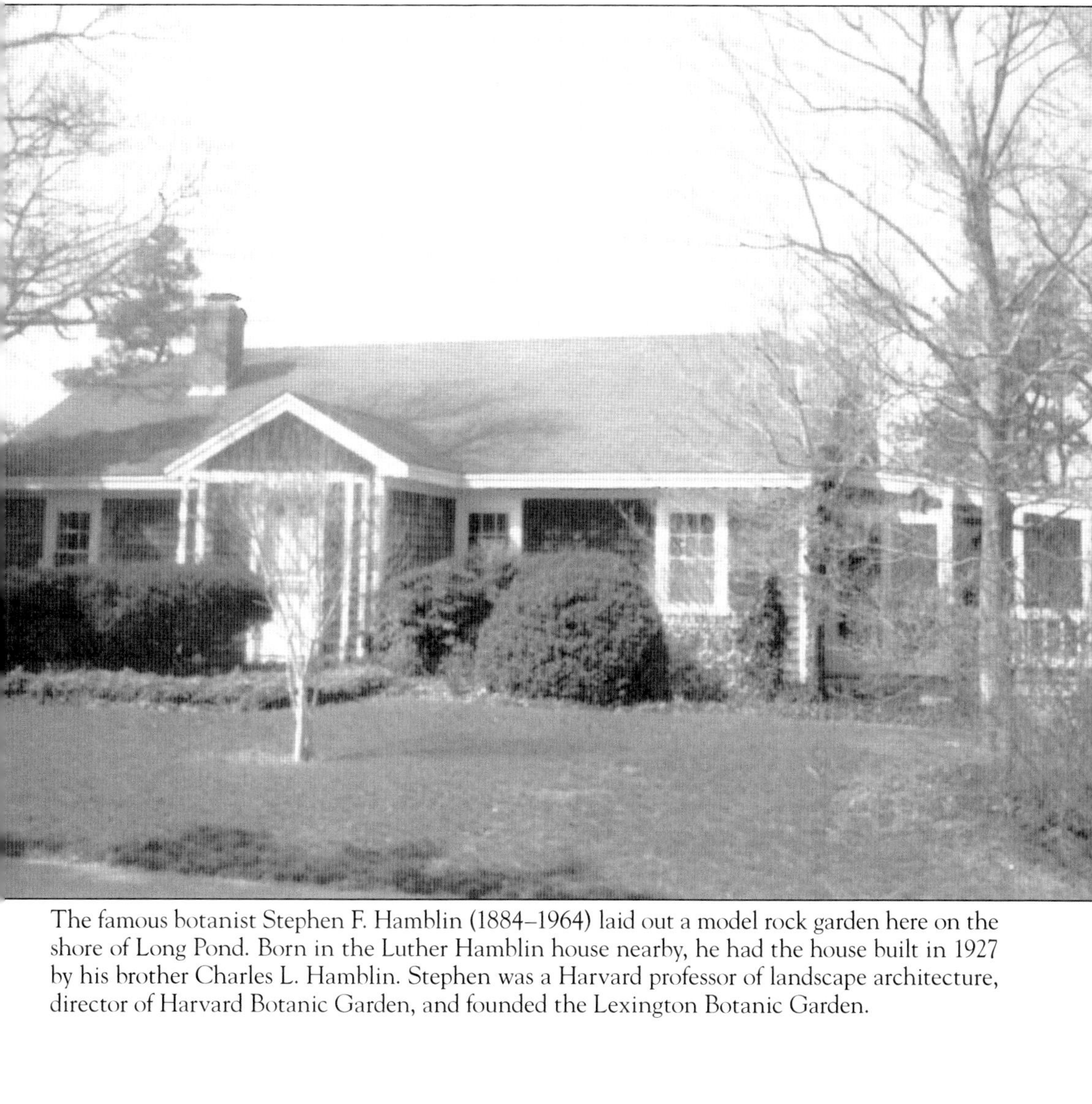

The famous botanist Stephen F. Hamblin (1884–1964) laid out a model rock garden here on the shore of Long Pond. Born in the Luther Hamblin house nearby, he had the house built in 1927 by his brother Charles L. Hamblin. Stephen was a Harvard professor of landscape architecture, director of Harvard Botanic Garden, and founded the Lexington Botanic Garden.

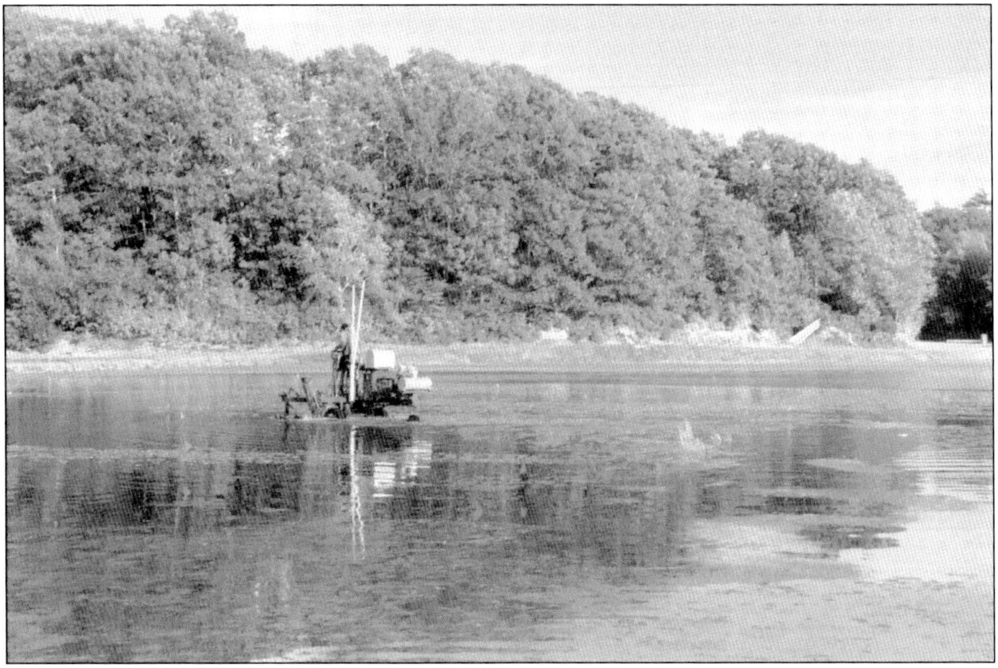

Dry picking of cranberries still persists, using machine harvesters. But most bogs are now wet-harvested, a process that dates from the 1960s. The bog is flooded, and scoured by a water-reel harvesting machine that whips through the vines and knocks loose the berries, which float to the surface. (Courtesy of Holly Hobart.)

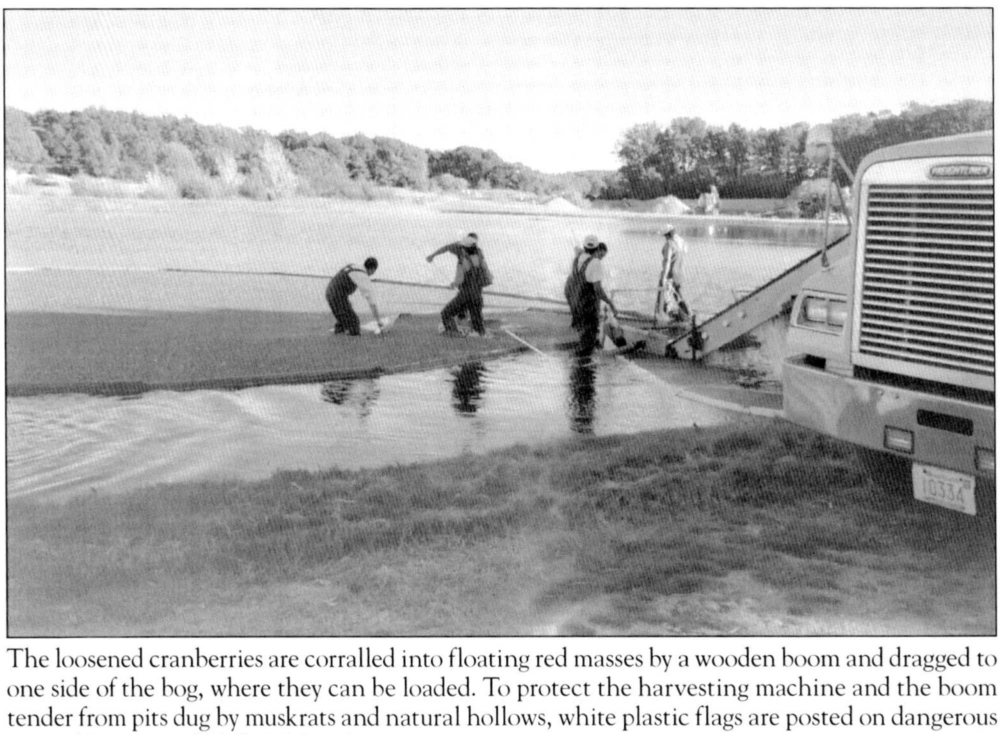

The loosened cranberries are corralled into floating red masses by a wooden boom and dragged to one side of the bog, where they can be loaded. To protect the harvesting machine and the boom tender from pits dug by muskrats and natural hollows, white plastic flags are posted on dangerous spots. (Courtesy of Holly Hobart.)

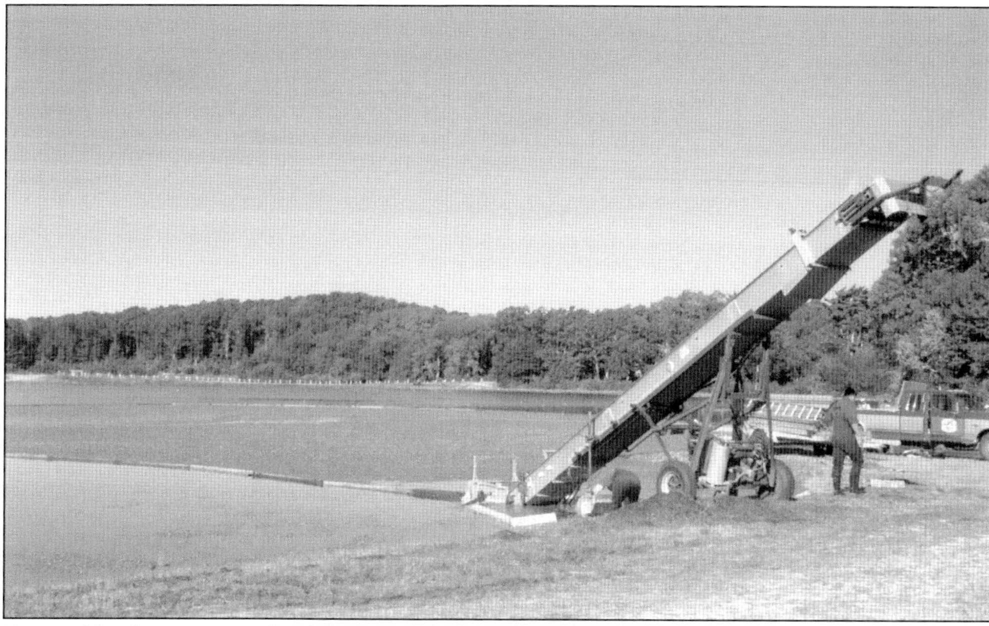

A portable elevator is used to lift the cranberries from the edge of the bog. The bogs in Marstons Mills are owned and worked by John Hamblin, fourth generation of the family that pioneered growing in the area. His great-grandfather Luther bought a marsh in 1858, where he began cultivation. His great-uncle Stephen constructed the large bogs for A.D. Makepeace. (Courtesy of Holly Hobart.)

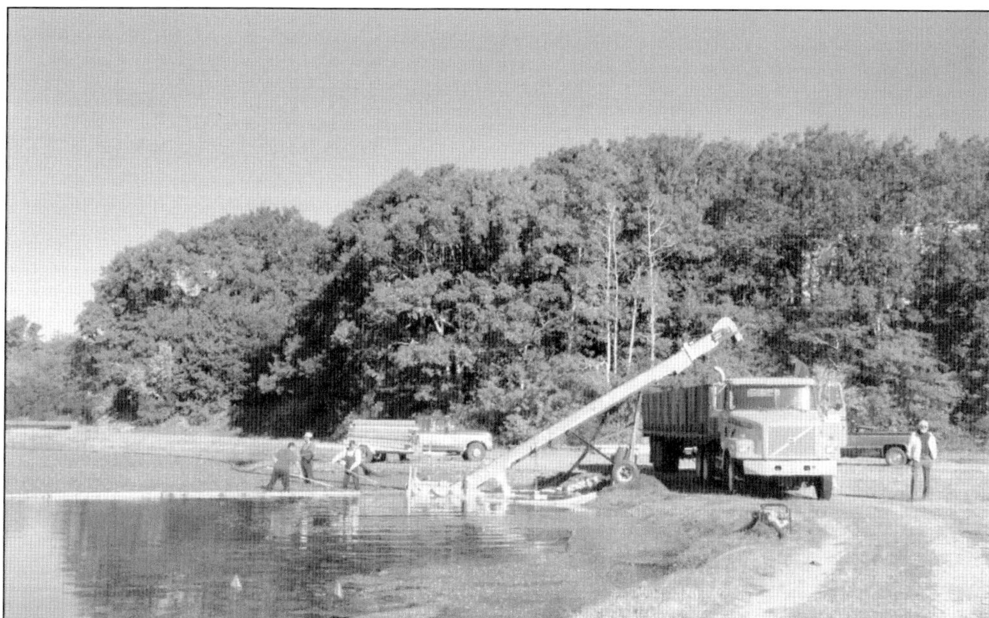

Cranberries are lifted on a conveyor belt to the top, where they are sprayed with water to remove the vines and debris, which can be seen below in piles of trash. As the truck fills with berries, it moves forward to even out the load. The loaded trucks cross the canal to deliver the load to a receiving center. (Courtesy of Holly Hobart.)

INDEX

About the Organization

The origins of the society lie in the mystery of the curious ridges that cross the landscape in straight lines, often connected by granite pillars. Marstons Mills residents Wilbur Cushing and Robert McClusky explored the woods, bogs, and fields, mapping and connecting them to Colonial land grants.

On January 30, 1983, the Marstons Mills Historical Society was founded at the home of Arnold and Irene Hadfield. Robert McClusky was elected president. Among early members were Vivian Cushing, Adele and Loring Jones Jr., Sue Davenport Johnson, and Barbara Hill.

The first project was to collect old photographs. In May 1983, the society merged with the Marstons Mills Village Association. Led by Hazel Meyer, the society helped to record historic houses in the National Register of Historic Places.

A ham-and-bean supper at Liberty Hall in 1984 raised $692 to restore the Hearse House at the cemetery. McClusky and Cushing laid a concrete foundation, and Michael Hill repaired and painted the frame.

The society reorganized on December 4, 1984, separating from the village association. Barbara Hill became president, serving for 21 years. Robert McClusky was vice president, Adele Jones continued as secretary, and Vivian Cushing was elected treasurer.

In 1985, Sue Davenport obtained a $4,500 state grant for the library to do a history of the village. Barbara Hill directed the living history project, interviewing old-timers for memories and displaying artifacts in the library.

The society's photo collection was used to print historical calendars in 1986 and 1987.

The society was legally established as a corporation under state law on April 22, 1987, with tax-exempt status. Bronze plaques were placed on the four principal public buildings in 1987; they were a gift from Joan Knowlton in honor of her husband, William Knowlton. The president's sketch of the buildings was reproduced on notepapers and letterheads sold to raise funds.

The historical society supported the preservation of the historic Burgess House in 1998. In 2001, the historic buildings and sites in Newtown were recorded for the National Register by James W. Gould.

Kevin Galvin was elected president in October 2005. He began digitizing the photographs, set up a website, revised the bylaws, revived the oral history project, worked to preserve the Isaac Crocker homestead, obtained the papers of Crocker Snow, and began the first count of herring.

In 2009, the Historic Sites Committee (Holly Hobart and Jim Gould) completed the inventory of every house in the village built before 1945. After Kevin Galvin's tragic death in January 2012, he was succeeded as president by Robert Frazee, a former chairman of the Barnstable Historical Commission, who has a degree in historic preservation from Roger Williams University.

The Marstons Mills Historical Society invites all to join the growing membership in pursuing its mission of recording the history of the village and preserving its historic sites.

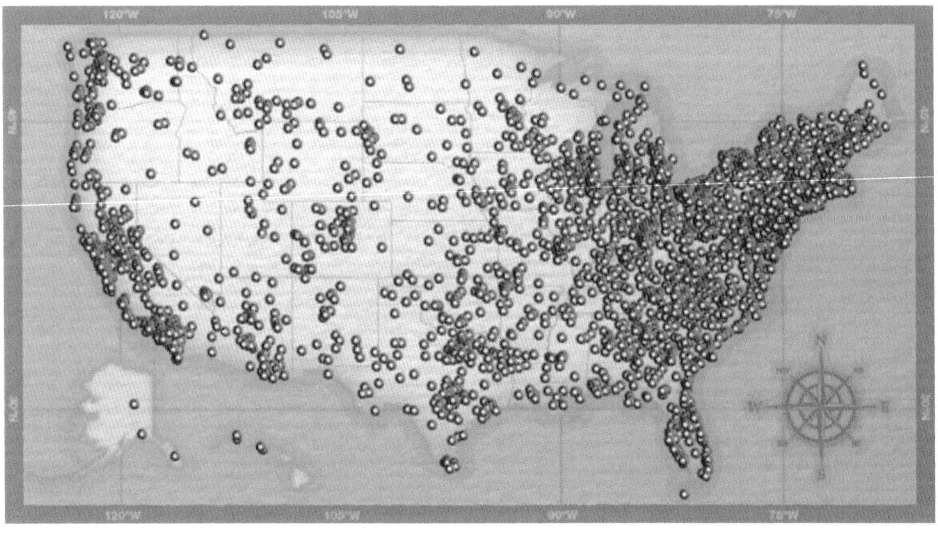